Characterization is a popular way to understand
forth by the various authors. What is often lackin
of historical appropriateness. Dr. Alukwe manage.
the apostle Peter in Acts, and by doing so furthers our knowledge of both Acts
and the Damascus Document of the Qumran community. Here Dr. Alukwe
has demonstrated that Peter's role and function fits the role of the "overseer" in
the Damascus Document, and that therefore the paradigm of Peter's role was
available to and probably known in the early church. Indirectly this helps us also
to trust Luke as a historian even further. Apart from the historical questions,
this study can be applied as a biblical model of how to lead and serve well by
simply noting how Peter fulfilled his apostleship.

Dirk Jongkind, PhD
Academic Vice Principal,
Tyndale House, Cambridge, UK

This fresh and interesting study fruitfully compares Peter's leadership in the
book of Acts to that of the Mebaqqer, the leader of the Qumran community.
This is an appropriate comparison because both the earliest Christians and
the Qumran community saw themselves as living in a new age as communities called by God to follow a founder, respectively, Jesus and the Teacher of
Righteousness. Dr. Alukwe carefully examines Acts and the Dead Sea Scrolls,
as well as other ancient writers' discussion of the Essenes, and offers a thoughtful and nuanced comparison which highlights key similarities in the style and
manner of leadership by Peter and the Mebaqqer, as well as significant differences that shine fresh light on the distinctives of the two communities. This is
a book which will benefit scholars and students of Acts, the early Christians,
and the Dead Sea Scrolls.

Steve Walton, PhD
Senior Research Fellow in New Testament,
Trinity College, Bristol, UK

The Characterization of Peter's Leadership and Ethics in Acts 1–12, 15

Echoes of the Mebaqqer at Qumran

Benea Alukwe

© 2024 Benea Alukwe

Published 2024 by Langham Academic (Previously Langham Monographs)
An imprint of Langham Publishing
www.langhampublishing.org

Langham Publishing and its imprints are a ministry of Langham Partnership

Langham Partnership
PO Box 296, Carlisle, Cumbria, CA3 9WZ, UK
www.langham.org

ISBNs:
978-1-83973-847-0 Print
978-1-83973-994-1 ePub
978-1-83973-995-8 PDF

British Library Cataloguing-in-Publication Data
A catalogue record for this book is available from the British Library

ISBN: 978-1-83973-847-0

Cover & Book Design: projectluz.com

To my parents, Stanley Amakhungu Walukwe and Florence Ayuma Amakhungu, and my parents-in-law, Joshua Aganda Achara and Robai Mmbone Aganda, and the Muyundi village community where my passion for leadership and ethics was born as a result of the leadership and ethical gaps I witnessed growing up.

Contents

Acknowledgments

I am heavily indebted to the communities that have contributed to who I am. My mother, Florence Ayuma Amakhungu, defied all odds to give me a chance at education. She literally carried me on her back to sit for my final primary exams. I owe the very roots and foundation of my academic life to her selfless love. I offer special appreciation to my dear wife Margaret Kigamwa, who loved me, believed in me, and risked a commitment that has brought me immense joy. My three little angels and my true treasure, Joan, Jeremy, and Jan, who have greatly endured many things to allow daddy to do his research.

To my friend and brother who persistently reminded me of the need to pursue this vision and lavishly supported me in prayer and kind, Bishop David Bwire. My first Hebrew lecturer Dr. Marcia Anderson, who saw a scholar in me way back at the undergraduate level and treated me like one, your prophetic utterances have been a source of strength in trying moments when giving up would have been a wise option. To Settna boys – you have amazingly funded my studies even without knowing it because you willingly accepted to shoulder what could have hindered my studies, not to forget the leadership and members of Gate of Light Chapel-Likoni who through their challenges and needs I was encouraged to seek solutions for both of us.

Last, to my two friends and supervisors, Dr. Andrew Mull and Dr. Joshua Harper, you accepted me as a brother and a ministry partner and guided me graciously as true shepherds. In addition, to all who have made this journey comfortable and a success, a big thank you. Finally, glory and honor be to God, the only one who favored me with the breath, health, and healing from a stroke (in March 2012) to carry out this research.

Abstract

This dissertation explores the narratives of Acts 1–12 and 15 with the goal of demonstrating that the characterization of apostle Peter's leadership and his ethics resonates with the leadership and ethics of the community discussed in the Damascus Document (CD). Engaging the lenses of narrative criticism, supplemented by intertextuality, this study highlights how Peter's leadership and ethics in Acts 1–12 and 15 resembles leadership and the ethics lived in CD's community. This we accomplish by setting forth our proposal in chapter 1. Chapter 2 discusses the method of study, narrative features of setting and rhetoric, with an explanation of intertextuality. Chapter 3 examines the proposed analogy from the Jewish histories in reading Acts 1–12 and 15. Chapter 4 focuses first on characterization of Peter's leadership and ethics in Acts 1–12 and 15, noting the areas of expansion of the community of believers, the handling of scriptures (by Peter), and the works of God (miracles, healings, and visions). It then demonstrates how these are similar to the Mebaqqer's leadership and ethics at Qumran. Chapter 5 draws parallels between the leadership and ethics of Peter and the Mebaqqer. Finally, chapter 6 discusses the findings and conclusions of the study.

Abbreviations

Standard abbreviations follow the *SBL Handbook of Style: For Ancient Near Eastern, Biblical, and Early Christian Studies*. Additional abbreviations not found in the SBL Handbook are listed here below.

AJEC	Ancient Judaism and Early Christianity
ASBT	Acadia Studies in Bible and Theology
BECNT	Baker Exegetical Commentary on the New Testament
BIS	Biblical Interpretation Series
CBR	Currents in Biblical Research
CBI	Currents in Biblical Interpretation
CD	Damascus Document
EBC	Expositor's Bible Commentary
ECC	Eerdmans Critical Commentary
EC	Epworth Commentaries
ESEC	Emory Studies in Early Christianity
JGRChJ	*Journal of Greco-Roman Christianity and Judaism*
JPTSup	Journal of Pentecostal Theology Supplement Series
JSJSup	Supplements to the Journal for the Study of Judaism
JSNTSup	Journal for the Study of New Testament Supplement
JSocSt	Jewish Social Studies
LCBI	Literary Currents in Biblical Interpretation
LHBOTS	Library of Hebrew Bible/Old Testament Studies
LNTS	Library of New Testament Studies
LSTS	Library of Second Temple Studies
MissSt	Mission Studies
NTM	New Testament Monographs

NT	New Testament
OT	Old Testament
PTM	Princeton Theological Monograph Series
SBG	Studies in Biblical Greek
SCJ	Studies in Christianity and Judaism
SNTW	Studies of the New Testament and Its World
TSAJ	Texts and Studies in Ancient Judaism / Texte und Studien zum antiken Judentum

CHAPTER 1

Introduction

Resilient leadership and ethics are crucial to the success and stability of governments, corporate bodies, and institutions. Often, it seems, the need to keep an institution afloat takes priority, and leaders learn to ignore the qualms of their consciences when ethics threaten to block their ascent up the ladder. The success of Christ's handful of followers, under the still forming character of the apostles, developing into a community of hundreds, thousands, and millions today – first in Jerusalem then to the ends of the world – is enough reason to attract serious inquiry into what constitutes the success of such a community. Irrespective of the aggression exhibited within by the Jews and without by the Roman government, the Christian community in Acts defied the odds to become a formidable and charming force in the first-century Greco-Roman world.

This study explores the narratives of Acts 1–12 and 15, a text produced in the early Christian community context. We seek to demonstrate that the characterization of Peter's leadership and ethics resembles the Qumran community's leadership and ethics as it is recorded in the Damascus Document.[1] These two communities, living in the same context less than a century apart, founded on similar beliefs, very similar in organization, and facing almost the same challenges, managed to set themselves apart by going against the grain of their time. Chapter 1 will set forth our proposal and its significance to scholarship, providing a statement of the problem, a survey of the Qumran scrolls, especially CD and New Testament research, and noting methodological considerations and content outline. In chapter 2, we will discuss

---

1. From here forward the Damascus Document will be referred to as CD.

the method underlying this study. In chapter 3, we will propose the analogy for understanding Acts 1–12 and 15, namely the Qumran community, and examine its history, organization, leadership, and ethics. Chapter 4 consists of a narrative study of the passages under consideration, focusing on their setting, rhetoric, characterization, and other narrative features. Chapter 5 will seek to draw parallels between the characterization of Peter's leadership and ethics in Acts 1–12 and 15 and Mebaqqer[2] of Qumran and the ethics lived in Qumran and its camps. The final chapter will draw conclusions from the findings made in this study and recommend further areas of research in Acts and Qumran.

It is anticipated that the outcome of this research will be of significance, first to the understanding of the structure of the early Christian community, but much more to the interpretation of the book of Acts through a new analogy within its Jewish milieu. This will enhance understanding of problematic texts in Acts which are pesher inclined. Reading Acts in the light of Qumran literature will illuminate some of these problematic texts by shedding light on how a Jewish community who believed themselves to be living in eschatological times would have envisioned the message of Acts.

In this study, Peter's leadership and ethics will refer to his ability to influence[3] the community of believers in Acts in achieving the goals set by Christ in Acts 1:8, and the moral principles that govern his behavior. In this study also referred to as character traits or virtues.

1.1. The Statement of the Problem

In contrast to other New Testament characters like Jesus, John the Baptist, John, Herod, and the Pharisees on the subject of characterization and parallels drawn between them and Qumran leadership, Peter has received minimal attention to date. In view of the key role Peter plays in the New Testament, this inattention prevents New Testament readers from seeing the valuable leadership and ethical lessons embedded in this round character.

---

2. The terms Mebaqqer of Qumran, Overseer and inspector of camps or many camps will be used interchangeably in this study from this point forward.

3. Bennis, *Invented Life*; Maxwell, *Developing the Leader*; Maxwell, *21 Irrefutable Laws of Leadership*.

Ben Witherington, F. Scott Spencer, and Timothy Wiarda, among other scholars, refer to Peter in their studies as the leader of Jesus's followers,[4] a role he occupies in the text under study (Acts 1–12 and 15). Wiarda contends that Peter's leadership relationship with Jesus could be compared to the Elijah-Elisha narratives.[5] He argues,

> Since the Old Testament writings were well known among the early followers of Jesus . . . the possibility that certain of their motifs or conventions may have influenced the gospel narratives must be considered [and in this case Acts].[6]

Reading Peter's leadership relationship with Jesus in light of Elijah-Elisha narratives is very interesting. Elisha as a student of Elijah ends up with a double portion of his master's anointing. The request for the double portion is subordinated to the condition, if Elisha sees Elijah depart, he will be granted his request. In contrast, Peter, who sees the master taken to heaven in Luke and Acts, displays an extraordinary anointing – even his shadow heals the sick laid on the streets (Acts 5:15–16).[7]

In the same vein, John J. Collins, Craig A. Evans, and Alicia Myers have taken the concept of parallels between the church and Qumran communities a step further. They not only show connections between the church and Qumran communities but they further point to an understanding of the very structures from which the early Christian community and its leadership emerges. Collins and Evans argue,

> We find that the very structure of the early Christian community grows out of a typology (or set of typologies) rooted in the sacred scriptures of Israel. This structure cannot be adequately understood without a careful and nuanced appreciation of the Dead Sea Scrolls.[8]

---

4. Witherington, *Acts of the Apostles*, 116; Spencer, "Sacred to Death," 68; Wiarda, *Peter in the Gospels*, 167, 170.

5. Wiarda, *Peter in the Gospels*, 184.

6. Wiarda, 183–84.

7. However, this should not be taken to imply a double portion of Christ's power for Peter also.

8. Collins and Evans, *Christian Beginnings*, 62.

Alicia Myers further argues,

> In a manner similar to other authors from Middle Judaism, New Testament authors appeal to the authority of Israel's scripture in order to bolster their rhetoric. Thus, even noting the consistent employment of scripture alone reveals the indebtedness of New Testament authors to developing Jewish traditions and warrants exploration into connections between contemporaneous Jewish practices and the New Testament writings.[9]

Therefore, the need to locate suitable analogies for reading New Testament texts cannot be overemphasized. Robert Maddox is more precise on the matter of a suitable analogy. He argues,

> Beyond Mark (and any other gospels he may have known), the best analogies for Luke's work are the historical works of the Old Testament, and perhaps post-Old Testament Jewish histories such as Maccabees. In this tradition, the aim of historiography is more unified than in the Greek world: it is a form of confessional proclamation . . . If Luke is to some extent shaped by the style and technique of Greek historiography, he is steeped in the motivation of biblical historiography.[10]

Maddox further argues,

> From the second century onwards, at least, there was among the Christians a strong ideology of martyrdom largely inspired by the memory of the Maccabees and, of course, by the passion of Jesus. While many martyrs suffered heroically in circumstances which they had done nothing to bring on themselves, others were driven to the fanatical desire for martyrdom out of their hostility towards Rome regarded as the center of idolatry. . . . The proper business of Christians is to live at peace with the sovereign power, so far as possible, and not to play the hero. In order to encourage such an attitude, it was necessary to hold up before his readers the example of their great leaders, especially

---

9. Myers, *Characterizing Jesus*, 10.

10. Maddox, *Purpose of Luke–Acts*, 16.

Jesus and Paul, and (like Paul and the author of 1 Peter) to take the best possible view of the regime.[11]

Although Maddox's proposal is more precise, the characteristics of the disposition of the Maccabean era may not be the best analogy for Acts. The Maccabeans were more aggressive compared to the peaceful Luke-Acts community. Even the author is persuading his audience to adopt a peaceful approach to their government as much as possible.[12]

Brian Capper argues, "Acts emerges as a source which reveals good knowledge of Palestinian cultural features of the earliest community, despite Luke's evident desire to stylize his material in a manner which appealed to those readers who shared the esteem for goods in Greek popular philosophy."[13] Collins concurs with this position in his work *Jewish Wisdom in the Hellenistic Age* by stating that Hebrew traditions are cast in a "Hellenistic dress."[14] Collins and Evans have strongly argued elsewhere that it is challenging to comprehend the structure of the New Testament writings without a good grip on Jewish history, such as found in the Dead Sea Scrolls.[15] As much as it is worth noting that the prologues in Luke-Acts (Luke 1:1–4; Acts 1:1–4) have similar traits to introductions in certain Greek or Jewish histories, these historians in antiquity focused on the clarity, conciseness, and credibility of their narratives,[16] which were intended to persuade their audience that the events and persons presented are believable accounts.[17] Still there remains the need to provide a suitable analogy for reading the text of Luke-Acts that lends itself well to Jewish histories.

Darrell Bock argues that the key theme in Jewish historiography is to demonstrate that "what people are experiencing is part of the way God has acted for ages."[18] If this be so, then we must read Acts through an analogy that is in concurrent with its message (an analogy portraying God's activities as they are presented in Acts). This study therefore proposes the Qumran community

---

11. Maddox, 16, 96–97.

12. Maddox, 97.

13. Capper, "Palestinian Cultural Context," 356; Capper, "Community of Goods," 1730–74.

14. Collins, *Jewish Wisdom*, 158–77.

15. Collins and Evans, *Christian Beginnings*, 62.

16. Kennedy, *Progymnasmata*, 96.

17. Myers, *Characterizing Jesus*, 33–34.

18. Bock, *Acts*, 12.

as discussed in CD as the closest and most fitting analogy we have in Jewish histories for reading Acts, especially the characterization of Peter's leadership and ethics in Acts 1–12 and 15. The two communities of Acts and Qumran see themselves as a people living in the eschatological times, a time when God divinely intervened in history by raising up a prophetic leadership to prepare his people in a wicked generation for his visitation (Acts 2:17 cf. CD 1:1–5; 4:4; 6:11). For Qumran, God raised the Teacher of Righteousness to whom God made known his mysteries that they might teach the holy ones in the time of wickedness; for Christians, God sent his Christ to save and preserve them as a bride for the day of the Lord. Habakkuk Pesher clearly indicates that everyone who is righteous is attached to the Qumran community and is living in the end times (QpHab VIII 1–3).[19] These two communities were proud of the leadership and ethical standards they advanced in their contexts. Therefore, a comparative study of the leadership and ethics they exemplified in their time would be a highly acceptable quest for progressive scholarship in biblical studies.

The first limitation of this study will be in discussing the purpose of Acts. Several scholars have done a credible job on the subject and can be consulted.[20] However, whenever it is necessary to mention matters on the purpose of Acts, this study will give brief summaries. Second, we will not seek to establish the custodians of the Qumran literature. A very healthy conversation exists that can be of help to interested readers.[21] Third, this study does not seek to demonstrate the literary dependence of Acts on Qumran scrolls; hence our parallels will be at the level of organization, ideas, and theology. Furthermore, our comparative study between the Acts and Qumran communities will primarily use the Damascus Document. Other Qumran Scrolls will be only referenced where the researcher finds the Damascus Document either silent or inadequate to provide the necessary information.

Acts can be easily structured around two main protagonists Peter and Paul. Both had doubtful backgrounds in the Jewish and Christian

---

19. Barrera, "The Essenes of Qumran," 73–74.

20. See for example, Witherington, *Acts of the Apostles*, 21, 69, 72; Keener, *Acts*, 164; Peterson, *Acts*, 26.

21. Boccaccini, *Beyond the Essene Hypothesis*; Collins, *Beyond the Qumran Community*; Dupont-Sommer, *Essene Writings*, Meridian Books MG44; Dupont-Sommer, *Jewish Sect of Qumran*.

communities – Peter denied Jesus and Paul persecuted the people of "the way."[22] The structure of Acts could be divided based on the ministry of Peter and Paul. The parallels that have been drawn between these two prominent figures in Acts are a matter of another conversation.[23] This research will seek to examine the characterization of Peter's leadership and ethics in Acts 1–12 and 15 in light of the leadership and ethics of the Mebaqqer in the Damascus Document. This study therefore, consequently argues that the leadership and ethics lived in the two communities resemble each other.

A study of this nature could prompt many pertinent questions. Would Luke have had contacts with the Qumran community?[24] Would that be possible considering the sect's rules toward outsiders especially Gentiles like Luke? Could it be that Luke had no contacts with Qumran but the church he was writing about was influenced by the sect? To which group (Sadducees or Essenes) would one connect the influx of the priests coming to faith (Acts 6:7)? Nevertheless, we reiterate that this study will limit itself to drawing conceptual parallels.[25]

---

22. Peter denied Jesus and even went back to fishing. It is not our goal to establish the extent of the denial, as to whether it amounts to denying the faith or not, although he categorically denies being a disciple of Jesus (Luke 22:58). For his part, Paul had persecuted the church and even symbolically approved of the people who stoned Stephen through their garments being laid at his feet (Acts 7:57–8:1, 1 Tim 1:12–15), painting him as a murderer (Acts 9:1; 22:4, 1 Tim 1:13). It will be a great risk for Luke and his work, which he asserts is intended to give certainty to Theophilus, to ignore the background of these two prominent leaders in Acts (a background that could be obvious to the readers).

23. Dunn, *Acts*, xiv.

24. On this colossal question, I hereby record a few thoughts. First, Luke as a historian and researcher (Luke 1:1–4) may have had a good grasp of the Jewish faith and sects. Second, if this information concerning the Qumran community was available to outsiders like Josephus, then Luke's association with the Jewish faith must have helped him to access the story of Qumran. Third, the Qumran community referred to themselves as בני צדוק sons of Zadok (the priests) (CD 3:21; 4:3); see Fitzmyer, *Dead Sea Scrolls and Christian Origins*, 253. Also Luke reports, Καὶ ὁ λόγος τοῦ θεοῦ ηὔξανεν, καὶ ἐπληθύνετο ὁ ἀριθμὸς τῶν μαθητῶν ἐν Ἰερουσαλὴμ σφόδρα, πολύς τε ὄχλος τῶν ἱερέων ὑπήκουον τῇ πίστει. (Acts 6:7). It may be possible that through these great numbers of the priests, who may have preserved their heritage, the author of Acts received information about Qumran or they themselves influenced the burgeoning church.

25. By conceptual I mean that our parallels will focus on structures, themes, and ideas that are similar between the two leaderships and the ethics lived in the communities. Our primary concern is not with actual quotations and technical terminologies used in the two texts but the structural matrix, themes, theology, moral principles, and ideas shared in the two texts.

1.2. A Survey of Previous Scholarship on the Apostle Peter

W. H. Thomas opens our survey. He outlines the apostle's life, character, and writings throughout the New Testament.[26] However shallow the outlines may be, they set us on a course that is discriminately traveled. Carsten Thiede decries this treatment of the apostle Peter. Thiede protests,

> Today, there is no shortage on every possible aspect of Peter's life (as well as some that seem frankly impossible!) but there seems to be a little commitment to the genuine historical Peter. Yet unlike Paul, who has somewhat overshadowed him in the history of Christendom, Peter remains the most tangible, the most humanly understandable of the apostles. It is Peter, not Paul who stands out most clearly as a character in his own right, with all his strengths and shortcomings.[27]

Thiede's observation can be extended further to studies in Qumran scrolls as we will see later in this study. Tim Wiarda classifies interpretations done in this area into three categories: the first is of approaches that evaluate the gospel narratives concerning Peter on the basis of historical persons and events (whether the accounts are considered reliable or not); the second category understands narrative as symbolic presentations of theological/ ecclesiological points or veiled portrayals of ecclesiastical situations; the last category understands narratives primarily as story worlds, which he admits overlap. He groups Thiede's work and that of Oscar Cullmann under the first category.[28] This first category is of primary interest to this study, albeit the other two categories may be engaged secondarily in the study.[29]

We now turn to a brief snapshot of Peter's life. He was born in Bethsaida, and his father's name was John (John 21:15–16). Andrew was his younger brother (John 1:41). It can be inferred that he was living in expectation of the

---

26. W. H. G. Thomas, *The Apostle Peter : Outline Studies in His Life, Character, and Writings* (London: Religious Tract Soc, 1954).

27. Thiede, *Simon Peter*, 9–10.

28. Wiarda, *Peter in the Gospels*, 12–13; Thiede, *Simon Peter*; Thiede, *Earliest Gospel Manuscript?*; Cullmann, *Peter*.

29. Other scholars who have done scholarly work in this area include, Perkins, *Peter*; Bockmuehl, *Remembered Peter*; Bockmuehl, *Simon Peter*; Bond, *Peter in Early Christianity*; Lowe, *Saint Peter*.

Messiah (John 1:41). Though not explicit, it is implied that Peter was John the Baptist's disciple (John 1:35–42). Based on his having a mother-in-law (Luke 4:38–39) and Paul's testimony in 1 Corinthians 9:5, he was married. Now Jesus calls the twelve and designates them as apostles with the goal of being with them and ultimately set them forth on a mission (Mark 3:13–14). This program did not flow as smoothly as might have been expected. At the end of his time with the disciples, it was not clear they would be available for the mission. It is apparent from Luke 22:54–62 that Peter, who was unmistakably a prominent figure of the group, ultimately repudiates Jesus and goes back to his old profession, fishing (John 21:3). Luke's account in the Third Gospel leaves the readers in suspense as to what may have exactly happened to Peter who was undoubtedly charged with the responsibility of leading the group (Matt 16:19–20; Luke 22:31–2).[30] We will now turn to how Luke characterizes Peter in the Third Gospel (Luke) in an effort to see how his character develops, but also to fill the gap between Luke 24 and Acts 1.

1.3. Peter in Luke

Although this study focuses on Acts, we will proceed on the assumption that Luke is the author of both texts Luke and Acts. We will refer to the former (Luke) as the first volume and the latter (Acts) as the second volume throughout this study. However, in spite of the continuing debate on the unity of the volumes, which is not within the scope of this study, we will trace Peter's characterization from Luke solely for the purposes of sensitivity to the narrative sequence. As John Darr rightly states,

> A pragmatic approach to characterization requires that we be especially sensitive to the narrative's sequence . . . Like all narrative elements, the *character is accumulative.* Thus, the means and timing of its accumulation must be taken into account by the interpreter.[31]

---

30. If the order of the presentation of the disciples list in Matthew 10:1–4, Mark 3:13–19, and Luke 6:12–16, is something to rely on narratively, and then, Simon is clearly presented as the leader of the twelve.

31. Darr, *Character Building*, 42.

M. D. Springer on the same subject rightly notes,

> The character is not given to us like a gift in the hand, or like a picture on the wall, but . . . it does in fact accumulate. This must make perfect sense since the story, unlike the picture on the wall, moves across time – we must turn the page in order to find out what else there is to know about the character, what new actions and choices there may be to expand or modify our knowledge, what decisions we are to make about whether the character is fixed or in change, individual or antithetical to another character, minor or main.[32]

The first volume of Luke ends with a characterization of Peter that James Resseguie refers to as "Peter with a material point of view that mistakes eagerness for discipleship."[33] This leaves us with the questions: Is this the same character we expect in Acts or has he changed? If changed, how and where? We will rely on intertextual information in the Gospel of John and Pauline writings as a way to fill this gap in Luke's presentation of Peter. This study will briefly seek to explain the change in Peter's character in Acts, where he is portrayed as already enjoying full narrative authority asserted by the narrator's references, authentication by the Holy Spirit, and the right to explain scriptures.[34] A brief overview of characterization will assist us in unveiling our character in this study

Robert Alter discusses a "scale of means," the lower end of the scale, the middle and the top of the ascending scale. At the lower end of the scale, Alter observes, "character is revealed through actions or appearance – this leaves us substantially in the realm of inference."[35] He further observes that at the middle categories the character is revealed by direct speech, either by the character themself or by other characters making direct statements on the character – this leaves us in the realm of weighing the claims made in the direct statements. Due to the unreliability of some of the characters, their statements cannot be trusted, hence a need to weigh their claims on

---

32. Springer, *Rhetoric of Literary Character*, 179.

33. Resseguie, *Strange Gospel*, 150.

34. Darr, *Character Building*, 50–53.

35. Alter, *Art of Biblical Narrative*, 116–17.

the basis of how they are portrayed in the narrative before establishing their traits. Furthermore,

> At the top of the ascending scale, we have the reliable narrator's explicit statement of what the characters feel, intend, desire; here we are accorded certainty, though biblical narrative . . . may choose for its own good purposes either to explain the ascription of attitude or to state it baldly and thus leave its cause as an enigma for us to ponder.[36]

Now, armed with Alter's "scale of means," we will turn to the first volume of Luke to see how he characterizes Peter in the attempt to fill in our stated gap. Peter is introduced in the narrative of Luke in a very remarkable way (Luke 4:38–39).[37] The narrator depicts Jesus as a guest in Simon's house.[38] We are left to infer both Peter's presence during this visit and his marital status. The sick person is addressed as Peter's mother-in-law. The architectural setting, Peter's house, is not a place of safety as it should be. Peter's mother-in-law is in the house yet attacked by a fever. The narrator is silent whether Peter is in the house or outside, leaving the reader to infer whether Peter is in a place of safety or danger. Jesus rebukes the fever, it leaves Peter's mother-in-law, and immediately she got up from her sick bed and served them. The final situation of the scene's plot constrains the reader to conclude that the high fever may have represented more oppression than just physical and health oppression. Daniel Marguerat observes,

> The handicap, which appeared between the woman and the master, has been removed by an act of healing. Information about the Jewish woman in the first century Palestine surprises the modern reader: women were forbidden to serve rabbis. The way in which Peter's mother-in-law serves bears witness to her

---

36. Alter, 116–17.

37. Thiede, *Simon Peter*, 24.

38. Mark reports inner details that Luke seems to be unconcerned with. Peter's house has become a center of Jesus's activity (Mark 1:33), Jesus heals many with various diseases; they leave for Capernaum but are back again (Mark 2:1), possibly Peter's roof broken to lower the invalid down through the tiles. The kind of gatherings at Peter's home tells us that Peter had a sizeable house yet simple enough that the roof could be broken into (Mark 2:2–5; Luke 5:18–20).

cure and attests freedom, which makes her go well beyond the social conditions of the time.[39]

Διηχόνει conveys the idea of the "table service," "wait on," which suggests the table etiquette of the time. This act of service establishes acceptance between Jesus and Peter's household. It moves them from the margin to the insiders exemplified in the joyous expression of social and spiritual hospitality through the shared meal.[40] However, it is difficult to conclude how Peter as an individual may have related to this guest (Jesus) in his house. Though his later confession in Luke 5:8, Ἰδὼν δὲ Σίμων Πέτρος προσέπεσεν τοῖς γόνασιν Ἰησοῦ λέγων· ἔξελθε ἀπ᾽ ἐμοῦ, ὅτι ἀνὴρ ἁμαρτωλός[41] εἰμι, κύριε, would paint him as one still on the margin in the society at the time of Jesus's visit to his home, though we can safely infer that he is receptive of the message of the kingdom.

In Luke 5:1–11, Jesus is standing at the lake of Gennesaret, τὸν ὄχλον ἐπιχεῖσθαι αὐτῷ καὶ ἀκούειν τὸν λόγον τοῦ θεου. He is depicted as crammed between the crowd (a seemingly uncontrollable force) and the lake that represents uncontrollable space.[42] ἐπιχεῖσθαι, which can be rendered "lie upon" (it is like the crowd was literally lying on Jesus) or "rage around," could be used to describe the state of the lake behind Jesus and the crowd before him. The lake as uncontrollable space and the uncontrollable crowd provides an ideal setting to interpret Peter's inner perspective.

The lake narrative begins in glaring and depressing scarcity. Jesus is almost crushed by a surging crowd. He sees an empty boat; the fishermen are out washing their (empty) nets that caught nothing after fishing the whole night. The crowds are raging around with empty hearts in need of God's word, and Jesus is in need of a place from which to preach. Simon's empty boat positions the only person (Jesus) who is able to tame the lake and the crowd. Resseguie aptly observes that Jesus "joins symbolically with the disciples/*fishermen*[43] in the common activity of fishing, but Jesus' fishing is uncommon."[44] Finally,

---

39. Marguerat and Bourquin, *How to Read Bible Stories*, 45–46.

40. Resseguie. *Spiritual Landscape*, 70.

41. Sinners, the poor, children, women etc., were considered outsiders.

42. Resseguie, *Spiritual Landscape*, 17.

43. The word in italics is my inclusion, at this time in the narrative the fishermen are not yet disciples, therefore Resseguie may have ambitiously given them a status they have not yet attained.

44. Resseguie, *Spiritual Landscape*, 17.

Jesus turns to Peter after taming the crowd. His suggestion to Peter to launch deep in the lake seems to provoke what is pressing on Peter's mind: ἐπιστάτα, δι' ὅλης νυκτὸς κοπιάσαντες οὐδὲν ἐλάβομεν. Peter who has been quiet now speaks for the first time in the narrative. Peter is characterized as oscillating between faith and doubt, a state that will define him most in the narrative. He is quick to object to Jesus's proposal yet quick to recant his position and obey (Luke 5:5). "The lake tests the limits of human endeavor and reveals the infinite power of God."[45] Peter eventually demonstrates his willingness to obey the Word of God. It is not the first time Peter is confronted by a situation that demands his commitment to the Word of God. Jesus had rebuked the high fever in his mother-in-law (Luke 4:38–9),[46] and so by virtue of this incident, he is aware of the power of God either by direct witness or by hearing from witnesses. His failure at night is turned into success during the day. Jesus succeeds in a situation that is humanly impossible. It is natural to fish in the deep sea at night, not during the day. Resseguie captures well the significance of this scene, "yet in this dreadful failure Peter's awakening begins, as Jesus tames the recalcitrant lake and makes it yield its bounty."[47] The reader who is aware of the two volumes clearly sees Luke foreshadow the happenings of Acts where Peter is instrumental in bringing large numbers to Christ.

The lake narrative as a setting foreshadows Peter's uncontrollable character in the rest of the meta-narrative of Luke. His outspoken disposition is clearly highlighted here. His confession of being a sinner locates him as a social outcast living on the margin. He is quick to humble and confess his shortcomings, something that many in Luke's narrative will find hard to embrace as the narrative progresses and even cause them to miss the kingdom

---

45. Resseguie, 17.

46. Peter, in the first place, shows willingness to let Jesus use his boat. However, just as Jesus is through with the crowds on the shore, he pushes Peter a little from the land just like his boat. "Put out in the deep sea and let down your nets for a catch." Peter objects, but after a reflection, perhaps on who Jesus was, especially after Jesus healed his mother-in-law, he lets down the nets. Wiarda suggests that Peter's character or responses should be read in the light of a beginning Christian. Wiarda's suggestion is right but gratuitous, Peter like any other human being believes in taking charge and being in control. Fishing is his trade and he knows how to come in and go out. It is reasonably challenging for him to offer himself to inexpert direction. Yet Jesus intends to move him from the dry land, and shallow waters of self, to the deep sea of profitability where obedience and reliance to God and his word works abundantly. See Wiarda, *Peter in the Gospels*, 100–101.

47. Resseguie, *Spiritual Landscape*, 17.

of God. Peter sees his state and he hears the word of God, a characteristic of those who are in the kingdom according to Luke. Jesus's response to his fear is highly instructive: μὴ φοβοῦ· ἀπὸ τοῦ νῦν ἀνθρώπους ἔσῃ ζωγρῶν. "Just as you have been catching fish in the uncontrollable lake so shall you be catching men alive from the uncontrollable crowds" Ἀπὸ τοῦ νῦν denotes a decisive separation from the past. Peter's spiritual awakening culminates with not only a realization of his unworthiness but also a clear break from his past evidenced in ἀφέντες πάντα ἠκολούθησαν αὐτῷ (Luke 5:11b). The narrative prop of an empty boat may have represented Peter's emptiness and unfruitfulness, which is now filled with fish. The reader must be now persuaded that Jesus is able to tame the uncontrollable sea and cause it to yield fruit for mankind when they obey Jesus's word.

The next time Peter is mentioned in the narrative is in Luke 6:14. However, he is only listed as among the apostles. His renaming and the order of the list points to the significance of the character in the narrative (Luke 6:14–15). The narrator's listing of his name first indicates the significance of his position among the chosen apostles. In Luke 8:45, Peter is portrayed as the spokesperson of the twelve, and now the narrator refers to him by his new name. The setting of this scene in chapter 8 is on the way to Jairus's home. It resembles the setting of Peter's calling although it is on the other side of the lake; the crowds are equally pressing, the space (lake) is uncontrollable, and the characters are a desperate woman and a needy man (Jairus). Peter mistakes οἱ ὄχλοι συνέχουσίν σε καὶ ἀποθλίβουσιν as the prompting of Jesus's question ἥψατό μού τις. It was something different because he attests to δύναμιν ἐξεληλυθυῖαν ἀπ᾽ ἐμοῦ. Peter will not only shift between obedience and opposition to the word, but he will be also be mistaken over a few significant issues. In Luke 9:33, "not knowing" what he was saying, he suggests erecting three tents. The booths seem to point to a mistaken messianic understanding of what Peter has seen on the Mount of Transfiguration. He further mistakes his ability to protect the master and follow him everywhere even to death (Matt 26:33–35; Mark 14:29–31). To turn back to the story about the woman, just as Peter had toiled without getting fish (Luke 5:5), the woman had toiled for her health without a solution. The narrative represents Peter and the woman as both afraid and fallen before Jesus (Luke 5:8; 8:47). There is no doubt that the falling of the two before Jesus depicts surrender; a state that positions them to receive mercy from the Lord even in their most devastating situations.

Peter responds to Jesus's inquiry appropriately by pointing out that he (Jesus) is the anointed one of God, demonstrating his ability to comprehend spiritual matters. Given reference, however, this ability seems to waver, for eight days later on the Mount of Transfiguration, Peter seems to speak inadvisably from what he sees (Luke 9:33). A voice from the cloud clarified what should be embraced: οὗτός ἐστιν ὁ υἱός μου ὁ ἐκλελεγμένος, αὐτοῦ ἀκούετε (Luke 9:35). Apart from the question Peter poses to Jesus in 12:41, we do not read of him in the journey narrative from Luke 9:51–19:44. He resurfaces again during passion events. Luke portrays Peter as a real human being, struggling with understanding the divine. He is up and down, strong and weak, silent and extremely talkative.

The narrator re-introduces Peter again, with Jesus making a prediction concerning him (Luke 22:31–34). The narrator leaves a gap for the reader to fill in. We are not told where and when Satan asked to sift Peter. Jesus addresses Peter by his old name, Simon, and prepares the reader for a possible lapse in Peter's life. Peter's instability like the waves of the sea persists. The absence (silence) of Peter and other disciples on the journey to Jerusalem and its effects on the disciples is now manifested. Jesus's statement, "Satan asked" may allude to Job's story (Job 1:6; 2:1, 6). Jesus establishes that Satan does not have free access to Peter's life, he needs permission. Jesus implies that it was granted; he prepares Peter for the time of testing that is coming. Marguaret refers to the theme of the way as "a place where the master is followed, and his word heard. . . . On the way Jesus is listened to."[48] Peter seems to display an attitude contrary to that expected from the wayfarer. Jesus predicts his eminent lapse and states that he has interceded for him and others. Peter is singled out for a responsibility that "when you have returned [turned to me again][49] establish [or fix firmly] your brothers" (Luke 22:32). What follows in Luke 22:54–65 demonstrates that Peter's understanding of the way of Jesus is still wanting. Peter's spiritual formation still calls for more attention. He has committed himself to a lifestyle that is demanding yet simple. He has yet to realize that he is called to follow Jesus where he leads. He will

---

48. Marguerat and Bourquin, *How to Read Bible Stories*, 38.

49. Words in square brackets are my own suggestions, alternatively: "when you have changed your way of thinking," or "when you are converted." See BDAG, 382.

soon realize that everything that the world provides – accomplishments, self-importance, wealth – are not only inadequate but also obstacles.[50] Resseguie rightly observes,

> The journey to Jerusalem outlines the itinerary of spiritual formation: the brokenness that enables the disciple to travel the hard road. . . . The securities of this life are left behind. The obligations that seem important – indeed essential to normal strategies of survival in this world – wane in comparison to following Jesus. . . . There are no possessions to stockpile and no ladder of personal success to climb.[51]

A look at Peter's actions in the light of this description may shed light on Peter's understanding and commitment that were found wanting at times in the face of the challenges that befell the disciples. He lacked the brokenness that would have enabled him to finish the journey successfully to Jerusalem. The securities of this life stood in his way. The distraction of what he left behind to follow Jesus in Luke 5 seemed to still have had a strong grip on his life, and it hampered his devotion to Jesus and the kingdom of God.

Luke ends Peter's characterization in the first volume with suspense – we are not told what happened later; we only find a rejuvenated Peter in Acts assuming a key leadership role. The reader is left wondering how this great transformation of Peter's character came about. Since Luke seems to have deliberately created this gap for the reader to fill in, we may need to consult other New Testament writers for information to fill in the glaring gap. Thus, we turn to John and Paul's writings for the information we need in filling this gap concerning Peter's transformed character.

1.4. Peter in the New Testament

Since our goal is to fill the gap between Luke 24 and Acts 1, we will limit ourselves to only two passages that will be profitable to this quest. The gospels according to Mathew, Mark, and Luke do not offer much in accounting for Peter's sudden transformation, they only assume it. The intertextual

---

50. Resseguie, *Spiritual Landscape*, 43.

51. Resseguie, 43.

information in 1 Corinthians only states that Jesus appeared to Cephas (Peter) after the resurrection (1 Cor 15:5). But the implications of that personal communication between the Lord and Peter are vast. Paul makes the point that Jesus restored Peter. That sets the stage for what John 21 expands.

In John 21:1–3, the narrator presents a topographical setting that is quite like the setting in Luke during Peter's call (Luke 5:1–11). The sea of Tiberias provides an ideal landscape for Peter and the other disciples' awakening. Peter's call in Luke 5:1–11 was characterized by "a spiritual awakening that includes an awed sense of unworthiness in the presence of the numinous and a radical break with the past."[52] The Sea of Tiberias reminds the reader of the uncontrollable space[53] as the background of this scene. Peter's patience is tested, and his limits exposed in his decision to go back fishing; six other disciples who voluntarily follow Peter in his pursuit embrace this lapse to his old life and profession. His calling in Luke was during the day, whereas the temporal setting in John 21 is just at daybreak. Just like in Luke, also in John, they caught nothing after fishing all night. Their unfruitful toil provides an appropriate stage for them to experience God's infinite power.[54] The disciples' endeavors in the uncontrollable sea do not bear fruit. They have to reckon with the fact that only God has the power to tame the sea.[55] Resseguie makes a significant observation that in the Synoptics, Peter denies having known Jesus; while in John, Peter denies being a disciple of Jesus (John 18:17, 25–27). He further observes that

> Peter's negation is the "gravest" of all the gospel accounts since it is an absolute denial of his discipleship and his οὐκ εἰμί ventriloquizes in an odd sort of way Jesus' ἐγώ εἰμι, spoken in the garden during his arrest. Peter's over-fullness in naming and extravagant desire to follow is matched by abundant failure.[56]

However, Peter's eagerness to follow Christ is rejuvenated after Jesus's resurrection; he races to the tomb and though outrun by the beloved disciple

---

52. James L. Resseguie, *Spiritual Landscape: Images of the Spiritual Life in the Gospel of Luke* (Peabody, Mass: Hendrickson Publishers, 2004), 17.

53. Resseguie, 17.

54. Resseguie, 17.

55. Resseguie, 43–44.

56. Resseguie, *Strange Gospel*, 153.

he is the first to go into the tomb (John 20:2–7). This eagerness is demonstrated at the sea of Tiberias when he plunges himself in the sea and swims toward Jesus (John 21:7). The table etiquette depicted in John 21:9–14 sets the occasion for Jesus to receive Peter and the other disciples back to himself.[57] Resseguie rightly states,

> The threefold pledge of love corresponds to his threefold failure and prepares him [Peter] to care for the sheep and give his own life (21:15–19). . . . Peter's prominence among the disciples is then fortified with his commissioning as shepherd of the sheep, and reinforced by the subtle reminder that the beloved disciple lags behind (John 21:20).[58]

Thiede echoes,

> In the presence of other disciples, the message is clear: if there was symbolism in the catch of fish, it was meant to show that the unbroken net, pulled ashore by Peter, was like the vast numbers of coming converts to the faith, to be gathered in under Peter's stewardship, in a developed confirmation of Lk. 5:10. If there is symbolism in the feeding and tending of the sheep, it is to show that Peter's authority over and responsibility for the budding communities is restored and enhanced with no shade of blemish.[59]

Reading the characterization of Peter in Luke alongside the final chapter of the Gospel of John aids in establishing the link in the process of how Peter became a church leader in Acts. Now that we have a full picture of the development of our character courtesy of intertextuality, we will now give a brief survey of previous scholarship on our proposed analogy for reading Acts 1–12 and 15.

---

57. Resseguie, *Spiritual Landscape*, 71.
58. Resseguie, *Strange Gospel*, 154.
59. Thiede, *Simon Peter*, 95.

1.5. Survey of Qumran Scrolls and New Testament

It was the late professor Eleazar L. Sukenik, professor of the Hebrew University of Jerusalem, who first linked the Qumran finds to the Essene community,[60] followed independently by Dupont-Sommer. This supposition prompted a heated exchange among scholars with divergent views on the subject.[61] Dupont-Sommer concurs with French scholars and others in drawing attention to the many parallels emerging from a comparative study. The comparative study between the Qumran community and the early church addresses both "institutional" as well as theological concerns, community life and constitution of the early church, ordinances of baptism and the Holy Communion, even the teachings of Jesus, Paul, and John, with the fundamental doctrines of justification and predestination, Messianism and eschatology.[62] Dupont-Sommer has shown many areas of contact and parallels between the Dead Sea Scrolls and the New Testament and early Christianity; in particular, he suggests parallels between the Teacher of Righteousness and John the Baptist and Jesus.[63]

John Collins examines the degree to which the Dead Sea sect envisioned a messiah comparable to Jesus and explores the possibility that the portrayal of the Teacher of Righteousness in the Teacher hymns of the Hodayot echoes the suffering servant of Isaiah.[64] His coeditor Craig Evans discusses the "three

---

60. Another limitation of this study is in attempting to identify the custodians of the Dead Sea Scrolls. This study will use Qumran and Essenes interchangeably. It is beyond the scope of our study to delve into the business of proving the true custodians of the Qumran literature.

61. Robert Eisenman, Professor of Middle East Religions at California State University in Long Beach, states that the members of the Qumran community were not Essenes, but proto-Christians cum Zealots, a theory that was first authored by John Allegro. This theory was expanded by Michael Baigent and Richard Leigh in *The Dead Sea Scrolls Deception*, 107–8. Though identifying the community is beyond the purview of this study, Lawrence Schiffman's work should, however, be noted as he is a well-reasoned proponent of the idea that the foundation of the community was by proto-Sadducees. Robert Eisenman and Barbara Thiering have been termed as the two main defenders of the fallacy of esoteric interpretation. They both believe that the Qumran writings and the New Testament are both coded and they have finally availed the code since two thousand years. Thiering connected John the Baptist with the Teacher of Righteousness and Jesus as his rival, whereas Eisenman linked James the brother of the Lord to the Teacher of Righteousness with Paul as his rival. To these hypotheses, Florentino and Julio have ably responded. Martinez and Barrera, *Dead Sea Scrolls*, 17–26.

62. Dupont-Sommer, *Essene Writings from Qumran*, 373.

63. Dupont-Sommer, 368–78.

64. "Having authored three of its eight essays. The book begins with two articles by him on Messianism: 'A Messiah before Jesus?' and 'An Essene Messiah? Comments on Israel Knohl, The Messiah before Jesus.'" See Collins and Evans, *Christian Beginnings*, 15–35, and 37–44.

typologies used in New Testament and Qumran literature that was invoked to describe the restoration of Israel: a wilderness typology, a water immersion typology, and a typology of the number twelve."[65] In expounding "the wilderness typology," Evans and Collins briefly bring to light a character mentioned in Acts – the restoration prophet Theudas (Acts 5:36).[66] Josephus writes,

> Now, it came to pass, while Fadus was procurator of Judea, that a certain magician,[67] whose name was Theudas, persuaded a great part of the people to take their effects with them, and follow him to the river Jordan; for he told them he was a prophet, and that he would, by his own command, divide the river, and afford them an easy passage over it; and many were deluded by his words. However, Fadus did not permit them to make any advantage of his wild attempt but sent a troop of horsemen out against them; who, falling upon them unexpectedly, slew many of them, and took many of them alive. They also took Theudas alive, and cut off his head, and carried it to Jerusalem.[68]

Evans and Collins point out connections between the Dead Sea Scrolls and the New Testament by highlighting the echoes of this theme in Acts 9:2; 19:9, 23; 24:14, 22, asserting that just like the disciples of Jesus, the community of Essenes referred to itself as "the way."

Joseph A. Fitzmyer also attests to this parallel:

> All of its twenty-seven books [the NT books] were composed in Greek, and almost all of them in places outside of Palestine;

---

65. Collins and Evans, 50–53.

66. The author's (Luke's) knowledge of Theudas is expressed through Gamaliel the Pharisees. This was a common style for historians to put words in the mouth of Prominent figures in the narrative to speak what was on their mind:

> As to the speeches which were made either before or during the war, it was hard for me, and for others who reported them to me, to recollect the exact words. I have therefore put into the mouth of each speaker the sentiments proper to the occasion, expressed as I thought he would be likely to expressed them, while at the same time I endeavored, as nearly as I could, to give the general import of what was actually said.

See Charles Foster Smith, trans., *Thucydides*, 1935), 39.

67. The way Theudas recruits his followers betrays him. The Essenes had a standard procedure of receiving their members (Josephus, *J.W.* 2.137–42) which seems to contradict the process explained by Josephus in this text.

68. Josephus, *Ant.* 20.97–98.

yet many writings in those Greek writings have been illu-
mined by these new Hebrew and Aramaic scrolls discovered
at Qumran. Even though none of them refers to any Christian
or mentions any Christians, they do give us firsthand evidence
of the Palestinian Jewish matrix from which ideas and phrases
found in these Christian writings emerged and to which they
are related.[69]

Fitzmyer's argument opens the door for the possibility of considering similarities between the characterization of Peter's leadership and ethics and
Mebaqqer of Qumran and the ethics lived in Qumran. Fitzmyer further
outlines four categories of material that point to possible parallels or influence in the New Testament: important Pauline teachings, christological titles
used in the New Testament, select passages in the gospels, and light shed on
Melchizedek in the epistle of Hebrews.[70] In 1966 he drew parallels from the
book of Acts.[71] Fitzmyer's contribution to our understanding of Christian
origins and their possible connection to the Qumran finds are greatly plausible. This study seeks to broaden the scope of parallels between Qumran
writings and the book of Acts and more specifically draw parallels between
the Mebaqqer in CD and Peter in Acts 1–12, and 15. The exegetical findings
from the characterization of Peter's leadership and ethics will ultimately be
compared with leadership of the Mebaqqer and the ethics lived in his community as presented in CD.

1.6. Methodological Considerations

The nature of this study commends itself to a method of study that approaches
the biblical text as a whole. Since we are looking at the characterization of
Peter and his ethics, it is imperative that the interpretive tool enables us to
build our character sequentially, progressively through the text. Narrative
criticism with its emphasis on the whole as opposed to parts of a text will be
best suited for this investigation. It will be significant that we are able to see

---

69. Fitzmyer, *Dead Sea Scrolls and Christian Origins*, 23. See also Fitzmyer, "Jewish
Christianity," 240.

70. Fitzmyer, *Dead Sea Scrolls and Christian Origins*, 24–28.

71. Fitzmyer, "Jewish Christianity," 240.

the development of Peter as a character and understand whether the ethics he represents are something to embrace or the author wants us to avoid imitating him.[72] By examining the complexities and nuances of texts through close reading, narrative criticism will be useful in analyzing setting, rhetoric, and characterization. These narrative techniques will be pursued and engaged as signaled from the text itself – not primarily from extratextual information. Further, this study will be alive to the fact that Acts is non-fictional narrative hence the method of study must adhere to the nature of the text.

1.7. A Proposal

This study, therefore, seeks to demonstrate the resemblance between Peter's leadership and ethics in Acts 1–12 and 15 and the Mebaqqer as exemplified in CD and the ethics lived in Qumran community, by comparing the findings of a narrative analysis of Acts 1–12 and 15 to the duties and responsibilities of the Mebaqqer (overseer of camps) and Qumran ethics as presented in the Damascus Document.

1.8. Conclusion

To summarize, this work seeks to contribute to biblical scholarship by breaking new grounds on drawing parallels in the book of Acts 1–12 and 15 and CD, which are lamentably few. This will provide a wider possible understanding of the Jewish milieu for reading Acts, and enhancing an understanding of some of the problematic texts in Acts 1–12 and 15 that do not lend themselves well to any available Jewish histories prior suggested. This in turn offers fresh analogy for Peter's leadership and ethics in Acts 1–12 and 15. The findings of this study will further provide a good window into understanding the leadership and practices of the early church.

---

72. Klein, Blomberg, and Hubbard, *Introduction to Biblical Interpretation*, 433.

CHAPTER 2

Methodology

2.1. Introduction

Mining is an appropriate analogy for drawing meaning from texts. The suitability[1] of the mining equipment in most cases guarantees the quality of returns. A suitable interpretive tool is essential to demonstrate that the characterization of Peter's leadership and ethics in Acts 1–12 and 15 resembles the Mebaqqer's[2] leadership and ethics as evident in CD. Acts is a literary work as well as a historical narrative. Thus, the genre of the text is a key factor in selecting our interpretive tool. However, before moving further, it is important to note that several critical presuppositions will undergird this study in Acts 1–12 and 15. First, literature functions rhetorically; the author of Acts has purpose in mind as he writes. Luke is very explicit in the prologues of both volumes that he is aiming to produce a literary work to ground the reader in the things Christ did and taught, in order to dispel doubt and establish the reader firmly into matters of faith and practice. Second, meaning is produced by dynamic interaction of both rhetorical strategies of the text

---

1. Suitability here refers to the appropriateness of the method in being sensitive to the genre, carefully attention to the syntax, semantics, and pragmatics of a given text, among other features that are embedded in the text.

2. Qumran community in this study will refer to the community or communities guided by the Dead Sea Scrolls and may not necessarily refer to the strict group at the Qumran headquarters. Whenever we refer to the stricter group in this study, we will always indicate. We reiterate still that this study will use interchangeably the nouns Essene and Qumran.

and the interpretive structures of its reader.[3] Third, texts are not produced in vacuums; they have producing and receiving contexts. Hence the historical, social, and literary contexts in which a work was first produced, received, and read remains significant for this study.[4] Fourth, the Bible will not be regarded as merely fiction in this research.[5] This study will be sensitive to the nature and function of the text in Acts 1–12 and 15. Cornelis Bennema in response to the truism that "there are no characters without texts" notes,

> While narrative critics tend to limit themselves to the text . . . many scholars regard the narrative material of the New Testament as nonfictional in nature and as referring to real events and people in history. This means we can fill the gaps in the narrative from knowledge of the socio-historical context of the first-century Mediterranean world (rather than our imagination).[6]

In the same vein, Merenlahti and Hakola's comments about the Gospels also apply to Acts:[7]

> The gospels are not art for art's sake . . . As ideological narratives, their task was to induce the reader to believe in the values shared by the Christian community from which they emerged. The fourth Gospel makes this quite explicit, as it reads: "these things were written that you may believe that Jesus is the Christ, the son of God, and by believing you may have life in his name" (Jn 20:31).[8]

---

3. This research will avoid the popular tendency among literary critics seeking to impose meaning on the text and will seek to understand the text on its terms as much as is possible. The reader is invited to enter the world of the text by attending to the text's rhetorical strategies. This involves a genuine exploration of the syntactic, semantic, and pragmatic textual relationships. Finally, since texts will make reference to other biblical texts, the reader will seek to explore references that Acts makes to other texts, see Alkier, "Intertextuality," 8–9.

4. Darr, *Herod the Fox*, 20–21.

5. Modern literary theory is primarily focused on fiction – epic, novel or short story. See Aune, *Westminster Dictionary*, 277.

6. Bennema, *Theory of Character*, 63.

7. Though their argument addresses the Gospels, it can as well serve Acts, which of course is noted as the second of the two volumes of the Lukan text.

8. Merenlahti and Hakola, "Reconceiving Narrative Criticism," 33–34.

We will come back to this issue under character and characterization later in this chapter but it suffices to state here that the truth claims stated in the Luke-Acts narratives set Acts apart from just any literary work. Luke's commitment to historical reliability in both Luke and Acts, points to their genuineness (Luke 1:1–4; Acts 1–3).[9] Hence, it is essential to treat the characters in the narrative as representative of real historical people and the events as true happening. We now turn to examine the literary tools fitting for our task in Acts 1–12 and 15.

2.2. Literary Lenses

The historical-grammatical method and Luke's theology have informed the vast preponderance of the studies on Acts.[10] While historical methods focus on the historical context that gave rise to the text, the predisposition to focus on isolated narrative sub-units rather than the unitary view of the book defeats the ultimate purpose of this study – the characterization of Peter's leadership and ethics in Acts 1–12 and 15 in light of CD. Since Acts is a literary creation, it is important to pay attention to the literary logic used to make it into a unified whole. A method that attempts to fragment the text of Acts into its constituent parts and then to examine them individually apart from their larger literary context will obscure the larger literary context within which this study seeks to read individual passages.[11] The historical-critical method, through whose lenses most scholars have viewed Acts, is insufficient for the current study. Literary criticism that seeks to understand the text based on its language and imagery, structure and development of thought, literary forms, character, and plot, will be our consideration for this work.

Aída Besançon Spencer defines literary criticism as

> the analysis of the meaning of a written text by means of the study of the style, and how that meaning is communicated by author(s) to a reader(s). It includes the analysis of how the form is related to meaning and the aesthetic effects of language. The

---

9. Merenlahti and Hakola, 35.
10. Porter, "Literary Approaches," 84.
11. Darr, *Herod the Fox*, 14.

goal of the literary study is not historical, but the study of form, narrative, or sentence for its own sake.[12]

Spencer, however, goes on to indicate that the goal of biblical criticism is historical in nature, affirming the importance of both history and literary features. She further cites 1 John 1:1, to underscore the historical nature of the New Testament, and thus calls for a different methodology when dealing with the New Testament. "*Literary Criticism* is actually an umbrella for a spectrum of critical tools to the reading and interpretation of literary texts."[13] It is to one of these critical tools of the literary criticism, narrative criticism, that we now turn to for analysis.

2.3. Narrative Criticism

In 1982, David Rhoads coined the term "narrative criticism."[14] However, the seminal works of Norman Perrin, Thomas Boomershine, Joanna Dewey, Werner Kelber, Norman Petersen, Robert Tannehill, and Mary Ann Tolbert already in the 1970s gave birth to narrative analysis of the New Testament texts.[15] This approach to analyzing text established itself as an interpretative tool in its own right in the 1980s – with Mark Allen Powell, Daniel Marguerat, and James Resseguie[16] making distinct contributions in developing the specific tools of narrative criticism. The most significant interdisciplinary work done in the field of narrative analysis after Robert Tannehill[17] are the monographs

---

12. Spencer, "Literary Criticism," 245; Black and Dockery, *New Testament Criticism*, 245.

13. Aune, *Westminster Dictionary*, 276.

14. Rhoads, "Gospel of Mark," 412.

15. Rhoads, "Narrative Criticism," 264.

16. Powell, *What Is Narrative Criticism?*; Marguerat and Bourquin, *How to Read Bible Stories*; Resseguie, *Narrative Criticism*; Alter, *Art of Biblical Narrative*.

17. Tannehill, *Narrative Unity of Luke-Acts*.

of Mikeal C. Parsons,[18] R. L. Brawley,[19] David B. Gowler,[20] William Kurz,[21] and John Darr.[22] Tannehill, in his classic work, is an ideal model of a suitable application of the principles of narrative criticism.[23] However, Tannehill's theological inquiries in Luke as a part of his literary investigations fall short of clearly addressing historical issues, with apparently purposeful references to a few historical events in Acts 7:44–50, Luke 13:32–35; 19:41–44; 21:5–6, 20–24; 23:27–31.[24]

Narrative criticism not only examines narrative literature as a whole but also focuses on the text itself. Its text-centered nature seeks to understand the Bible on its own terms rather than in reference to something else. This method provides some insight into biblical texts for which the historical background is uncertain. Unlike the historical-critical method that requires specialized training, narrative criticism interprets the text from the perspective of the implied reader. Powell well notes, "Narrative criticism unleashes the power of biblical stories for personal and social transformation."[25] Therefore Acts as a story lends itself well to this interpretive tool.

---

18. Parsons, *Departure of Jesus*. Parsons, drawing from Torgovnick and Boris Uspensky's models, investigates Luke 24 and Acts 1: the ascension narratives, probing the various contexts for understanding the ascension stories, with a focus on how the stories independently serve as climax in Luke and commencement in Acts. See Parsons, 199. See also Spencer, "Acts," 396–97.

19. Brawley, *Centering on God*.

Brawley draws eclectically on five voices in literary studies: the hermeneutical voice focusing on pertinent questions raised in the text; "voice of Semes" examining the significance of characters in the text; the "Proairetic," symbolic and Barthes voice; to define the contours of a literary text of Acts (Brawley, 17–20).

Brawley enlists the necessary repertoire in engaging Acts:

Popular medicine, magic, soothsaying, the Roman military, the Olympian gods and their priesthood, Epicurean and Stoic philosophy, judicial and political systems, every biblical citation and allusions, Jewish eschatological expectations, commandments, purity laws, feasts, marriage customs. The nature and meaning of table fellowship, the functions and significance of the temple, and the social status of women, shepherds, priests, Sadducees, Pharisees, and toll collectors[, Essenes and Qumran community]. See Brawley, *Centering on God*, 162

20. Gowler, *Host, Guest, Enemy*.

21. Kurz, *Reading Luke-Acts*.

22. Darr, *Herod the Fox*; See also Darr, *Character Building*.

23. Tannehill, *Narrative Unity of Luke-Acts*. See also Spencer, "Acts."

24. Spencer, "Acts," 393–95.

25. Powell, *What Is Narrative Criticism?*, 85–90.

Narrative criticism is concerned with a particular type of literature. Acts as a narrative has two parts: story and discourse. A story consists of events, characters, and setting whose interactions comprise of the plot. Discourse refers to the rhetoric of the narrative, how the story is told.[26] Every story has events, characters, and settings.

This study will therefore seek to analyze the incidents that happen to Peter in different settings of Acts and note the Leadership traits and ethics he evidences in those circumstances and places. The results of these analyses will be compared and contrasted to those of the Mebaqqer in CD. We will now turn to a survey of some of the narrative strategies that will be engaged in this study.[27]

2.3.1. Setting in Acts

The setting in narrative criticism provides the background against which the narrative activities take place. The setting may be geographical (Jerusalem, Judea, Samaria), topographical (mountain, sea, desert), religious, or architectural among others.[28] It describes the traits of a character in their setting(s) and develops the character's mental, emotional, or spiritual landscape in response to the setting. The setting may also foreshadow the choices to be made in the narrative, and it provides the structure in which the story should be understood.[29]

The settings of Acts 1–12 and 15 are numerous. They can be grouped under the following categories: geographical (Jerusalem, Samaria, Lydda, Joppa), topographical (Mount of Olives and the journeys made by the apostles from Jerusalem to other places), architectural (the upper room [1:13, 9:36, and 10:13], the temple [3:1], the door [5:9]). The temporal settings (including Sabbath, Pentecost as well as days and nights), sociocultural settings (Gentiles, Samaria, unclean and clean), and props of chains (crowd, disciples and bed) among other settings, contribute immensely to enabling us to describe the

---

26. Powell, *What Is Narrative Criticism?*, 23.

27. Powell, 412–13.

28. Resseguie, *Narrative Criticism*, 87.

29. On setting in the New Testament see Rhoads, Dewey, and Michie, *Mark as Story*; Powell, *What Is Narrative Criticism?*, chapter 6; Resseguie, *Revelation Unsealed*, 15–19, 70–102; Resseguie, *Strange Gospel*; Resseguie, *Spiritual Landscape*, chapters 1 and 2.

character traits of Peter, foreshadow his choices, and describe the growth of Peter's mental, emotional, or spiritual landscape.

Geographical, sociocultural, religious, and even political settings are historically based and require knowledge of the socio-historical context to be able to make sense of the meaning of such texts. An example here will suffice. The geographical setting of Joppa in Acts 9:36–43 sheds light on the Tabitha narrative. Teresa J. Calpino states, "Joppa not only had a cultural resonance through associations with Greek mythology but also through the book of Jonah . . . one of the major motifs of the book of Jonah is rescue."[30] The setting of Joppa provokes much more than rescue. It reminds the reader of the hatred and animosity that existed between Israel and the Assyrians (Ninevites). The setting symbolically foreshadows the struggles Peter will go through to accept what God is sending him to do at Cornelius's house. Just as Jonah found it difficult to proclaim the deliverance of the Ninevites, perceived enemies of Israel, so Peter and the entire "circumcision party" will find it inconceivable for Gentiles to be saved by faith alone. Joppa as a Jewish socio-historical setting echoes the Ninevites. The setting (Joppa) is a reminder of additional narratives that are significant sub-texts. These include the city, religious and political settings of Assyria and Israel antagonism.

> For as Jonah became a sign to the people of Nineveh, so will the Son of Man be to this generation. . . . The men of Nineveh will rise up at the judgment with this generation and condemn it, for they repented at the preaching of Jonah, and behold, something greater than Jonah is here. (Luke 11:30, 32).

Jesus discusses his resurrection in the light of Jonah's stay in the belly of the fish for three days, "For just as Jonah was three days and three nights in the belly of the great fish, so will the Son of Man be three days and three nights in the heart of the earth" (Matt 12:40). Though Luke is not as specific as Matthew, a comparison of Matthew 12:40 and Luke 11:29–30 shows that they are speaking of the same incident, though with different wordings. Luke demonstrates that Tabitha's resurrection is well situated in Jewish history as presented in the story of Jonah and the resurrection of Christ.[31] Using Joppa

---

30. Calpino, *Women, Work and Leadership*, 149.

31. This reinforces our resolve to read Peter's characterization in Acts in light of the Mebaqqer. A careful examination of the New Testament may lead us to more relevant Jewish

for a setting alerts the sensitive reader to the possibility of the presence of such symbolic associations; this setting foreshadows Tabitha's miraculous resuscitation and rescue from death and furthermore prepares the audience for Peter's vision in Acts 10.[32]

This example brings several methodological issues to light. First, the setting may point the reader to historical, sociocultural, and religious connections; thus, our methodology must be sensitive to such narrative features in order to interpret a text fully. Second, narrative features may point to more than one analogy; those reflecting the Jewish milieu will be most preferred. Last, narrative criticism "is alert to rhetorical devices that may thicken and deepen the nuances of a text. The LXX undergirds much of the New Testament writers' use of OT quotes and allusions, such as Acts 2:14–28.[33] Studying it is part of the textual pursuit. Here, for instance, the setting of Joppa alerts us to the symbolic associations with the Old Testament book of Jonah, which further connects us to the Gospel texts.

2.3.2. Rhetoric in Acts

Rhetoric as the art of persuasion in narrative analysis involves numerous devices found in the biblical literature.[34] These devices include repetition (verbal repetition), the sequence of actions, framing, rhetoric questions, and irony.

2.3.2.1. Repetition

This stylistic device reiterates words, phrases, themes, patterns, situations, and actions for emphasis. It is employed intentionally to add force and clarity to a statement or motif.[35] Repetition in biblical literature helps in identifying norms, values, beliefs, and points of view the narrator considers significant. Repetition occurs in both small units and large units.

---

analogies for our characters than the more popular Greek analogies. This said, we still appreciate the work done in these areas and encourage more, and even in this study where possible we will fall back to the Greek figures yet with seated longing for a more Jewish one.

32. Calpino, *Women, Work and Leadership*, 149.

33. Fitzmyer, *Acts of the Apostles*, 251–61; Darr, *Herod the Fox*, 61–63.

34. Resseguie, *Narrative Criticism*, 41–42. For definition of various rhetorical terms see Abram, *Glossary of Literary Terms*; Aune, *Westminster Dictionary*.

35. Resseguie, *Narrative Criticism*, 42.

Luke employs the reiteration of keywords and phrases to tie together different episodes in Acts, to elaborate his theme or to present his ideological point of view in the narrative. The Ananias and Sapphira episode (Acts 5:1–11) seems to have little in common with Simon the magician (8:9–24) and the Jerusalem council (15:1–20). However, Luke uses a verbal thread to tie the three narratives together so that they illuminate one another. Peter confronts Ananias concerning their sale proceeds. He asserts that Satan has filled Ananias's heart to lie to the Holy Spirit. In the same vein, as he confronts Sapphira later he redefines the conspiracy as Satan has filled their hearts with "testing the Spirit of the Lord." Later as he confronts Simon the magician, the verbal thread of "the heart," "money," and "the Holy Spirit" is echoed again (Acts 8:20–23). Satan has planted deceit in the hearts of all three people in order to attack the Spirit of the Lord, and Luke wants his readers to understand that God and his Spirit perfectly know the state of men's hearts. In the Jerusalem council, although the thread of money is now missing, the thread of the "heart" and "God/Spirit" is maintained. After precisely conveying God's visitation to the Gentiles, Peter poses a rhetorical question to the assembly in an attempt to reveal their lack of understanding of what is happening. "Why are you putting God to the test by placing a yoke on the neck of the disciples that neither our fathers nor we have been able to bear?" (15:10). The audience cannot avoid seeing Luke's point of view concerning the matter being discussed at the council by allowing the first two narratives to illuminate the debate at the council. God has been established in the narrative as one who knows the hearts of men; thus, challenging salvation by faith among the Gentiles is testing God. If those who hear the recommendations of the council allow Satan to control their hearts, no doubt God will judge them, just as he has in the previous narratives of Ananias and Sapphira and Simon the magician.

2.3.2.2. Point of View

Point of view is one of the rhetorical devices in narrative criticism. Every author has a point of view that they expect the reader will adopt. The author establishes norms and values that ultimately serve as standards of judgment by which readers are led to evaluate the events, characters, and settings that comprise the story. In Acts we will be concerned with evaluative point of view. Acts depicts a world that includes supernatural beings and events. It presupposes an ethical position that distinguishes right and wrong responses to the acts of God. As readers of Acts, we must accept the implied author's evaluative point of view, which is in line with God's evaluative point of view. In Acts God's point of view is evident when he speaks directly but also when he speaks through agents such as angels and apostles. He is presumed to act through dreams and visions and the working of events that would otherwise be incomprehensible (e.g. Acts 10; 12:4–18, 20–25). The other point of view in Acts is Satan's point of view, which is of course negative. In Acts, Satan mostly works indirectly through agents, namely, the demons and sometimes through human characters who oppose God and his agents (e.g. Acts 4:1–7; 5:1–10; 8:9–24; 12:1–5). Powell posits, "The creation of a narrative world in which God's evaluative point of view can be determined and must be accepted as normative is a powerful rhetoric device."[36] Therefore, in reading Acts' narrative, we are constraint to accept that the apostles are the legitimate representatives of God and not the leaders of the people. We may have to believe that the baptism in the Spirit is God's new sign of God's covenant people and not circumcision.

2.3.2.3. Symbolism and Irony

Symbolism and irony are other rhetorical devices employed in narrative criticism. By these strategies, the reader is encouraged to reject certain interpretations and to accept or at least engage other alternatives.[37] Animals such as pigs, serpents, lambs, and birds such as doves may function as symbols. Powell observes that "sometimes entire actions or events are symbolic . . . Settings such as mountains, deserts, weddings and feast are fraught with symbolic meaning."[38] In Acts, numbers like 40, 120, 7, and others have sometimes been interpreted symbolically, but more specifically the temple is the most powerful symbol witnessed in Acts.

Another literary technique that has received much attention in biblical studies is irony. Symbolism and irony are related insofar as both engage in detection of multiple meanings. Symbolism implies recognition that something means more than it initially appears to mean, whereas irony implies

---

36. Powell, *What Is Narrative Criticism?*, 25.
37. Powell, 27.
38. Powell, 29.

that the true interpretation is actually contrary to the apparent meaning. Something like a great sheet descending, being let down by its four corners upon the earth (Acts 10:11–17), and the command to Peter to kill and eat are symbolic for they not only signify uncleanliness but also represent the inclusion of the Gentiles in the new community of believers. Ananias and Sapphira's responses to Peter in Acts 5:1–9 are ironic for they are contrary to what is true. Scholes and Kellogg state that "in its basic sense, then, irony is 'always the result of a disparity in understanding.'"[39] Acts is filled with ironic moments. Some of the devout men in Acts 2 mocked the apostles saying, "They are filled with new wine" (Acts 2:13) without realizing that what was happening was a fulfillment of Joel's prophecy. The man at the beautiful gate asked for alms without realizing God had destined that he walks. Peter told the Lord he had not eaten anything unclean not knowing that God was speaking about the inclusion of Gentiles in the kingdom.

2.3.3. Character and Characterization

Another essential narrative element beside setting and rhetoric is character. S. Chatman defines character as a "Paradigm of traits."[40] Whereas Joel Williams defines traits as "any distinguishable way in which one individual differs from another . . . an adjective which labels a personal quality of a character which persists over a part or the whole of the story . . . It emerges earlier or later in the narrative and may disappear or be replaced in the course of the story."[41] Wayne Booth points out that "character traits are revealed by 'showing' and 'telling' that is, they are surmised from the character's interaction with other characters and from the information mentioned by the narrator."[42] Characters can be dynamic[43] when they exhibit growth but

---

39. Scholes, Phelan, and Kellogg, *Nature of Narrative*, 240.

40. Chatman, *Story and Discourse*, 126. Character attempts to understand persons in the narrative and how the reader can reconstruct character from indicators in the text, whereas characterization refers to the author's techniques of constructing character, how the various indicators have been put along the text continuum. See Williams, *Other Followers of Jesus*; Rimmon-Kenan, *Narrative Fiction*.

41. Williams, *Other Followers of Jesus*, 58. Also Chatman, *Story and Discourse*, 126

42. Booth, *Rhetoric of Fiction*, 3–9; Resseguie, *Narrative Criticism*, 126–28. This will be further discussed in detail under the means of characterization section.

43. Dynamic or round characters manifest diverse qualities denoting that they are real people whereas flat characters have few traits and are more predictable in behavior. See Forster, *Aspects of the Novel*, 46–47.

static when they do not.[44] Forster contends, "The test of a round character is whether it is capable of surprising in a convincing way. If it never surprises, it does not convince, it is flat pretending to be round."[45]

Cornelis Bennema raises pertinent questions: What constitutes a trait? How many times must we see a trait before we refer to it as a trait proper? There are characters in Acts who appear only once, and they do not have an opportunity to show certain traits again. For example, the two disciples nominated to replace Judas (Barsabbas and Mathias) (Acts 1:23), Ananias and Sapphira (5:1–10), Ananias the disciple in Damascus (9:10–18), Rhoda, the young girl who was over excited about Peter's release from prison (12:13). In such circumstances, Bennema suggests, "A character may be established by different means. Sometimes a character may show a particular feature once but, within the theological framework of the narrative, this feature may be significant and therefore identified as trait."[46] Thus, Rhoda (12:13) appears once in the narrative of Acts, exhibits overwhelming joy and never appears again (12:14). Her joy viewed within the theological framework of the narrative, demonstrates that people who positively encountered the message of the kingdom expressed joy as an evident feature. Rhoda is not the only one who exhibited such joy; there is the lame man at the beautiful gate (3:8); the apostles, when they were beaten for preaching resurrection (5:41); when Philip preached Christ to the city of Samaria (8:8). In all these accounts joy is expressed as a feature demonstrating solidarity with the works of God. These should not be seen as random actions but as constituting an inherent quality – a trait.[47]

The narrator of Acts does not only choose what to convey about Peter as a character in Acts[48] but also arranges how and when to present this information to the audience.[49] Williams notes that this makes understanding people

---

44. Aune, *Westminster Dictionary*, 92.

45. Forster, *Aspects of the Novel*, 54. See Kingsbury, *Matthew as Story*.

46. Bennema, *Theory of Character*, 74.

47. Bennema, 74.

48. A trait is a personal quality that persists over time. Sometimes such traits are explicitly named in a narrative. Frequently they are inferred from words and actions, as suggested previously. Some characters are portrayed with only one trait. Others are given a number of traits, or developing traits, or even conflicting traits. See Flessen, *Exemplary Man*, 12.

49. Sternberg, *Expositional Modes*, 96–97.

in a narrative more challenging than understanding living people,[50] a fact a number of literary critics confirm.[51] The reader's questions are limited to the internal world of the text, and the narrator strictly controls and shapes what is available for the reader's consumption. Against this somewhat pessimistic view, Merenlahti and Hakola, argue:

> Because a non-fiction narrative claims to refer to events and circumstances of the "real" world, it is natural that the reader tries to fill any gaps the narrative may have, making use of all available information about the events and circumstances in concern. What readers of a non-fictional narrative think of a character depends not only on what the narrator reveals but also on what else the readers may know about the person who is portrayed as a character in the narrative.[52]

Characters as the *dramatis personae* are recognized by their speech, actions, clothing and their gestures and postures or by the narrator's direct evaluation of the character.

The prologue of Acts reveals its nature as nonfictional literature (1:3). The characters and events recorded in Acts refer to real events and people in history.[53] Thus, our methodology must encompass matters of socio-historical context of the text, as signaled by setting of the narrative.

In reconstructing characters based on textual clues and extratextual repertoire, Frank Kermode writes,

> School children are expected to be able to infer something called the character of Macbeth from indices scattered about Shakespeare's text. There is room for disagreement even at this level . . . There is institutional agreement that there exists an abstract-able entity called the character of Macbeth, with which all views must conform in some measure if the candidate is to pass the examination; yet there is always the possibility of being

---

50. Williams, *Other Followers of Jesus*, 55.

51. Culpeper, *Anatomy*, 105; Darr, *Character Building*, 47; Hochman, *Character in Literature*, 59–85; Forster, *Aspects of the Novel*, 69–99; Price, *Forms of Life*, 44–45.

52. Merenlahti and Hakola, "Reconceiving Narrative Criticism," 39–40.

53. Bennema, *Theory of Character*, 63.

original about the subject, for the institution urges examiners to reward originality highly.[54]

In Kermode's statement, the student has the task of reconstructing the character Macbeth using indices scattered in Shakespeare's text. On innovation, Kermode notes that in addition to characteristics mentioned in the text, readers supplement "them by inferring from the repertoire of indices characteristics not immediately signaled in the text, but familiar from other texts and from life."[55] The rubric for originality here rested on reconstructing a Macbeth that is highly impressive, syntactical, and has a semantical flow without reference to the indices in Shakespeare's text. Now, originality for the school children meant character reconstruction with disregard to the indices in the text but supplementing them by inferring from other texts and life. Kermode encourages readers to be creative, "drawing from their own experiences outside the text but familiar from other texts and from life,"[56] Though Bennema encourages literary critics to investigate socio-historical issues of the text, Kermode's approach is insensitive to the Bible as nonfictional text, since the purported originality ignores "the indices of the text and supplements it with human creativity and experience."[57] Although this may be helpful in some areas, it exposes the biblical text to reader-response approaches that heavily rely on the readers' presuppositions.

We will however study the characterization of Peter's leadership and ethics in Acts 1–12 and 15 in context by investigating its textual clues and the extratextual repertoire they signal in the text. Luke uses devices and techniques in writing Acts that if followed should lead his readers to the proper interpretation of his work. But it suffices to state here that this study will interact with CD in the effort to provide a suitable extratextual repertoire in understanding Acts 1–12 and 15.

---

54. Kermode, *Genesis of Secrecy*, 77.
55. Kermode, 77–78.
56. Bennema, *Theory of Character*, 63.
57. Kermode, *Genesis of Secrecy*, 78, and Benemma, *Theory of Character*, 63

2.3.4. The Nature and Means of Characterization in Acts 1–12 and 15

We have defined character as a network of traits.[58] However, "characterization refers to the elements in a narrative text which state or presents the traits of a particular character."[59] We will draw together various character indicators embedded in Acts that will aid us in exploring Peter's leadership and ethics in Acts.

First, the narrator or the character may directly state the trait of a character.[60] The narrator of Acts 1–12 and 15 is outside the narrative. He has the privilege of accessing the characters' thoughts and feelings, a fact that is depicted in how he refers to the characters by name and the third person pronouns. He is omniscient, able to know the thoughts of the characters and make comments on characters. Therefore, his comments will be taken at the highest level in Alter's scale of means; consequently, we will treat the narrator's comments as certain.[61] Comments like, there were ἄνδρες εὐλαβεῖς (2:5), the multitude was συνεχύθη (2:6), they ἐξίσταντο καὶ διηπόρουν (2:12), others διαχλευάζοντες (2:13), κατενύγησαν τὴν καρδίαν (2:37), the man at the beautiful gate was χωλὸς (3:2), Rhoda, τῆς χαρᾶς οὐκ ἤνοιξεν τὸν πυλῶνα, (12:14), Cornelius was a εὐσεβὴς καὶ φοβούμενος τὸν θεὸν (10:2), will be understood as reliable indicators of character traits. Further, Peter and the apostles are portrayed as agents of the Holy Spirit in Acts. That legitimation is by the Spirit or a person who is portrayed as his true agent. The comments of the apostle and saints will be weighed seriously in this study and generally treated as reliable for the purposes of characterization. In sum then, direct statements and evaluation of Peter by the narrator, the apostles, or other saints will be treated as certainly underlining a character trait of Peter.

Second, the narrator or a character may express an evaluation of what a character is like without directly stating a trait.[62] In this particular evaluation

---

58. Williams, *Other Followers of Jesus*, 60.

59. Williams, 60.

60. Bar-Efrat, *Narrative Art*, 53–54. Also see Berlin, *Poetics and Interpretation* 34–36; Gowler, *Host, Guest, Enemy*, 55–59; Rimmon-Kenan, *Narrative Fiction*, 59–60; Sternberg, *Poetics of Biblical Narrative*, 476.

61. Powell, *What Is Narrative Criticism?*, 26.

62. Sternberg, *Poetics of Biblical Narrative*, 476–77; Alter, *Art of Biblical Narrative*, 117; see also Bar-Efrat, *Narrative Art*, 56–58.

of the character, the narrator describes an action or other indirect clues to a character trait.[63] Instead of the narrator of Acts openly stating that Peter was bold, he portrays him as standing up and lifting up his voice and addressed them (2:14). This is done against the backdrop of the confusion and scorn in verses 12 and 13. Similarly, at the beautiful gate, the narrator depicts Peter as giving the lame man his hand to lift him up, an evaluation that shows him as supportive, kind and caring (3:7). In Acts 5:40–42, the narrator does not directly refer to the apostles' godly defiance of the council. Although the council had forbidden them to speak in the name of Jesus, the apostles "did not cease teaching and preaching that the Christ is Jesus" 5:42. Moreover, they were "rejoicing that they were counted worthy to suffer dishonor for the name" (5:41), thus demonstrating the depth of their commitment to Jesus. In all these incidences, the narrator's evaluation is a reliable indication of the apostles' character.

Third, a character may express an evaluation of another character through the use of drastic action that speaks for itself.[64] If God can be described as a character in Acts, then when the apostles are in prison, God remains silent but sets them free (12:7–10). Thus, God communicates. The religious leaders lock up the apostles in prison and God says nothing but sets them free by his agent – an angel of the Lord (5:19–21; 12:7–10). Hence God communicates his understanding of these characters through deeds rather than through words.[65]

Fourth, a narrator may show the traits of a character by presenting the character's inward thoughts.[66] The narrator of Acts in several places shows the traits of characters by this means. He shows the inward thoughts of the beggar at the beautiful gate – ὁ δὲ ἐπεῖχεν αὐτοῖς προσδοκῶν τι παρ' αὐτῶν λαβεῖν (3:5); he also shows the inward thought of Ananias and his wife Sapphira – καὶ ἐνοσφίσατο ἀπὸ τῆς τιμῆς, συνειδυίης καὶ τῆς γυναικός, καὶ ἐνέγκας μέρος τι παρὰ τοὺς πόδας τῶν ἀποστόλων ἔθηκεν (5:2); and of the high priest and

---

63. Williams, *Other Followers of Jesus*, 61.

64. Sternberg, *Poetics of Biblical Narrative*, 476–77.

65. Williams, *Other Followers of Jesus*, 63.

66. Sternberg, *Poetics of Biblical Narrative*, 477–78; Rimmon-Kenan, *Narrative Fiction*, 63; Alter, *Art of Biblical Narrative*, 117.

the party of the Sadducees – Ἀναστὰς δὲ ὁ ἀρχιερεὺς καὶ πάντες οἱ σὺν αὐτῷ, ἡ οὖσα αἵρεσις τῶν Σαδδουκαίων, ἐπλήσθησαν ζήλου . . . (5:17–8).[67]

Fifth, the narrator may show the traits of a character by presenting the character's actions.[68] When Peter went to Cornelius's house, Cornelius fell down at his feet and worshipped him. Yet Luke presents Peter's action of raising him up to show Peter's humility. The lame man's action, καὶ ἐξαλλόμενος ἔστη καὶ περιεπάτει καὶ εἰσῆλθεν σὺν αὐτοῖς εἰς τὸ ἱερὸν περιπατῶν καὶ ἀλλόμενος καὶ αἰνῶν τὸν θεόν (3:8), demonstrates his character trait of joy. Though chapter 7 is not within our scope in the study, Luke presents the actions of the characters who stoned Stephen in the manner described here (7:57). The action, Κράξαντες δὲ φωνῇ μεγάλη, συνέσχον τὰ ὦτα αὐτῶν, καὶ ὥρμησαν ὁμοθυμαδὸν ἐπ᾽ αὐτόν· (7:57), depicts the intensity of their trait of anger toward Stephen.

Sixth, the narrator may show the traits of a character by presenting the character's speech.[69] Luke employs both words and actions of his characters to show their traits. He uses the speeches of the apostles to demonstrate their boldness (2:14–41; 4:5–12; 7:16–60). Peter's speech denotes an honest and truthful man whereas the speeches of Ananias and Sapphira denote their character trait of deception. The speeches of Peter and Simon the sorcerer likewise reveal their character traits (8:19, 24; 20–23). The helplessness of the rulers of the people to punish the apostles shows their lack of power and weakness, portraying them as rulers lacking in authority (4:21).

Seventh, the narrator may show the traits of a character by presenting the character's appearance.[70] This device is not explicit in Acts. Nevertheless, Stephen's θεὶς δὲ τὰ γόνατα (7:60) shows his surrender and submission to God. Correspondingly in the same setting, Saul appears as one with the people who stoned Stephen. This portrayed by the act of laying their clothes at his feet, denoting that Saul was one in authority. Probably the most fitting appearance here for this device of detecting traits is Herod's appearance in his

---

67. More of this could be seen in Acts 5:33; 12:1–4 etc., and in this situation, a reader is left to make inferences because the evaluation is not certain.

68. Bar-Efrat, *Narrative Art*, 77–78; Alter, *Art of Biblical Narrative*, 116; Rimmon-Kenan, *Narrative Fiction*, 61.

69. Bar-Efrat, *Narrative Art*, 77–78; see also Alter, *Art of Biblical Narrative*, 116.

70. Bar-Efrat, *Narrative Art*, 48–53; Alter, *Art of Biblical Narrative*, 116; Rimmon-Kenan, *Narrative Fiction*, 65.

kingly robes and taking his seat upon the throne (12:20–23). This appearance is viewed against the background of his anger toward the people of Tyre and Sidon who had come to make peace in the light of their dependence on the king for food. It is followed by an address (the contents of the speech are not given) and the response from his audience. God's judgment portrays Herod as arrogant and proud (12:23).

Eighth, the narrator may highlight the traits of a character using an analogy.[71] Luke employs this device shrewdly in placing the leaders of Israel and the apostles in similar circumstances and draws the reader to their diverse ways of approaching the issues of interpreting the word of God (4:5–7; 5:17). The contrast between Barnabas and Ananias and Sapphira seems to set this device on stage for the reader to infer the traits of these characters and decide what they adopt (4:32–33; 5:1–11). The juxtaposition of the power of God and magic power in Samaria, and Peter and Simon the magician depicts the operation of this device in Acts. The traits of Peter, such as faithfulness and integrity among others, are demonstrated.

Then last, the narrator may influence the reconstruction of a character's traits through the order of presentation. Resseguie suggests,

> The arrangement of events in a plot can be ordered to achieve rhetorical, emotional, or artistic effects. A plot can be ordered to convince the reader of a new point of view or persuade the reader to adopt a different set of values, beliefs, or norms, or catch the reader by surprise creating delight or frustration. Ordering alone is not the only way to convince, persuade, or move the reader to a particular end.[72]

Williams further states, "First impressions are important in life, but they are more important in narratives because in narratives they are controlled by the narrator."[73] The narrator of Acts portrays Peter as presiding over the official inception of all new communities of believers from Jerusalem, Samaria, Judea and the Gentile world, thus depicting his leadership trait. He presents Peter and John but never allows John to speak, subordinating him to Peter to

---

71. Berlin, *Poetics and Interpretation*, 40; Rimmon-Kenan, *Narrative Fiction*, 67–69; Sternberg, *Poetics of Biblical Narrative*, 479–80.

72. Resseguie, *Narrative Criticism*, 208.

73. Williams, *Other Followers of Jesus*, 66.

show the leader of the two. The narrator places the presentation of the lame man at the beautiful gate, and the rebuke of Ananias and Sapphira before the council, hence vindicating the apostles as faithful representatives of God over the unfaithful leaders of Israel.

Before we sum up this study on character and characterization, it is vital to engage the subject of how to categorize and label the various traits we observe in the characters in Acts. Chatman argues, "Characters as narrative constructs do require terms for description, and there is no point in rejecting those out of the general vocabulary of psychology, morality, and any other relevant area of human experience."[74] This is true for the study of character in both ancient and modern narratives. Acts 1–12 and 15, does not provide names for all the character traits we hope to infer. Thus, it becomes the responsibility of this study carefully to name every character trait inferred. Questions arise when readers find themselves in such complex situations. How many times should a trait show up to determine a character? What perimeters guide the naming, since one sentence, appearance, and action may mean one thing in this community and completely the opposite in the other. Chatman rightly observes that "It is interesting to consider how traits acquire names. It turns out that they are culturally coded."[75] Since we have promised to read our text in the culture of the general text, the Bible, it will be imperative that we adopt a naming that is relevant to this culture. In the same vein, Chatman observes that:

> The introduction of trait-names can be seen to follow this principle of cultural (not psychological) determination to a striking degree. Presumably, human beings through countless ages had displayed such qualities as *devotion*, *piety*, and *patience*, but these terms were not established with their present meaning until the church made of them recognized and articulated Christian virtues.[76]

---

74. Chatman, *Story and Discourse*, 138; Bennema, *Theory of Character*, 54. See Allport and Odbert, *Trait-Names: A Psycholexical Study*, 17, cited in Chatman, *Story and Discourse*, 124

75. Chatman, *Story and Discourse*, 123.

76. Chatman, *Story and Discourse*, 123; See Allport and Odbert, *Trait-Names: A Psycholexical study*, 2.

Chatman goes ahead to name more sources of trait-names – astrology, Galenian medicine, Neoclassicism, reformation, romanticism, psychology, and psychoanalysis. However, of interest to this study is the cultural source labeled Christian virtues by the church. Contrary to the fiction narratives Chatman consults to conclude that there are no clear names for traits, Acts has some clear places where the narrator gives the trait-name. Still in many scenes and episodes, we must infer as accurately as possible and within the culture. It is worth noting that some trait-names have a rich family of synonyms; where possible, two trait-names may be provided for clarity. Regarding the frequency of a trait's appearance necessary to be considered a reliable character trait, Chatman states,

> The relative persistence of a trait is critical. The narrative audience does not perform statistical analyses, but their evidence is empirical. And the observation that traits generally overlap is equally significant, at least for classical narratives. It contributes to that sense of the verisimilar consistency of characters that is the cornerstone of fiction, at least of the social variety.[77]

Bennema has also suggested that a trait may be considered stable and certain when it appears once yet within the theological framework of the narrative or the narrator's ideological point of view.[78]

2.4. Approaching Acts as a Literary Work

The intratextual investigation in this study will closely examine Acts, focusing on the indices the author has embedded in the text – plot, setting, rhetoric, point of view. After establishing any signals that point to connections to other texts, we address the second phase of our study of Acts, intertextual analysis. Darr indicates,

> The text of Luke-Acts contains crucial indicators of the type of extratextual repertoire (including the intertext) . . . that the reader had to know in order to engage it properly . . . [the reader should] have a good grasp of the LXX as well as a solid

---

77. Chatman, *Story and Discourse*, 122.
78. Bennema, *Theory of Character*, 74.

grounding in the Greco-Roman literary and social conventions
of the late first and early second centuries . . . basic facts about
Jesus' life and death and the beginning of the church (i.e. "the
things you have been told," Luke 1:4).[79]

Rather than setting aside the text to pursue extratextual indices, we will rely
on the text to point to the extratextual repertoire that our text may signal
through setting and other embedded devices. This will define how we will
reconstruct our character without drifting into imagination and imposing
our own extraneous presuppositions onto the text. Darr continues,

The characters of Luke-Acts are delineated to a certain degree by
the geographical and cultural settings within which the readers
encounter them. That is, such setting furnishes valuable clues
as to how to the reader should assess the significance of the
characters and evaluate their relationships one to another . . .
locations such as Bethlehem, Galilee, Jerusalem, the area of
the Jordan river, Samaria, Athens, and Rome as well as topographical features such as mountains, plains and deserts carry
theological connotations (often extratextual) and thus prove to
be meaningful contexts for understanding characters and their
relationship in Luke-Acts.[80]

These arguments are readily applicable to our text of study – Acts 1–12 and
15, and we have already demonstrated how setting is directly applicable to
our study in the discussion of Joppa above.

The subject of proper interpretation is fundamental to the characters of
Acts. The authority to interpret the word of God repeatedly seems to trig-
ger conflict between the leaders of the people and the apostles in Acts (Acts
4:18–22; 5:27–42; 7:1–60). The two groups both claim to speak for God. They
both enjoyed the authority to interpret Scripture to their communities yet
with highly incompatible meanings. They greatly disagree and the reader is
in limbo as to whom to follow in Acts. The subject of how God validates the
correct point of view in reading the biblical narratives of Acts is a matter of
concern. Darr inquires, "How, then, is the reader made aware of God's actions

---

79. Darr, *Herod the Fox*, 61–62.
80. Darr, 70–71.

and will? How does one determine what God – this invisible, mysterious super-agent – has done? The answer, of course, is that the readers are provided with carefully-authenticated oracles which explicate how the divine impinges on personages, events and natural forces."[81] In Acts, Jesus emphasized the need for the disciples to wait in Jerusalem for the father's promise (1:6). We will elaborate on this in chapter 4 but notice that it is the Spirit who authenticates the works of God in Acts. In the same vein of thought, Darr maintains,

> Every speech that purports to represent the divinity (especially prophetic or predictive words) must bear the Spirit's stamp of approval or else it remains subject to suspicion. Those sayings that are authorized by the Spirit are always borne out in the narrative (i.e., they are fulfilled). Even sayings of relatively minor figures . . . take on great significance when the narrator informs us that they are inspired by the *Pneuma tou theou*.[82]

Darr continues,

> The scriptures are a primary oracle through which the divine impinges upon the characters and events of Luke-Acts. In Luke's hierarchy of authority, however, even the promises, predictions, and prefigurations found in scripture are placed under the aegis of the Spirit . . . The scriptures alone are not sufficient to legitimate anything; they too must be "accredited" in each case by the Spirit or by a figure who has the Spirit's sanction.[83]

Joel B. Green raises a very thoughtful argument against this kind of approach to legitimation of authority. Though I will not deal with the details here, Green contends that the commonly held view in reading Acts 6:1–4 that "the apostles hit upon delegation as a key ingredient of effective leadership is problematic because of its failure to work theologically with what Luke has given us."[84] The first of his two problems is of interest to this study for it impinges on the means of legitimation introduced above. Green cautions,

---

81. Darr, *Character Building*, 51.
82. Darr, 51–52.
83. Darr, 52–53..
84. Green, *Practicing Theological Interpretation*, 65.

Legitimacy justifies the position of a person or group, but at the same time it sets boundaries around that person or group's behavior; their status is legitimate insofar as they operate within the boundaries of their legitimation.[85] Rather than representing the nature of the gospel, the apostles, I am arguing, have transgressed the good news.[86] Indeed, rather than presuming that the apostles are above reproach, we ought to wonder about the opposite.[87]

Green presents a strong theological argument here that deserves serious consideration. Green opines that the apostles transgressed the good news in prioritizing prayer and the word[88] to serving tables. We will interrogate Green's position conclusively in chapter 4 when we examine the passage in question (6:1–6).[89]

Back to our validation of God's point of view in Acts, "The scriptures alone are not sufficient to legitimate anything; they too must be 'accredited' in each case by the Spirit or by a figure who has the Spirit's sanction."[90] The scope of this study presents a number of problematic passages (5:1–11; 6:1–6; 8:4–24; 15:6–22) that scripture alone may not be sufficient to validate unless the Spirit or a person sanctioned by him also accredits them. For example, let us consider the Jerusalem council scene. On one hand the "circumcision party" has scriptural basis for their line of thought that circumcision is a sign

---

85. See Green, *Practicing Theological Interpretation*, 66. Seymour-Smith, *Macmillan Dictionary of Anthropology*, 166.

86. See Green, *Practicing Theological Interpretation*, 66. That the Jerusalem apostles are in need of ongoing conversion is transparent later in the narrative of Acts, 11: 1–18, where their criticism of Peter for sharing in the hospitality of gentiles is overturned by Peter's explanation.

87. Green, *Practicing Theological Interpretation*, 65–66.

88. Green, *Practicing Theological Interpretation*, 65–67. The leaders of the people had been entrusted with authority; however according to Green, "Legitimacy justifies the position of a person or group, but at the same time it sets boundaries around that person or group's behavior; their status is legitimate insofar as they operate within the boundaries of their legitimation." Having lost a character that is consistent with one sanctioned by God, these leaders forfeited their legitimation consequently the authority to speak for God as seen in Acts 3–5.

89. Green seems to have overstretched his argument against Parsons' view (see Parsons, *Acts*, 83–84) by challenging the apostles decision as untheological and inconsistent with "what Luke has given us." The decision to focus on prayer and the ministry of the word is equally theological and I would posit that serving tables, as much as it is theological, is subordinate to the latter; see Green, *Practicing Theological Interpretation*, 65–66.

90. Darr, *Character Building*, 52–53.

of promise to Abraham and his seed (which Israel naturally and Gentiles spiritually claim to be). The stipulations of that covenant demand that any of Abraham's seed who does not observe this rite should be cut off. On the other hand, Peter has had a vision (Acts 10) with clear instructions, and Paul and Barnabas have prophetic worship in Antioch (Paul also has the Damascus road experience in Acts 9) that set them apart for the Gentile mission (Acts 13:1–3). Scripture alone could not resolve these issues, but the clear evidence that God is giving the Gentiles the Spirit just as the Jews had received it is what stilled the assembly (15:12).

At this point, it is to summarize the many things we have stated in this chapter Narrative criticism looks at Acts as a whole and the text is autonomous. Nevertheless, we have clarified that independence is not isolation; we will read Acts as literature but non-fiction. Acts is the word of God and thus we will treat it indeed as God's expressed will to man. However, we will attend closely to the embedded devices and patterns that contribute to proper interpretation. A close reading of its settings and the socio-historical contexts is required. Drawing out verbal threads tying dissimilar episodes together allows them to illuminate each other.

Luke has a burden for persuasion and so his language is loaded with rhetoric strategies. His chosen "original reader" is a potential/incipient believer (friend of God – Theophilus), whose very name implies that he is well disposed toward, receptive of, and indeed eager to witness and understand the divine agenda as it is set forth in the text.[91] Theophilus's anticipation is heightened; what Jesus began to do in the first volume continues noticeably in his absence in the second volume. Jesus's followers are under command not to leave Jerusalem until the promised gift comes (1:4). The promise of the Father is elevated above service and situated in a place of indispensability for the characters. As the subject of the kingdom seems to linger, Jesus evidently embraces it yet subordinates it to the promise of the Father. Luke has set the stage for his reader. What Jesus began to teach and do calls for the ears of the student and the eyes both to see what he does and hear what he teaches.[92] Our characters will be analyzed in relation to how they hear and see what the apostles teach and do. When the Holy Spirit has come upon them, they will

---

91. Darr, 55.
92. Darr, 56.

become witnesses. The reader is persuaded already by the significance of what the Spirit brings into the witness's life and the community. It might not be Luke's purpose to portray the leadership and ethics of Peter. Yet Theophilus who is now acquainted with Jesus's leadership and way of life will be interested to see how the community of believers functions – now that Jesus has ascended to heaven – and what the apostles' daily lives and normal dealings with people will look like. Luke shows how characters respond to God's spokesperson, Peter. Characters are evaluated on the basis of their response or rejection of God's message as presented by the one of the apostles (Peter). Beverly Gaventa states, "Luke presents and assesses these human characters in relationship to their place in and reception of the larger story of God (or story of Israel). What makes human characters interesting or important for Luke pertains to their response or resistance to God."[93] My main rule of judgment for evaluating characters in this study is how they respond to (or resist) Peter as the emerging leader of the believing community and the ethics he models in Acts. As we have stated in our nature and means of characterization, we will infer character traits that are revealed in the interactions of our character, Peter, coupled with what the narrator shows or tells us about Peter's leadership and ethics. These character traits will be given terms of description that reflect the Christian culture.

The results of this reconstruction of Peter's leadership and ethics will ultimately be compared to the Mebaqqer of many camps as discussed in CD and the ethics lived in the community. We reiterate that Qumran community discussed in CD is the best and closest analogy possible for reading Acts 1–12 and 15, since both communities believed that they lived in the eschatological times. At this time, God intervened by providing leadership that would guide both communities in living a life worthy of his holiness in readiness for the day of his visitation.

In spite of the potential benefits that narrative criticism has to offer in biblical studies, a number of objections have been raised among its critics concerning its legitimacy and advisability of using it in the study of Gospel, and consequently Acts. We will note here three of the objections that are relevant to this study. First, narrative criticism imposes on ancient literature concepts drawn from the study of modern literature. Second, it seeks to

---

93. Gaventa, *Acts of the Apostles*, 27.

interpret New Testament narratives through methods devised for the study of fiction. Third, narrative criticism lacks objective criteria for the analysis of texts. Petri Merenlahti and Raimo Hakola contend,

> The literary unity of the Gospels should not be exaggerated. . . . While we emphasize that the Gospels are non-fictional narratives by nature, we do not take this to mean that narrative criticism should stop making any questions that concern the "literary" aspects of the Gospels and replace such questions for "historical" and "sociological" ones. . . . that narrative analysis of the Gospels should be methodologically as inclusive and comprehensive as possible.[94]

Some of the objections raise valid points. However, cognizant of the fact that none of our methods of analysis in biblical studies are without defects, and more so most of the objections are directed at the larger literary study and not specifically narrative criticism, we will proceed albeit warned of the pitfalls involved. This study will seek to examine our text, engaging the many potentials benefits that narrative criticism brings to biblical studies.

Here, we briefly turn our focus to comparative study. Having done a character study of Peter's leadership and ethics as it is presented in Acts, the results of the study will be compared to the Mebaqqer's duties and responsibilities and the ethics lived at Qumran. Since the discovery of the Dead Sea Scrolls seventy-one years ago, parallels are constantly being adduced and held in different areas of biblical studies especially the New Testament. Some scholars have argued that the Dead Sea Scrolls will go a long way in demystifying the structure of the early Christian community.[95] However, Samuel Sandmel in his SBL presidential address for 1961 under the title "Parallelomania,"[96] sternly

---

94. Merenlahti and Hakola, "Reconceiving Narrative Criticism," 47–48. Merenlahti and Halako acknowledge that their approach parallels not only Bakhtin's early translinguistics but also recent sociolinguistics and socio-rhetorical approaches to early Christian literature, e.g., Robbins, *Texture of the Texts* and *Tapestry of Early Christian Discourse*. See Merenlahti and Hakola, "Reconceiving Narrative Criticism," 47fn84.

95. Evans, "Jesus, John," 62.

96. Sandmel admits to have forgotten the author and the book where he first encountered the term parallelomania. However, he points out that A. T. S. Goodrick, *The Book of Wisdom* (New York, 1913), 405, apparently attributes the phrase to Menzel, *De Graecis in libris Koheleth et Sophiae vestigiis*, 40. Goodrick gives neither the place nor the date of publication. Perhaps it is Menzel, cf. Charles, *Apocrypha and Pseudepigrapha*, 533.

cautions scholars against these exaggerations. However, he concluded his article on a superb note describing the ideal scholarly atmosphere present then.[97] We embrace Sandmel's warning fully and similarly his encouragement. We will vigorously yet carefully present our viewpoints, freely, as we vie with each other for acceptance in the scholarly society. His article remains very significant to this study as we seek to move this discussion further by pointing out similarities between Peter's leadership and ethics and the Mebaqqer and the ethics lived in Qumran. We applaud Sandmel for his objectivity in acknowledging that there is a level of utility and worth to the scrolls. He further opines, "I shall continue to believe, respecting the scrolls and early Christianity, that they contribute a few more drops to a bucket that was already half-full."[98] It is the goal of this study that we will be able to contribute a few more drops to the bucket by drawing accurate and full depth similarities which are historically recognizable and concrete.

This study is indebted to the significant interdisciplinary work done in the field of narrative analysis by Robert Tannehill,[99] and thereafter the monographs of Parsons, Brawley, Gowler, William Kurz, and Darr.[100] More significantly the characterization paradigms of character reconstruction by Seymour Chatman, Shlomith Rimmon-Kenan, Mieke Bal, John Darr, Alicia Myers and Cornelis Bennema among others upon whose work this methodology stands.[101]

---

97. Sandmel, "Parallelomania," 13. Sandmel notes "our Society should be host to differences of opinion, and even acute ones. We do not want to arrive at some pallid unanimity, but rather to be the market place in which vigorously held viewpoints, freely expressed, vie with each other for acceptance."

98. Samuel Sandmel, "Parallelomania," *The Society of Biblical Literature* Vol. 81, no. No. 1 (March 1962): 13.

99. Tannehill, *Narrative Unity of Luke-Acts*.

100. Parsons, *Departure of Jesus*; Brawley, *Centering on God*; Gowler, *Host, Guest, Enemy*; Darr, *Herod the Fox*; see also Darr, *Character Building*.

101. Chatman, *Story and Discourse*; Rimmon-Kenan, *Narrative Fiction*; Bal, *Narratology*; Darr, *Character Building*; Darr, *Herod the Fox*; Myers, *Characterizing Jesus*; Bennema, *Theory of Character*; Resseguie, *Narrative Criticism*; Resseguie, *Spiritual Landscape*; Resseguie, *Revelation Unsealed*; Alter, *Art of Biblical Narrative*; Bar-Efrat, *Narrative Art*; Powell, *What Is Narrative Criticism?*; Springer, *Rhetoric of Literary Character*, 179.

2.5. Conclusion

For the reasons noted above narrative criticism is the best suited method in examining Acts 1–12 and 15. As a method that upholds the autonomy of the text, it relies on the rhetorical clues embedded in the text that point to the relevant socio-historical context of the text.

CHAPTER 3

The Qumran Community

3.1. Introduction

In this chapter, we will set forth the proposed analogy for Acts in this study. We have alluded to the significance of the extra-biblical repertoire in this process. Iser notes, "The repertoire consists of all familiar territory within the text. This may be in the form of references to earlier works, or to social and historical norms, or to the whole culture from which the text has emerged – in brief to what the Prague structuralists have called the 'extratextual' reality."[1] Darr further summarizes Iser's familiar territory in what he calls four overlapping regions: "common known historical facts and figures, classical or canonical literature, literary conventions such as stock characters, type scenes, and topoi and the like; and social norms and structures."[2] This chapter will focus on the first, second, and the fourth section in Darr's summary since the third one has been discussed in the methodology at length.

I propose the Qumran community[3] as an excellent comparison in seeking to understand Acts. The early church in Acts echoes the Qumran community's social life and their theological predispositions in several ways.

---

1. Iser, *Act of Reading*, 69.
2. Darr, *Herod the Fox*, 92.
3. As previously stated, Qumran community will be used interchangeably with Essenes in this work. Thus, we proceed on the presupposition that the custodians of the DSS were the Essenes. We will indicate when referring to the stricter Qumran community class that seems to have been resident at Qumran. Qumran was at most one among the many camps or settlements of the Essene community see Collins, *Beyond the Qumran Community*, 10.

Both communities are responding to almost identical challenges in similar communities, though at different times. The two communities of Acts and Qumran, see themselves as a people living in the eschatological times, when God would divinely intervene in history by raising up prophetic leadership to prepare his people in a wicked generation for his visitation (Acts 2:17; cf. CD 1:1–5; 4:4; 6:11). For the Qumran community, God raised the Teacher of Righteousness to whom God made known his mysteries that he may teach the holy ones in the time of wickedness. To Christians, God sent his Christ to save and preserve them as a bride for the day of the Lord. The Habakkuk Pesher clearly indicates that everyone who is just is attached to the Qumran community and is living in the end times (1QpHab VIII 1–3).[4] These two communities were esteemed of the leadership and ethical standards they advanced in their contexts (Josephus, *Ant.* 18.20; Acts 5:13). Therefore, a comparative study of their leadership and the ethics they postulated in their time would be helpful for progressive scholarship in biblical studies.

This behooves us to stay true to the Jewish historical overtones that pervade the text of Acts, even as it resonates with the Greco-Roman literary patterns at the same time.[5] Prior to the discovery of the Dead Sea Scrolls in 1947, information concerning the Essenes community was limited to the writing of Philo, Pliny, and Josephus.[6] Dupont-Sommer, Fitzmyer, and Collins, among others, have connected the Qumran community to the Essenes.[7] This said, it should be noted that there are still dissenting views on the identification

---

4. Barrera, "Qumran Texts," 73.

5. This study is aware of a strong argument for Luke's audience as being Gentiles. The argument is strengthened by the fact that Luke's recipient of both volumes is Theophilus a Greek. However, it is significant to note, Luke is writing to a community that houses both Greeks and Jews and though it is not within the scope of this study to establish Luke's audience but suffices to state here that even if Luke's audience is Gentile, the story he is recording is primarily Jewish hence the need to ensure that as he endeavors to engage his Gentile audience, it is imperative that he stays true to the Jewish history and analogies that will enable his Greek audience to understand.

6. See Philo, *Every Good Man Is Free* (1.75–91) and *Hypothetica* (1.1–18, preserved in Eusebius, *Praeparatio Evangelica*); Pliny, *Natural History* (5.73). Beall, *Josephus' Description of the Essenes*, 1; see also Josephus, *Life* 1.10–12; *J.W.* 2.119–61; *Ant.* 18.11, 18–22.

7. Dupont-Sommer, *Essene Writings*, Meridian books MG44; Fitzmyer, "Jewish Christianity," 233–57; Fitzmyer, *Impact of the Dead Sea Scrolls*; Collins and Evans, *Christian Beginnings*; see also Collins, *Beyond the Qumran Community*, 78–79.

of the Essenes as custodians of Dead Sea Scrolls.[8] It is not the goal of this study to establish the identity of the custodians of the Dead Sea Scrolls. The community at Qumran was governed by two documents, the Damascus Document[9] (popularly referred to as CD) and the Community Rule (*1QS*).

This study will focus on CD and only refer to *Yahad* in insistences where CD seems to provide little or no guidance. However, we acknowledge Collins's conclusion on this discussion:

> It makes little sense to distinguish between "Qumranic" and "pre-Qumranic" or "non-Qumranic." With the possible exception of the passage in 1QS 8, we have no literature that can be said with confidence to have been composed specifically for the Qumran settlement. There is no evidence at all that the Qumran settlement resulted from a schism within the *Yahad*, or that Serek ha-yahad and the *Damascus Rule* reflected the two sides of a "split."[10]

In this study, we will proceed on the presupposition that CD was used among the camps (a camp was a settlement community made up of at least ten people with a leader referred to as overseer). Whereas the *Serek ha-yahad* was probably mainly used at Qumran, which seems like the headquarters of the communities or the camps. Furthermore, the two documents could as well have served different levels of members within the one group at Qumran. For example, the general membership could have found CD comfortable while the leadership that might have operated on higher level of integrity and commitment would have found the seemingly strict *Serek ha-Yahad* appropriate for their discipline.

---

8. For instance, G. Margoliouth, R. North, L. H. Schiffman argue for the Sadducees(Dupont-Sommer, Essene Writings, 395–397). ; C. Rabin propose Pharisees(Dupont-Sommer, Essene Writings, 403–405). ; C. Daniel, Herodians; S. Zeitlin and P. R. Weiss argue for Karaites (Dupont-Sommer, Essene Writings, 393–395). ; while R. H. Eisenman and B. Thiering connect the DSS to the early Christians and O. Cullmann and J. L. Teicher proposing Ebionites (Dupont-Sommer, Essene Writings, 396–398).

9. CD reflects the primitive form of the Essenes's community organization. It is primarily concerned with households. And they were multiple communities organized in groups of the minimums of ten, they provided for perfect holiness with scanty information on the actual way of life for this group.

10. Collins, *Scriptures and Sectarianism*, 158–59.

CD is believed to have been composed prior to the AD 66–70, is one of the significant works of the Essene community at Qumran. The community may have been forced to disband due to the Jewish revolt. CD consists of two major sections, the exhortation and the Statutes.[11] Two medieval manuscripts dating 10th and 12th century that were discovered in 1896–7 and published under the title Fragments of Zadokite point to the Essenes as their custodians, since the Essenes referred to themselves also as the sons of Zadok, the righteous one.[12] A brief examination of previous scholarship in this area will suffice at this point.

3.2. Previous Scholarship

Dupont-Sommer notes that the theory attributing an Essene origin to Christianity was wide spread among the eighteenth-century philosophers of the Enlightenment. He asserts,

> The documents from Qumran make it plain that the primitive Christian church was rooted in the Jewish sect of the New Covenant, the Essene sect, to a degree none would have suspected, and it borrowed from it a large part of its organization, rites, doctrines, "patterns of thought" and its mystical and ethical ideas.[13]

While the idea was repugnant to the nineteenth- and twentieth-century church historians, both Catholic and Protestant,[14] Dupont-Sommer registers the resilience of this idea in his statement: "Today a negative attitude such as this is quite impossible."[15] In summarizing the discussion on the subject, Dupont-Sommer echoes the words of Father J. Daniélou:

---

11. The 'exhortation' sets forth the sect's" leader and its "religious teaching, emphasizing fidelity to God's covenant with Israel and strict observance of the Sabbath and other holy days. The list of statutes contains guidelines for community assemblies, the selection of judges, and the duties of the Guardian." See https://www.britannica.com/topic/Damascus-Document.

12. Https://www.britannica.com/topic/Damascus-Document.

13. Dupont-Sommer, *Essene Writings*, trans. G. Vermes, 373.

14. Dupont-Sommer, 10–18.

15. Dupont-Sommer, 377.

Of the immediate environment in which Christianity came into being (i.e. the *Essene milieu*), the Qumran discoveries resolve a considerable number of problems which exegesis had not been able to solve. . . . The utilization of all these documents, and the comparisons to which they lead, will doubtless considerably augment the number of solved enigmas. It can therefore be said that this is the most sensational discovery ever made.[16]

Dupont-Sommer notes the advent of this nature of work among dissimilar authors in France. He observes,

All of them . . . punctiliously draw attention to the many parallels emerging from a comparative study, whether it be with regard to the community life and constitution of the primitive church, with the very concept of the church, with the fundamental rites of baptism and Eucharist, with the sermon on the mountain, with the writings of the apostle Paul and the Johannine Gospel, with the fundamental doctrines of justification and predestination, or with the beliefs relative to Messiah and the end of the world.[17]

Dupont-Sommer himself notes that the preaching of repentance, baptism, confession of sin, expectation of the kingdom, the motif of the way, and Judean wilderness in which the prophet's voice sounded in the New Testament, are all indicative of the Qumran community.[18]

Julio T. Barrera asserts, "The New Testament texts show many parallels and points of contact with the texts from Qumran."[19] However, he cautions that it is not possible to reduce this fact to matters of detail. Barrera observes that the Qumran writings are more ancient, and thus it is more probable that they may have influenced the New Testament writings (if there was contact

---

16. Daniélou, *Manuscrits de La Mer Morte*, 123.

17. Dupont-Sommer, *Essene Writings*, trans G. Vermes, 373.

18. Dupont-Sommer, 371. See also some of Dupont-Sommer's work on the DSS related topics in Dupont-Sommer and Rowley, *Dead Sea Scrolls*.

19. Barrera, "Qumran Texts," 203.

at all).[20] Moreover, he posits the possibility of the Qumran texts and New Testament texts running together without the likelihood of the first influencing the second directly; just as two parallel lines would run without meeting.[21] He further argues, "Study of comparative literature and comparative religion has often fallen into what Sandmel refers to as parallelomania, which confuses parallels with tangents and similarities of form or content with direct contacts or influence."[22] He rightly observes:

> Although they offer no direct evidence about Christian origins, the importance of the texts from Qumran for the study of the New Testament is absolutely conclusive. They provide much rich and valuable information about Judaism of the period and as a consequence allow us to know what has been called the Jewish matrix of Christianity (Käsemann). Up to the moment of the Qumran discovery there was no other resort except to compare early Christian literature with contemporary Hellenistic literature or with rabbinic literature of a later period (Billerbeck). Today we have at our disposal material which comes from just before the Christian period or is strictly contemporary with the period of Jesus.[23]

Barrera proceeds to highlight points of contact between the New Testament and the Qumran texts: John the Baptist and Jesus of Nazareth (the titles of the person of Jesus). He then examines the Gospel of Mathew (Matt 5:3–11, 43, 48; 7:13–14; 16:16–9; 18:15–17), the Gospel of John, the Epistles of Paul (Romans, Corinthians, Ephesians, and Colossians) and partially mentions Acts 26:18 in relation to the baptismal exhortation.[24] Barrera's work is commendable as it provides direction to this study.

Despite Florentino Garcia Martinez's pessimistic beginning in section six of his article "The Dead Sea Scrolls,"[25] he turns around and makes significant

---

20. Luke as an author under inspiration, wrote from whatever sources he had under the guidance of the Holy Spirit, in that only what God willed to be included in Luke's report was written down.

21. Barrera, "Qumran Texts," 203.

22. Barrera, 203.

23. Barrera, 204.

24. Barrera, 205–31.

25. Martinez, "Dead Sea Scrolls," 13.

observations on the significance of the Qumran manuscripts. On one hand he lauds the contribution of the Qumran scrolls for studying the New Testament compared to the Old Testament, and on other hand he presents the collection of Italian journal articles dedicated to the Gospel of Mark based on Spanish papyrologist Jesuit José O'Callaghan's contentious discovery.[26] Martinez contends that the real contribution of the scrolls to knowledge of primitive Christianity and New Testament affects all levels of New Testament study: linguistic, literary, legal, historical, and theological. Concerning these Scrolls, he writes,

> We can now discover real meaning of enigmatic sentences and expressions in the New Testament unintelligible in a Greek context and now documented in a contemporary Jewish milieu . . . we can now trace the origin of certain insertions we find incorporated in various New Testament writings . . . we now have available precise literary parallels to some pericopes as important as the Beatitudes . . . we can understand certain New Testament prescriptions, such us brotherly rebuke or the arguments over Sabbath observance. . . . Qumran manuscripts make the theological thinking of the recipients of certain New Testament writings, such as the letter to the Hebrews, less bewildering to us. They also prove that certain theological ideas about the priestly character of the expected Messiah.[27]

According to Martinez, the Qumran documents afford us a better comprehension of the composition of Judaism, putting rabbinic Judaism into proper perspective and understanding Christianity in its inception as a new Jewish sect among others. However, this should not reduce Christianity just to another sect of Judaism. As much as we acknowledge its Jewish roots, it is noteworthy that Christianity enjoys a distinct identity of its own.[28]

---

26. The discovery concerned certain fragment of papyrus found that could contain remains of what had been the oldest copies of the books of the NT: Fragments of the Gospel of Mark, of the Acts of the Apostles, the Epistle to the Romans, 1 Timothy and even 2 Peter and the Epistle of James. These fragments would provide proof that towards the year 50 CE in Palestine the Gospels and the whole New Testament had already acquired the form we know. See Martinez, "Dead Sea Scrolls," 12; Martinez and Barrera, *Dead Sea Scrolls*, 12.

27. Martinez, "Dead Sea Scrolls," 15.

28. Martinez, 16. The same as Martinez and Barrera, *Dead Sea Scrolls*, 16.

The Hayward Lectures delivered in March 2004 discussed several pertinent issues in regard to the contribution of the Dead Sea Scrolls to understanding the New Testament and Christian origins.[29] Craig Evans examines three OT typologies: wilderness, immersion, and twelve used in Qumran and NT writings. He concludes that the very structure of early Christianity grows out of typologies rooted in Jewish scriptures and appropriate comprehension of this structure requires a diligent examination of the nuances of the DSS.[30]

George Brooke (in his essay "Luke-Acts and the Qumran Scrolls") compares Luke-Acts with MMT (Miqṣat Maʿaśe Ha-Torah). Though he seems to focus on Luke more than Acts, Brooke makes insightful comments on Acts scholarship. He states,

> Since the early days of research into the meaning and significance of the scrolls found at Qumran, parallels with the Gospel of Luke and the Acts of the Apostles have been pointed out frequently and in detail. . . . For the Acts of Apostles the story has been the same. Numerous parallels have been noted. Among the most important has been the common ownership of property by the respective communities.[31]

The strength of Brooke's argument is dependent on the neatly summed up work of Fitzmyer in "Jewish Christianity in Acts in Light of the Qumran Scrolls."[32] However, Fitzmyer's opinion on the issue seems inconsistent with Brooke's observation. Fitzmyer notes, "In our opinion, the influence of Qumran literature on Acts is not as marked as it is in other New Testament writings (e.g., John, Paul, Matthew, Hebrews). The parallels that do exist, striking though they may be, are not numerous."[33] Fitzmyer precisely summarizes parallels between Qumran and Acts.[34] He even suggests modifying

---

29. Collins and Evans, *Christian Beginnings*. Contributors on this topic included, Abegg, "Paul and James," 63–74; Wilson, "Dead Sea Scrolls," 121–28; also Collins', "Messiah before Jesus," 15–35, "Essene Messiah," 37–44, and "Apocalyptic Theology," 129–33." For Qumran origins also see Boccaccini, *Beyond the Essene Hypothesis*, and *Enoch and Qumran Origins*.

30. Evans, "Jesus, John," 62.

31. Brooke, "Luke-Acts," 72.

32. Keck, Schubert, and Martyn, *Studies in Luke-Acts*, 233–57.

33. Keck, Schubert, and Martyn, 253.

34. He draws parallels on the use of "the way" in both groups, as well as koinonia, organization structure, the casting of lot to determine the will of God, the communal and common meal of the Essenes.

S. E. Johnson's judgment on the subject in the light of his findings. Fitzmyer has drawn many valuable parallels and contacts between the texts of Qumran and the New Testament, between the Qumran community's ethics and the early Christian movement and particularly in, the book of Acts.[35] We will return to these parallels at a later point in this study.

3.3. New Covenant

Collins observes, "The Damascus Document only provides oblique evidence of the history of the movement it describes."[36] This best known historiographical or quasi-historiographical passage[37] is found in the opening column of CD:

ועתה שמעו כל יודעי צדק ובינו במעשי ²אל. כי ריב לו עם כל בשר¹

ומשפט יעשה בכל מנאציו. ³כי במועלם אשר עזבוהו הסתיר פניו מי-

שראל וממקדשו ⁴ויתנם לחרב. ובזכרו ברית ראשנים השאיר שאירית

⁵לישראל ולא נתנם לכלה. ובקץ חרון שנים שלוש מאות ⁶ותשעים

לתיתו אותם ביד נבוכדנאצר מלך בבל ⁷פקדם. ויצמח מישראל

ומאהרן שורש מטעת לירוש ⁸את ארצו ולדשן בטוב אדמתו. ויבינו

בעונם וידעו כי ⁹אנשים אשימים הם. ויהיו כעורים וכימגששים דרך

שנים עשרים.¹⁰ ויבן אל אל מעשיהם כי בלב שלם דרשוהו¹¹ויקם להם

מורה צדק להדריכם בדרך לב (CD-A: 3–11).

He turned away from Israel and from His sanctuary and gave them up to the sword. But when He called to mind the covenant He made with their forefathers, He left a remnant for Israel and did not allow them to be exterminated. In the era of wrath three hundred and ninety years at the time He handed them over to the power of Nebuchadnezzar king of Babylon He took care of them and caused to grow from Israel and from Aaron a root of planting to inherit. His land and to grow fat on the good produce of His soil. They considered their iniquity and they knew that they were guilty men, and had been like the blind and like

---

35. Fitzmyer, "Jewish Christianity," 233–57.

36. Collins, *Beyond the Qumran Community*, 34.

37. Collins, *Scriptures and Sectarianism*, 120.

those groping for the way twenty years. But God considered their deeds, that they had sought Him with a whole heart. So He raised up for them a teacher of righteousness to guide them in the way of His heart (CD-A 3–11).[38]

Collins argues elsewhere,

The Damascus Document is not concerned with chronology (although the twenty years of groping has some value of understanding the way in which the movement developed). Rather, it is concerned to illustrate the ways in which God works in history, and to suggest that the author's group represented the elect of the last days.[39]

These opening verses in CD hark back to the pre and post-exilic periods.

The post-exilic period was one of the most daunting times for the nation of Israel. The promise of restoration to Israel meant going back to their own land, having their own king and renewed sense of the presence of God once his temple was re-established. The returnee exiles did all they knew to do yet things did not resemble the hope yearned for. They were still slaves on their own land. Ezra, Nehemiah, Esther, Daniel, Haggai, Zechariah, Isaiah 56–66, and Malachi addressed some of these challenging issues. The promise of God blessing Israel and giving them a king to deliver them from their enemies remained elusive.

The author of 1 Maccabees helps us to understand the state of the nation of Israel. They reformed all that called for reformation, family, community, and worship, but the situation did not change much. The post-exilic prophets proclaimed a more apocalyptic interpretation of Scriptures so as to make sense of the promises of prosperity and peace. They grappled with the question as to why God's promises to the returnees were not fulfilled. Malachi suggests that the nation is struck because the priests and the people have fallen short of God's standards (Mal 1:6–2:17); restoration has not come about and will not come about due to the breaking of the law (Mal 4:4). However, if they obey the law, they will be a blessing and a delight in the land (Mal 3:6–12).

---

38. Wise, Abegg, and Cook, *Dead Sea Scrolls*, 52.

39. Collins, *Scriptures and Sectarianism*, 120.

He said, Woe is me! Wherefore was I born to see this misery of my people, and of the holy city, and to dwell there, when it was delivered into the hand of the enemy, and the sanctuary into the hand of strangers? Her temple is become as a man without glory. Her glorious vessels are carried away into captivity; her infants are slain in the streets, her young men with the sword of the enemy. What nation hath not had a part in her kingdom and gotten of her spoils? All her ornaments are taken away; of a free woman she is become a bondslave. And, behold, our sanctuary, even our beauty and our glory, is laid waste, and the Gentiles have profaned it. To what end therefore shall we live any longer? Then Mattathias and his sons rent their clothes, and put on sackcloth, and mourned very sore.[40]

This condition informs the emerging of several groups in Israel in the efforts to win God's favor and full restoration as envisioned by the exiles. The Jewish literature that emerged during this period (Second Temple) can be classified in four categories: theocratic,[41] apocalyptic,[42] apologetic,[43] and sectarian apocalyptic.[44] It suffices to note here that these perspectives break away from the traditional Jewish norm. This served to caution that "a ritualistic obsession with the Torah did not, in fact, sustain the covenant with God. Neither did a xenophobic attitude square with the divine intention to convert the nations of the world."[45] Of these four, the literature related to the community under study is the fourth one: sectarian apocalyptic literature.

---

40. 1 Maccabees 2:7–14.

41. Works in this category emphasized only a return to entire Mosaic codes would pave way for Israel's deliverance and a re-enthronement of God as their king. Writings like Maccabees, Sirach, Baruch, and psalm of Solomon fall under this category, literature which informed the Pharisees and Sadducee philosophy.

42. The texts in this category expressed the belief the kingdom will be ushered from heaven, preceded by unparalleled suffering that Yahweh's faithful were expect to endure at the hand of their enemies. See Dan 12:1–3; 1 Enoch 80:4–5, 91:7; Jubilees 23:14–23; Testament of Moses, Ezra and Maccabees.

43. This group focused on defending Judaism in Hellenistic categories and Gentiles. See Wisdom of Solomon, the Third Sibylline Oracle, The letter of Aristeas, The Testament of the Twelve Patriarchs, 4 Maccabees, and Philo.

44. Writings such as the Enoch literature, Jubilees and the Dead Sea Scrolls fit this sectarian apocalyptic literature.

45. Pate et al., *Story of Israel*, 116–17.

The Qumran community believed in separation and particularity. Everett Ferguson, states:

> The Qumran community lived under a strong eschatological expectation. They believed that they were living in the last days, and they interpreted the prophets as referring to their times. They looked forward to the coming of prophet and the Messiahs (Anointed) of Aaron (the eschatological Priest) and of Israel (the Messianic king) . . . As the community awaited God's action they spent their time in intense study of Scriptures.[46]

3.3.1. Historical Background

This leads us to a brief examination of the historical background of the Qumran community focusing on the Hasmonean clan, the new covenant, their literature, community life, social structure and leadership. The earliest mention of the Essenes is in Philo of Alexandria *Every Good Man is Free* (§§75–91). Of our interest here will be §76–77, which sheds light on the subject of separation. Prior to discussing the reasons Essenes separated from Israel, Philo writes:

> These men, in the first place, live in villages, avoiding all cities on account of the habitual lawlessness of those who inhabit them, well knowing that such a moral disease is contracted from associations with wicked men, just as a real disease might be from an impure atmosphere, and that this would stamp an incurable evil on their souls. Of these men, some cultivating the earth, and others devoting themselves to those arts which are the result of peace, benefit both themselves and all those who come in contact with them, not storing up treasures of silver and of gold, nor acquiring vast sections of the earth out of a desire for ample revenues, but providing all things which are requisite for the natural purposes of life.[47]

It is not the goal of this study to establish whether the reason for the movement rose as a result of moral issues as in Philo's testimony, or a dispute

---

46. Ferguson, *Backgrounds of Early Christianity*, 491.
47. Philo, *The Works of Philo*, 689.

over the priesthood, or even the divergence in interpretation of the Mosaic law (1QS VIII 12–16).[48] However, the ancient testimonies about the Essenes portray a high level of piety and holiness which confirms that their reason for separating may have been an effort to preserve virtue and godliness. The sect subscribed to clearly stipulated principles that governed their community and personal lives.

We will now examine selected features of the Essenes as a community. The activities of Antiochus IV Epiphanes between 169–167 BC in Jerusalem set the scene for our quest. These events are recorded in Daniel 7–12;[49] 1 Maccabees 1:2; 2 Maccabees 3–7; Josephus *Jewish War* 1.31–35 and *Antiquities* 12.237–64.[50] During this time, the Hasidim, translated as "holy ones," "pious ones," "faithful ones," "devoted ones," sparked a revolt against their Syrian overlords.[51] Their efforts won religious liberty under Judas Maccabeus. However, it was not until the reign of Simon in 143 BC that secular freedom was achieved, though considerable grounds toward this independence was covered in Jonathan Maccabeus's tenure. This temporary victory was celebrated as the fulfillment of the promise of restoration after exile.

The political and religious freedom presented a moral challenge to the Hasmoneans (who were also referred to as the Maccabeans). The pious Maccabean family lost their grip of the very religious ideals that had modeled their vision and greatness. It must have been this time in their history that CD refers to: "they were guilty men, and had been like the blind and like those groping for the way for twenty years" (CD 1:6–9).[52] Dupont-Sommer in discussing the wicked priest observes,

> There is, I think, no doubt that this apocalypse envisages definite historical reality – seven priests following one after another, succeeding one another as in a dynasty. Which sacerdotal dynasty can this be? It has a holy and glorious beginning, and a miserable and criminal end: does this not suggest, first and foremost, that

---

48. Martinez, "Dead Sea Scrolls," 34; Dupont-Sommer, *Essene Writings*, 359.

49. In this study, we will use the dating of the sixth century BC for Daniel. We proceed on the assumption that the contentious chapter 11 of Daniel is not recording history but rather (accurate) prophecy.

50. Eshel, *Dead Sea Scrolls*, 13.

51. Brownlee, *Meaning of the Qumrân Scrolls*, 131.

52. Brownlee, 131–32.

the author has in mind the Hasmonaean dynasty which began so well with Judas Maccabee, continued honorably under Jonathan, fell into decadence with Simon and John Hyrcanus, and completed its decline with Aristobulus I, Alexander Jannaeus and Hyrcanus II the three priests who dared assume the title of the "king"?[53]

Dupont-Sommer captures well the succession in the Hasmonaean dynasty. He has clearly described their rise and fall. His identification, however, of Hyrcanus II as the wicked priest who may have executed the Teacher of Righteousness is doubtful. A few reasons would suffice for this doubt. First, Hyrcanus had a very unstable tenure during his mother's reign and was almost vanquished by his brother Aristobulus II. He was not properly established in the office of the high priest and his efforts were focused on battling his brother Aristobulus II more than the Teacher. He was inclined to the sect of the Pharisees that was not hostile to the Essenes as such. Second, identifying him as the wicked priest will situate the Teacher of Righteousness close to Pompey's reign in the 60s BC when Qumran community fled their camp never to return again.

Alexander Jannaeus father to Hyrcanus II and son of John Hyrcanus, ruled as king-priest 103–76 BC.[54] Brownlee describes Jannaeus as,

A man given to self-indulgence and his rule was marked both by wars of conquest and internal dissensions and civil war, as he supported the view of the worldly Sadducean priests and sought to crush all Hasidic elements, both the Pharisees and Essenes. Many of the devout fled the country, taking refuge in neighboring countries.[55]

It is assumed that this may be the time the Teacher of Righteousness fled to the region of Damascus,[56] a situation probably cited in the Hymns.[57] Due to

---

53. Dupont-Sommer, *Essene Writings*, 354–55.

54. Josephus, *J.W.* 1.85–106; Josephus, *Ant.* 13.320–406. See also Brownlee, *Meaning of the Qumrân Scrolls*, 132; Collins, *Beyond the Qumran Community*, 104.

55. Brownlee, *Meaning of the Qumrân Scrolls*, 132.

56. Though, we will discuss the interpretation of the Damascus "space" in CD at a later stage in this chapter.

57. 1QH 4. 8.

differences in calendars in observing the Day of Atonement, Jannaeus had the opportunity to pursue the Teacher of Righteousness, with the goal to "swallow the Teacher" and make his followers "stumble." However, on his death bed he counseled his wife Salome to make peace with the Pharisees,[58] a decision that brought the Pharisees back to power and the Sadducees were left to contend for the political supremacy. The state in this Second Temple era denotes tension between the Pharisees and the aristocratic Sadducees while the Essenes contended with the tension of staying true to their separation spirit or to get involved in the scramble for earthly power.[59]

3.3.2. The Damascus Document

The Teacher of Righteousness modeled an ascetic life among his followers. We may safely infer that his ethical ideals may have put off many of the Hasidim and caused a rift between them. Those who braved the commitment of the Teacher of Righteousness became the Essenes; the majority who preferred a more moderate halakhic course became the Pharisees, who were referred to as "seekers after smooth things."[60] There was also a third religious party, Sadducees, for Josephus pointed out that there were three philosophical groups among the Jews: "At this time there were three sects among the Jews, who had different opinions concerning human actions: the one was called the sect of the Pharisees, another sect of the Sadducees,[61] and the other sect of the Essenes."[62] Weighed down with the daunting presence of the overlords and the seeming confusion among the Jews on how to restore her glory (evidenced in the scramble for power and wealth),[63] the Teacher of Righteousness separated himself and the Essenes to the desert to seek Yahweh and observe

---

58. Collins, *Beyond the Qumran Community*, 104.

59. Howlett, *Essenes and Christianity*, 92–104.

60. CD 1:14–21 see also Collins, *Beyond Qumran community*, 113,

61. The Sadducees were largely priests and held to the strict observance of the law. They were less attracted to the Essenic pesher with its tendency to reapply the scriptures to the community or the needs of the later generations; they rejected the emerging oral traditions associated with the law mainly practiced by the Pharisees.

62. Josephus, *Ant.* 13:171

63. I propose the possibility of the Essenes having been aware of the skirmishes around priesthood in Numbers 16 and 17 and the judgement that followed Korah and his group. This may have restrained them from the fights over priesthood. Presumably they may have believed that God vindicates his true priests who are holy and pure.

the Torah with the intention of winning back God's favor and a restoration of the kingdom as he had promised their forefathers.

The Damascus Document is concerned with the law of Moses and how it should be applied in daily life in all Israel. However, it is also concerned with the Essenes as a separated group. The Essenes saw themselves as true Israel, set apart in the wilderness to appropriately observe the Law of God and usher in the fulfillment of an overdue restoration of the nation of Israel to her promised glory. This, they believed was only possible not just by casual obedience but by proper interpretation of the Law and a cutting of a new covenant with God (Jer 31:31).[64] Though the covenant was still based on the Law of Moses, the conditions of entry were transformed. Every individual was to take an oath before the Mebaqqer (overseer or inspector of the camps), with a further commitment to introduce his son at the appropriate age of admission. Both Israelites by birth and proselytes were eligible to be participants of the covenant. There was no automatic entry for Israelites based on birth as it was stipulated among the Jews.[65] These conditions for admission and devotion at Qumran, suggests Qumran as fitting comparison to Peter's leadership and ethics in Acts 1–12 and 15. We will examine some of the new provisions of enrollment.

3.3.3. Leadership and Admission in the New Covenant

The admission and enrollment oath were administered by the Mebaqqer, unlike when one only needed to be born into a Jewish family. Membership entailed: "no one who is a fool or insane may enter; and no simpleton or ignoramus or one with eyes too weak to see or lame or crippled or deaf or minor child, none of these shall enter the congregation, for the holy angels are in your midst."[66] Members live in camps, with a minimum of ten and an interpreter of the law among the ten. It is a family-based movement. Members were prohibited from the vices that characterize the sons of darkness and there was an assembly of all camps possibly patterned after the Jewish gathering for the Day of Atonement. It was believed that obeying this order guaranteed

---

64. Such concern for the word of God resembles Peter's concern in Acts 6:1–3 at the time when daily distributions in the primitive church threatened devotion to God and his word. Hence, making Qumran community a suitable comparison to the community in Acts 1–12,15.

65. CD 15:5–12.

66. CD 15: 15: 15–17.

the blessings of God upon the sect and its members. The law was divided into the general revelation to all Israel and the hidden things that could only be known by the members of the "holy ones" who had separated themselves for appropriate living and interpretation of the Torah.[67] Collins argues that there is an obvious relationship between CD and the Community Rule and hence no reason to attribute the difference between the rules to schism. He states,

> The popular theory that the Damascus rule represents an order that practiced marriage while the Serek was the rule for the celibates, requires some qualification, but is substantially correct. The Damascus Rule is primarily concerned with households. It allows for some other members who walk in perfect holiness, says little about their way of life, and it is possible that the one passage that distinguishes this groups was a secondary addition. The Serek, in contrast, is primarily concerned with those who walk in perfect holiness, while it allows for multiple communities with quorum of ten members, in the manner of the "camps" of the Damascus Rule; it makes no mention of women and children . . .[68]

Not only is the new covenant based on Torah, but the camp setup resembles the camp of Israel in the wilderness as in Numbers 2.[69] This organization hints at two possible OT contexts. The first may echo the camping of Israel in the wilderness under the original Teacher of Righteousness, Moses. The second might be Jethro's counsel to his son-law to divide Israelites into smaller units to enhance efficiency and effective leadership (Exod 18).[70] The arrangement of the tribes as given in Numbers 2 might also be of interest.

---

67. Schiffman, *Reclaiming the Dead Sea Scrolls*, 247. More of Schiffman's work on DSS see Schiffman, *Eschatological Community*; Schiffman, "Law of Vows," 199–214.

68. Collins, *Beyond the Qumran Community*, 78–79.

69. CD12:22–23, however, the Qumran camps consist of a minimum of ten people one must be a priest and they could go to tens, fifties, hundreds and thousands (CD13:1–3). This philosophy of camps echoes the significance of priests during this period in the life of Israel in the wilderness. They insured the purity and holiness of the nation and the people of God in a hostile desert and the honor due to the presence of Yahweh amidst them symbolized by the Ark of the Covenant. The tribe of Levi was God's chosen tribe and lot among the children of Israel and the undisputed priesthood of Aaron and his sons.

70. Compare Exodus 18:19–27 and CD 12:23–13:1–3, "this is the rule for those who live in camps, . . . then the allotment shall proceed in all its ways at his command, all the members of the camp."

The new covenant stipulates the duties of the Mebaqqer. The Mebaqqer hears evidence in criminal cases (CD 9:18–22); instructs the priest in the law (CD 13:5); teaches the many about works of God, examines, teaches and admits new members in the camp(s) (CD 13:11; 15:8–14); exercises control over the community's commerce (CD 13:16); and receives wages to be disbursed to the needy (CD 14:13–16).

Another title, *pāqîd*, is used in 1QS 6:14 to refer to the overseer or the inspector of the camp. It seems like the *pāqîd* and the Mebaqqer have the same duties as shown in 1QS 6:14 and CD 13:11 and 15:8–14; they both examined potential new members. Beall observes that the *pāqîd* of CD 14:6 is a priest, while the Mebaqqer is presumably a lay person, since in CD 13:5 he instructs the priest in the law.[71] A careful examination of the texts in question reveals that Beall may have confused the ignorant priest for a Mebaqqer:

> But if it is a case of the law of skin diseases, then the priest must come and be present in the camp, and the Overseer shall instruct him in the details of the Law, and even if the priest is ignorant, it is he who must isolate the one suffering from skin disease, because that duty is the priests' alone. This is the rule for the Overseer of a camp.[72]

It would be problematic for the revered office of the Mebaqqer in CD to be occupied by a lay person. This text seems to speak of a priest who is ignorant of the law of God yet is the only priest authorized to deal with matters of purity and rituals like the one in question above (probably leprosy or some skin disease). Hence, it is necessary that the priest be instructed by the overseer (Mebaqqer) in the law to understand what is required by the Torah in such situations.

J. Priest argues, "the *pāqîd* was originally the real leader of the community, with the Mebaqqer initially only a minor official (overseer of the property 1QS 6:20); only later was the Mebaqqer equal to the *pāqîd* (1QS 6: 12–24?); and finally, superior to the *pāqîd*."[73] Priest's argument is notable and possible

---

71. Todd S. Beall, *Josephus' Description of the Essenes Illustrated by the Dead Sea Scrolls*, SNTSMS 58 (Cambridge: Cambridge University, 2004), 47.

72. CD 13:5.

73. Priest, "Mebaqqer," 55–61. Also Priest, "Messiah," 95–100. Beall suggests that if Priest's argument is right, then early *Mebaqqer* corresponds exactly to Josephus's ἐπιμελητηζ.

but with reservations. We have made reference in this study of the possible additions in *Serek* which may account for some of the variances, but it is suitable noting that CD consistently uses Mebaqqer to refer to the overseer of the camp and of many camps. Thus, he seems to be overall leader of the community inspecting all the camps of the community or communities.[74]

3.3.4. Models of the New Covenant

New covenant at Qumran was based on the Law of Moses and informed by the prophecy of Jeremiah 31:31. The fact that it is new provokes our memory of the old. The Qumran community separated themselves to focus on proper interpretation and keeping of the Torah. The keeping of the law in Israel was tied to staying in the land (Deut 4:25–26; 4:39–40). One reason for this is that the primary way other nations would come to know of Yahweh and be drawn to follow him is by the Israelites living faithfully by the law in the land. So, the land is not a gift in the abstract but a necessary backdrop for the flourishing of mission through worship and action. Deuteronomy provides the rationale for viewing and interpreting the history of Israel, the meaning of the sequence of events that had befallen her ending in the destruction of Jerusalem and the deportation of her people. What is more, in all probability, there are direct references to Deuteronomy in the reforms of Josiah (2 Kgs 22–23) and in the ministry of Ezra (Neh 8). Deuteronomy becomes the framework within which the prophets preach and prophesy.[75] Righteous and wicked kings in Israel are evaluated considering Deuteronomic norms. The reforms of Asa (2 Chron 15:9–15) and Josiah in the pre-exilic period (2 Kgs 22–23) and the Second Temple covenants of Nehemiah (Neh 10:29–39) were prior attempts to call Israel to observe the law, however not much was transformed. The remnant had regained opportunity to live according to the Law and its precepts.[76] Under the Sinai covenant Israel was called and commissioned for this purpose and they failed by polluting the land with their rebellious acts. Davies contends,

---

74. CD 14:8–9.

75. Ideas drawn from lecture notes in Biblical Theology class by Peter Nyende at Africa International University, January 2014.

76. Lied, "Another Look," 111.

The purity which the Holiness Code enjoins is intrinsically bound up with the present defilement of the land and its future re-possession; it is a code written by exiles who believed that the disaster which occurred resulted from Israel's previous pollution of the land it had been given, and which had now been purged of its inhabitants to "enjoy its Sabbaths."[77]

The land of promise was expected to be a place of demonstrating God's ideal community, exemplified by Israel's obedience to the Law through which, by their way of life, the nations would be drawn to Yahweh. Regrettably, the Israelites failed to live by these divine injunctions and forfeited the opportunity to restore God's rule on earth in a restored Eden. Unlike the failures of their ancestors, the adherents of CD saw an opportunity for a new exodus and a newly reconstituted Israel. CD here seems to present a new theological framework of reflecting on the Old Testament motifs of Exodus – Israelites camping in the wilderness, desert, exile, Canaan, kingdom and king, among others. G. Vermes concerning this new theological context envisioned in CD argues,

> In "the land of Damascus" they were able to observe the law according to its true meaning. They lived in camps, the Israelites after the exodus, and they made a new covenant as their forefathers had done on Sinai. Their exile would last for about forty years to correspond with the wandering in the wilderness before conquest of the Promised Land and with its end would come the dawn of the messianic era.[78]

Lied also observes,

> A tendency within CD-A 6–7 towards making space mobile must be understood in this context. The description of camps, the references to the presence of God, and the law as central forces among the remnant group operating independent of the institutions of Palestine, all point to the flexible and mobile spatial patterns characteristic of the Exodus story. By recalling the camps of Exodus, CD-A brings a powerful set of paradigmatic

---

77. Davies, *Damascus Covenant*, 133.
78. Vermes, *Scripture and Tradition*, 45.

events into play as central arguments for the redemption of the remnant group. Just as the first exodus once saved Israel, a similar set of events will again save the remnants (CD-A 5.19).[79]

CD 6–8 presents three biblical spaces as spatial paradigms: exile, camp, and land. The Second Temple view of exile and land-spaces pose a challenge to interpreting CD passage above. Judah (Palestine) is definitely a place of promise and blessing. To be banished from the geographical land of promise is an exile, yet presently the remnants living in the land are precisely exiles. These returnees going to Damascus, outside Palestine and its institutions (temple and city), automatically meant exile.

Liv Ingeborg Lied, using Edward W. Soja's theory of Thirdspace, re-interprets the Damascus space in CD. Lied argues that Damascus must be understood as a place of the remnant during evil times, hence a place of both exile and blessing. She re-examines the spaces of punishment, exile, camp, and land. Limiting her focus to CD-A 6:2–7:8, she applies Soja's social identity theory in conversation with the spaces indicated above. She further states,

> The presence of notions associated with Land-space within CD-A 7:6–8 is also indicated by the assertion that married life in the camps should be regulated by the rule of the Land. Thus the spaces brought about by life according to the law make the camps equivalent to Land. As lived realities the spaces of exilic camps and Land become interchangeable.[80]

The Damascus rule provides the choice of celibacy or family life with an admonition to live in camps according to the rule of the land.

> In short, for all who conduct their lives by these laws, in perfect holiness, according to all the instructions, God's covenant stands firm to give them life for thousands of generations (Geniza B adds: as it is written, "He keeps the covenant and loyalty to those

---

79. Lied, "Another Look," 118. The tendency may also shed light on the interpretation of the "king's booth," "the king" "the כיון of images," "the star" and "the staff" in CD-A 7:14–20. In the Damascus setting CD-A address them all as institutions detached from Palestine (cf. also Brooke, "Amos-Numbers Midrash," 400–402; and Davies, *Damascus Covenant*, 123–24. For an alternative view, see Rabinowitz, "Reconsideration of 'Damascus,'" 25–27. See also 4QFlorelegium 1. 11–12 and Baruch 85.3.

80. Lied, "Another Look," 120.

who love Him and keep His commandments for a thousand generations" [Deuteronomy 7:9]). But if they live in camps according to the rule of the land (Geniza B adds: which existed in ancient times) and marry women (B adds: as is the custom of the Law) and beget children, then let them live in accordance with the Law, and by the ordinance of vows according to the rule of the Law, just as it says, "Between a man and his wife, and between a father and his sons" [Numbers 30:17].[81]

In sum, given that the arguments of Davies, Vermes, and Lied are acceptable, then new socio-theological paradigms underlying CD present far-reaching implications on how the space of land and the institutions that are dependent on land should be perceived and conceived by readers of the Old and New Testaments. For example, if the spaces of exilic camps and the land become interchangeable in this transformative perspective, it should be conceivable that the temple and temple worship, the priesthood, the kingdom along with the king and the royal city Jerusalem, as well as other symbolic elements that defined Israel will be transformed into this new understanding. The composition of a renewed Israel and admission into it would also experience this paradigm shift.

3.4. Qumran and Early Christianity

Now I must briefly show how Peter and the disciples are depicted as constituting a community similar to the remnants of the Damascus community (under the new covenant instituted by Jesus Christ) in readiness to usher in the new temple and the inception of the kingdom of God in Acts chapter 1. The patterns of re-interpreting and re-appropriating the history of biblical Israel for contemporary practice found in Qumran are similar to those ascribed to Peter and the disciples in Acts 1. The early Christians, under a new covenant instituted by Jesus, their Messiah, were ready to usher in the kingdom of God and looked toward a new temple. They also drew upon notions of Israel in the wilderness under Moses. These and other echoes will be examined further in chapter 5 of this study. Commenting on J. W. Parkes'

---

81. CD 7:4–9 (Wise, Abegg, and Cook, *Dead Sea Scrolls.*)

work,[82] Gabriel Boccaccini notes, "The Qumran community offers the first example of the notorious 'theology of supersession' that the church would use to define itself in relation to the Synagogue. The sectarians believed that they had superseded Israel in this world as the 'eternal Planting' celebrated in Enochic literature."[83]

When the inhabitants of Qumran left in haste for their safety, preserving what could be preserved in light of the urgency of the Roman advance in AD 70, little did they know that their actions would be the genesis of exposing the literature they held so close to their hearts. The discoveries of the late 1940s opened the door for those whom the Essenes could have regarded as outsiders to read and examine their once jealously guarded literature. Dupont-Sommer writes,

> It should not be forgotten that the Essene sect was strictly eso-
> teric in character; according to Josephus, the new member swore
> never to reveal any of the sect's doctrines "even if subjected to
> violence unto death," and the Qumran documents echo this
> rule of secrecy. In unhoped-for manner, the Dead Sea Scrolls
> disclose, authentically, the very doctrines and rites whose di-
> vulgence was severely proscribed.[84]

We cannot overemphasize the significance of the Qumran discoveries. For they have shed light on the religious background of the New Testament, its terminology and concepts, emerging as the closest analogies to much of the language of the New Testament literature that had always been analyzed in the light of the mystery cults of the Greco-Roman world.[85] Brownlee perfectly captures that situation: "Scholars of the New Testament have long been seeking the religious background of its terminology and concepts, for every literary work requires examination in the light of current literature if it is to be fully understood."[86]

---

82. Parkes, *Conflict of the Church*.

83. Boccaccini, *Beyond the Essene Hypothesis*, 155. The Enochic literature (1 En. 93:10); Jubilees (23:26); Daniel and Pseudo-Daniel text are some of the witnesses that speak of the emergence of an elect group within Judaism.

84. Dupont-Sommer, *Essene Writings*, 369.

85. Brownlee, *Meaning of the Qumrân Scrolls*, 122.

86. Brownlee, 122.

3.4.1. The Teachers of Righteousness

One way in which the Qumran documents illuminate the early Christian community is in describing the pioneers of the two groups. The Teacher of Righteousness was central to the organization and structure of the Qumran community. This section will briefly discuss the pioneers of the two groups. We are not told much about the birth and growth of the Teacher[87] but he appears on the scene of the remnant's narrative to meet an expectation. The remnant of true Israel has been groping in the dark for twenty years. Likewise, remnants were living in a state of uncertainty concerning the Messiah. For the Christian community, Luke indicates that Jesus comes into the world to meet an expectation that is evident in Anna's and Simon's responses in Luke 2:22–38. Both the Teacher of Righteousness and Jesus began their ministries in the wilderness, which hints at the eschatological hopes of the Jewish communities they served. The Teacher builds his holiness and purity around the injunctions of the Torah. Jesus, though he does not base his holiness and purity on similar foundations, nevertheless upholds the Torah (Matt 5:17–8).

The Teacher is portrayed as an ardent reformer and faithful priest to the law, a resolute opponent of the Pharisees and the Sadducees; he reproves these fellow Judaistic sects and ultimately separates himself and his followers from them and their temple. Jesus may not have been addressed as a reformer but he had a reform agenda; he was not a priest by birth but he was called a priest according to the order of Melchizedek (Heb 7). He did not separate himself and his followers from the temple,[88] yet he spoke against its evils and against the Pharisees and Sadducees, leaders of the people of Israel. The Teacher established a communal society that viewed itself as a renewed Israel; this was accomplished by entering a new covenant on a personal basis as opposed to former adoption by descent. Jesus also established a group of followers, but it was not strictly communal; it was founded on a personal commitment to him as a Master. The followers of the Teacher were committed to the Torah whereas the followers of Jesus were committed to him, and they modeled their lives, speech and actions after his own. Thus they were in pursuit of a

---

87. In this section that follows, I will refer to the Teacher of Righteousness simply as "the teacher."

88. Though later his disciples are also seen as having stopped going to the temple.

relationship rather than rituals (although he did inaugurate sacraments for them to observe as acts of loyalty).[89]

Both were persecuted constantly by the sects, the Pharisees and Sadducees, and were unjustly judged, maltreated, and put to death.[90] Followers of both leaders emphasized the significance of baptism as a major sign of identification with the group only allowed for those who demonstrated unchallengeable commitment to the group.[91] The four Gospels in alluding to the presence of John the Baptist in the desert (Matt 3:3; Mark 1:3; Luke 3:3; John 1:23) use Isaiah 40:3 which is also significant to the *Serek ha yahad* (1QS) 8:12–16.

Elsewhere in this study, I argue for possible parallels in the Gospels, the Epistles of Paul, John the Baptist, and others.[92] Here we will focus on the community in Acts and the Qumran Scrolls. The extent of the influence of one community over the other is highly debatable. This study will not attempt to demonstrate whether the influence was direct or indirect or whether it was exerted upon the church or upon the New Testament authors themselves. It is highly probable that the preaching of the early Christians in Jerusalem may have touched a chord with the Essenes communities settled around Jerusalem. In fact, an investigation in this direction may result in a reasonable explanation of the sudden conversion records in Acts at Peter's preaching[93] (Acts 2:41, 47b; 4:4) in and around Jerusalem. These may have been the result of similarities between the community in Acts and the Essene community. The Essenes who converted to Christianity may have influenced the early church directly, while the thought of the surrounding Essene communities may have had a more indirect effect. Second, by the time Acts is being written, even if we argue for an early date of AD 64–70, at the very least thirty

---

89. Water baptism (Matt 28:18–20); the Lord's table (Matt 26:26–29) and feet washing (John 13:1–20).

90. Brownlee, has drawn some informative contrasts between the teacher and Jesus in Brownlee, *Meaning of the Qumrân Scrolls*, 126–51.

91. For Jesus's followers it was a demonstration of faith and trust in the master, Jesus Christ.

92. Barrera, "Qumran Texts," 204–20; Robinson, *Twelve New Testament Studies*, 11–27; Brownlee, "John the Baptist," 71–90; Fitzmyer, "Jewish Christianity," 234 (see Fitzmyer's eighth endnote for further reference). See also Section 3.2 pg 58 of this study.

93. They preached Jesus as the Messiah (2:36), a man certified by God of Abraham, Isaac, and Jacob by mighty works and wonders, and that God had raised him from the dead, and they are witnesses (1:6). This kind of Christology would certainly endear them to the messianically inclined Essenes known to have lived at and around Jerusalem; see Fitzmyer, "Jewish Christianity," 235.

years had elapsed since the inception of the church. In those three decades (or longer), converts may have come with stories of the Essenes influencing writers like Luke. This line of thought is strengthened by the fact that Pliny,[94] another outsider, writes about the Essenes.[95]

Luke in his first volume informs us that he is embarking on a project of writing an orderly account among other existing accounts. By the time he is writing, several versions must be public, including some that may be friendly to the Essenes. I suggest that the discussion should be shifting from whether he was influenced to how much he was influenced by the DSS. If he used sources, which he certainly did (Luke 1:1–4), and if the Essenes were being converted, which is highly plausible, then the Essenes who are reputed for excellent record keeping, would be in a good position to supply orderly and reliable texts that may have been resourceful in shaping the historiography of Acts, focused as it was on its readers' faith as was the case of their predecessors Essenes.

Our present focus, however, remains drawing parallels between Peter's leadership and ethics and the Qumran's overseer and ethics. Since the two communities, the church in Acts and that represented by the Qumran texts, seem to be responding to the same situation in their respective contexts, Fitzmyer posits,

> Acts vaguely suggests that the Christian group looked on itself as the New Israel; this seems at least implied in the disciples' question about the restoration of the Kingdom to Israel (1:6) and in the need felt to reconstitute the twelve (1:15–26). The corporate character of the Jewish Christians is formulated for the first time in the word κοινωνία (2:42).[96]

However, Fitzmyer's argument that the disciples' question in Acts 1:6 indicates that they believed themselves to be the renewed Israel may present a complex situation.[97] If Acts were a tree, the shoot from the ground would be clearly

---

94. It should be noted that this Latin writer died in A.D 79. However, it is presumed that he may have accompanied Titus to Palestine during the Jewish war in A.D 70, see Dupont-Sommer, *Essene Writings*, 37.

95. Dupont-Sommer, *Essene Writings*, 38.

96. Fitzmyer, "Jewish Christianity," 236.

97. The disciples are not sure if Jesus/the Father will restore the kingdom when the promise comes. As much as it is true that the disciples looked at themselves in the later

Jewish. The author of Acts has included Jewish keynotes in the first chapter. In his first volume, Luke wrote about Jesus, who fulfilled the prophecy of Isaiah 61:1–2. The gospel is preached to the poor, liberty to captives, sight is given to the blind, freedom to the oppressed and the acceptable year of the Lord is decreed (Acts 1:1). This resounds with Israel's desire for the Messiah, their deliverer, until the day Jesus was taken up after he had given commands through the Spirit to the apostles concerning their mission as witnesses. This provokes memories of the Elijah-Elisha narratives at a very critical time in the history of the nation of Israel. Just as Elisha stayed gazing upward for the mantle of Elijah so were the apostles found by the angels who promised his return; the apostles will have to tarry in the upper room waiting for the promised Holy Spirit (Acts 1:2, 2:1–4).

The commands mentioned (Acts 1:2) appeal to memories of the Torah. The setting of this departure being the Mount of Olives is like the scene at Mount Sinai and the covenant of Moses, reinforced by the reference to forty days symbolic of the forty years in the wilderness. Moreover, Jesus and the disciples spoke about the kingdom undoubtedly the kingdom of Israel vis-à-vis kingdom of God (Acts 1:3). These, and other parallels pointed out by Fitzmyer and others, are indicators that the movement that follows is typically Jewish and thought of itself as renewed Israel. We will argue later in the study that they considered themselves a renewed Israel in distinction to the old Israel represented by the leader of the people, who bluntly rejected the followers of Jesus as a strange sect in Israel. Just like their Leader – who came from a despised town, Nazareth, of suspected descent, scandalous family (his mother got pregnant while only betrothed), and seemingly a law-breaker who died a shameful death – the followers were similarly misunderstood and persecuted when they tried to blame the leaders of Israel for Jesus's undeserved death.

Fitzmyer has rightly observed seeming fundamental differences that would outweigh the resemblances between the early Christian movement in Acts and the Essenes. He suggests that these differences emerge more clearly when the character and the goal of the two communities are in focus. Although we propose Qumran as suitable comparison to Acts 1–12 and 15, it is prudent to note that the two communities did not just have similarities but differences

---

chapters of Acts as renewed Israel, it would be too presumptuous to read this notion in 1:6 in relation to that.

too. We will examine these contrasts in chapter 5 of this study. In the same vein Fitzmyer observes,

> The difference is more manifest when the Jewish Christians are compared with the Qumran Essenes. The discipline there laid stress on celibacy, obligatory communal ownership of property, common meals, regulated prayer, study and esoteric interpretation of the Torah, probation of candidates, fines and forms of excommunication, and a structured organization in which monarchic and democratic elements were admitted. Such a strictly organized community the early Jewish Christian church never was. Nor did it have the exclusive character of the Essene movement; it did not retire to the desert or to the "camps." It adopted an attitude toward the Law of Moses that would have been wholly inadmissible among the Essenes.[98]

It is the goal of this study to draw contacts between Qumran scrolls and the book of Acts, which may offer new light to studies like Fitzmyer's, to reconsider such differences between Essene and early Christian community in Acts.

It is worth noting that the Acts of the Apostles was written more than a quarter of a century after the actual inception of the early church at Pentecost. In addition, some of the Pauline Epistles predate Acts, which narrates the history of the establishment of the various churches. Moreover, Jerusalem probably served as a headquarters for the early church just as Qumran – often referred to as "mother group" – may have served the larger Essene communities in the camps. We see Peter and John sent from Jerusalem apparently to validate the Samarian church (Acts 8:14); Peter explains his actions among the Gentiles to the apostles and brothers at Jerusalem (Acts 11:4–18); the council in Acts 15 is held in Jerusalem. Paul, in defense of the distinctiveness of his ministry, alludes to the centrality of Jerusalem in the whole process (Gal 1:11–2:14).

It is important, however, not to forget Barrera's caution on parallelomania. This caution could as well be extended to other spheres related to comparative studies. It is not attainable that the parallels will be a simple verbatim exercise; neither should they be suspiciously imprecise. We will briefly examine the

---

98. Fitzmyer, "Jewish Christianity," 239–40.

guidelines of drawing our parallels in chapter 5 of this study. However, most of the differences cited by Fitzmyer – the practice of property ownership and communal meals – should be understood in this light.

Here, we will briefly compare some of the differences raised. The issue of celibacy at Qumran is of special interest, but not without its own inconsistencies. The residents of Qumran are believed to have separated themselves from the other Essenes for the purpose of seeking "perfect holiness." This provokes questions on how this was achieved and still strictly observe the law of Moses. In Genesis, the community at Babel suffers God's wrath and confusion of their languages in part for deliberately ignoring the command to fill the earth and choosing to unitedly dwell in the same space. The first part of that command to Adam was in relation to procreation. How, then, did celibates at Qumran view this command? Similar uncertainty is demonstrated around the lives of the apostles. In Matthew 19:27–30 and Luke 18:28–30 Peter states categorically that they have left everything. This could be understood as they abandoned families and divorced their wives, but a more appropriate reading would be that leaving everything in favor of Jesus means that they have placed Jesus as master over everything. There is a mild reservation toward married life among Jesus's followers though not to the level expressed at Qumran (Matt. 19: 11–12, 1 Cor 7:1–40; 1 Cor 9:5).[99]

In responding to the widows' need in Acts 6, the apostles prioritized the ministry of the word and prayer over serving tables. Acts is replete with gatherings for prayers and daily house fellowships around breaking of bread and the apostles' teaching (Acts 2:42–47; 3:1; 4:31; 10:9; 12:5). These means of grace may not have been regulated in Acts as we see in Qumran, but there is clearly similarity in this area between the two groups. The Jerusalem council in Acts 15 and the power entrusted to Peter, and at some point to James (Jesus's brother), mirrors the monarchic and democratic structures present in Qumran. Acts 5 records a severe level of discipline taken against Ananias and Sapphira for dealing deceitfully concerning their property. Moreover, while there are no clear guidelines in Acts on probation for candidates, there were clear norms expected for any that would become a member of the church (Acts 2:38–9; 8:9–25).

---

99. Josephus, *J.W.* 2.120.

A recap of Lied's conclusions is helpful at this point. "The spaces brought about by life according to the law make the camps equivalent to Land. As lived realities the spaces of exilic camps and Land become interchangeable."[100] Moreover, being "in the Wilderness" entails one's participation in the messianic age, which would first dawn in the Judean desert. The early church is evidently a participant in the messianic age, though it espouses a backward look as opposed to the Essenes' forward look.[101] Now, as obedience to the law in the Essene camps was equivalent to observing the law in the land (Palestine), and thus the two spaces have become interchangeable, it may be helpful to examine Jeremiah 31:31 to demonstrate the resemblance of Essene and early Christian obedience to the law.

The new covenant at Damascus was based on the Torah, but in response to Jeremiah 31:31. A look at verse 33b ushers one into the transformative exercise that takes place in effecting the practice. Yahweh promises to make a new covenant with his people but not as he did with Israel at Sinai. He promises to write his law in their hearts. The process of observance of the law transitions from Israel in the promised land to the camps of the Essenes in Damascus and now to the Christians in their hearts as Jeremiah prophesied. However, a careful examination in practice reveals that the observance of the law among Essenes is closer to the observance of the law among Christians in Acts. For example, the Essenes did not offer animal sacrifices like Israel, the Christian community also did not offer animal sacrifices. Both communities at some point abandoned the temple worship, which attracted animosity from the temple priests. Observance of the law has moved from tents made with hands of men (tabernacles), to a dwelling place made by God himself (2 Pet 1:13). Paul even goes further in equating the body with the temple of God, thus giving the Christian body the same function as the Jerusalem temple (1 Cor 6:19–20). The full exegesis in the next two chapters will demonstrate further the resemblance between the two communities and show where the author may have defamiliarized the act (of observing the law) with the goal of transforming it and imbuing it with new meaning, as Dupont-Sommer remarks:

---

100. Lied, "Another Look," 120.

101. The church believes in a Messiah who came in bodily form and died on the cross and rose again. While the Essenes look forward to the messiah to come in future.

But it is a recognized fact in history of religion that when a new sect comes into being it distinguishes itself from the old sect from which it emerges by certain innovations which are directly opposed to it, and yet at the same time betray its source origin: this is the law of all dissidence. Even though the historian may, in a sense, be led by the importance of the resemblances and borrowings to consider the primitive church as a para-Essene sect, a sort of derivative or variety of Essenism, he feels in no way disposed to set aside or underestimate the differences, and even the contrasts, between the church and classical Essenism.[102]

It is true that as much as we seek to draw parallels between Peter's leadership and ethics in Acts and the overseer of many camps in Qumran and his ethics, the differences between the two will not be ignored.

3.5. Conclusion

Although previous scholarship has not devoted much study to the parallels between the Qumran community and the church represented in Acts, an investigation of this sort is quite profitable. The Qumran scrolls depict a community that is similar in organization, leadership, and ethics to the community in Acts 1–12 and 15. Both communities share similar devotion to the word of God, require commitment for admission, and believe that they live in eschatological times in which God was intervening in their affairs by raising charismatic leaders to instruct them in the ways of Yahweh. Before embarking on the full-scale study of these parallels, we will turn to a narrative study of the text of Acts 1–12 and 15, which will provide a foundation for the subsequent comparative study.

---

102. Dupont-Sommer, *Essene Writings*, 375.

CHAPTER 4

Peter's Leadership and Ethics in Acts

This chapter will focus on the characterization of Peter's leadership and ethics in Acts. We will discuss this in four sections. Section one will look at Peter's leadership and ethics in the Jerusalem community (Acts 1–6), section two will examine Peter's leadership and ethics in the communities in Samaria and Judea (Acts 8–9), section three will look at Peter's leadership and ethics among the Gentiles (Acts 10–12, 15), and the fourth section will summarize the exegetical outcome in Acts 1–12 and 15.

4.1. Peter in Jerusalem (Acts 1–6)

4.1.1. Continuity of the Narrative (1:1–11)

The author of Acts seeks to maintain continuity in his two volumes. This he does by tying together Luke 24 and Acts 1 through the ascension narratives.[1] Traditionally Acts 1:1–5 has been viewed as the preface or prologue to Acts, with verse 8 serving as the programmatic statement to the narrative.[2] However, Walton in his article "Where does the Beginning of Acts End?" suggests a remarkable approach to the beginning of Acts.[3]

The mention of Theophilus in verse 1 and the repetition of the ascension narrative in verse 2 connect the Acts of the Apostles to the Third Gospel. Parsons and Walton concur that this is due to the author's efforts to keep the

---

1. Parsons, "*Departure of Jesus.*" 13–25
2. Rackham, *Acts of the Apostles*; Marshall, *Acts of the Apostles*, TNTC, 55; Munck, *Acts*, 4; Williams, *Acts*, 1.
3. See Walton, "Beginning of Acts," 447–67.

continuity of the Lukan narrative.[4] However, the author seems to be doing much more than just maintaining the continuity of the narrative. The themes of the fulfillment of God's promises, God's superintendence over history, as well as Jesus's suffering, resurrection, ascension, exaltation, and authority,[5] connect Acts more broadly to the narrative of the Bible and Israel's salvation story in particular.[6]

Chapter 1 of Acts is replete with settings, geographical, temporal, spatial, and topographical among others. After his resurrection, Jesus spends forty days speaking of things concerning the kingdom. These spatial and political settings no doubt echo several of Pentateuch narratives referring to the giving of the law and the establishment of the kingdom of Israel. The Mount of Olives as a setting is symbolic of Mount Sinai. A mountain is often the setting of divine-human encounters.[7] The narrator fills these verses with language and symbols of Israel at Mount Sinai. Jesus gives them commandments (ἐντειλάμενος Acts 1:2) by the Holy Spirit. Moses received the commandments on Mount Sinai from God. Israel's life in the wilderness is depicted in the forty days Jesus appeared to his disciples (1:3). Moses gave Israel the law and Jesus, a prophet like Moses (Deut 18:15–19), is presented in verse 2 as giving the disciples commandments through the Spirit.[8] The author not only uses flashbacks, but he also foreshadows the activities of Acts. The gathering in verse 4 is exhorted to wait in Jerusalem for the Father's promise to Israel. The apostles, like Israel, will wander through the world as their wilderness space,[9] and by the power of the Holy Spirit will model the Christian life as witnesses in a hostile world. This will subject them to pain and suffering. Discussing the wilderness, Resseguie writes,

---

4. Lukan narrative here refers to both Luke and Acts as a unit. Parsons, "Departure of Jesus." 13–25

5. Walton, "Beginning of Acts," 447–61.

6. Spencer, *Journeying through Acts*, 34–35.

7. Resseguie, *Narrative Criticism*, 98. Spencer notes that Mt. Olive was a place of revolution against oppressive kingdoms (Zech 14:1–4), see Spencer, *Journeying through Acts*, 37.

8. Spencer, *Journeying through Acts*, 35.

9. Cohn, *Shape of Sacred Space*, 14. For further information on wilderness or desert in biblical literature see *TDNT Vol 1*, 657–60; W. Radl, ἔρημος *EDNT* 2:51–52; Mauser, *Christ in the Wilderness*; Malbon, *Narrative Space*, 72–75; Talmon, "Dessert Motif," 31–63; Lane, *Solace of Fierce Landscape*; Resseguie, *Spiritual Landscape*, 12–16; *Revelation Unsealed*, 80–81.

The desert or wilderness is in-between space. It is neither here nor there, neither Egypt nor Promised Land. It is space between captivity and freedom, between past oppression and future freedom . . . the desert is life at the edge, distant from the security of human structures in the desert. There are no houses in the desert, only temporary dwelling places, and there are no marketplaces, only divine sustenance. It is a nomadic, unsettled, and rootless existence. It is also threatening space, a dwelling place for the satanic and demonic and every foul creature.[10]

The apostles' and the believers' wilderness space is the world. They are freed from the bondage of sin and death yet still contending with the power and presence of sin. They are in the world and not of the world, citizens of heaven and not yet in heaven. The subject of the forty days touches on the kingdom of God.[11] Notable is the shift of focus that follows from the kingdom of Israel to the kingdom of God. The repetition of the kingdom in verses 3 and 6 denotes the emphasis and significance of the theme in Acts. The focus shifts from David (as we will later see) to the God of David. It is not on Israel but on the God of Israel.

καὶ συναλιζόμενος παρήγγειλεν αὐτοῖς ἀπὸ Ἱεροσολύμων μὴ χωρίζεσθαι (Acts 1:4). συναλιζόμενος could be rendered "while staying, meeting or eating with them." Ἀλίζω echoes the salt of the covenant in Leviticus 2:13. In verse 3, the perfective aorist form παρέστησεν "signals arrival of the harvest and therefore its presence *has come*; compare with perfect παρέστηκεν ἐνώπιον ὑμῶν *stands before you*."[12] This serves two purposes. First, it is a pointer to the Feast of Tabernacles ahead of Pentecost; moreover second, Jesus could be viewed as having presented himself as a firstfruit offering before the Lord, an offering that was companied with salt (Lev 2:12). In this case, the latter is more salient for it foreshadows the apostles as a renewed Israel on the Mount of Olives just as the old covenant had been given on Mount Sinai.

---

10. Resseguie, *Narrative Criticism*, 95–96.

11. The forty years of wandering in the wilderness were also formation years of a nation that was supposed to model the ways of God to the world. Closer to Acts is the analogous forty days of prayer and fasting in the wilderness that preceded the inauguration of the proclamation of the kingdom of God in Luke's Gospel. Jesus has been with the disciples for forty days after his resurrection speaking about the Kingdom of God (Acts 1:3).

12. *BDAG*, 633.

The obsession of the disciples with the kingdom of Israel seems to have dulled their understanding and blinded their eyes to what Jesus spoke and did. The apostles' point of view of the restoration of the kingdom of Israel is stated in verse 6. The narrator portrays Jesus's point of view as the acceptable and right view. He emphasizes that the focus should be on the mission from Jerusalem, Judea, and Samaria to the uttermost parts of the world and not times which the father has fixed by his own authority. Having clarified the issue of the kingdom, a theme that will become challenging to some of the believers in Acts – such as the leaders (temple guards, Pharisees, and Sadducees), Ananias and Sapphira, and Simon the sorcerer among others – Jesus was taken up: he was received in the cloud as they watched. Two men in white robes, angels, are introduced in the narrative as trusted characters. Their comments are weighty.

The Mount of Olives had become an incredible space for the disciples. Remarkable experiences had taken place here. It had been a place of prayer and transformation but also a place of pain and separation. In antiquity, king David experienced here the pain of his own son wrestling the throne from him (2 Sam 15:30). In the same place Jesus's own disciples betrayed him. In verse 11, Luke sets forth his eschatology. The ascension sets the stage for the angels to explain this incident.

> While they were looking intently at the sky as he was going, suddenly two men dressed in white garments stood beside them. They said, "Men of Galilee, why are you standing there looking at the sky? This Jesus who has been taken up from you into heaven will return in the same way as you have seen him going into heaven." (Acts 1:10–11 NAB)

The apostles are not only charged with the responsibility to proclaim the kingdom of God but also to live in expectation of Christ's return. This similarity in eschatological expectations and holy living between the believers in Acts and the Essenes contributes to the goal of this study.

4.1.2. Renaissance of Peter as a Leader and Renaissance of the Community (1:12–26)

Verse 13 introduces the apostles into the narrative by name, and Peter's name comes first. All of them – even the women, Jesus's mother, brother, and sisters – are portrayed as devoted to prayer. Peter stood up among the brethren and drew their attention to the need of replacing Judas in the effort to have a community that reflects a true Israel.[13] Howard Marshall states "In Jewish law a minimum of 120 men was required to establish a community with its own council."[14] Therefore, it follows that in Jewish terms Luke establishes that the disciples were a body with sufficient numbers to legally form a new community (true Israel).[15] Citing the fulfillment of Scripture, Peter assumes his position as a shepherd of his brethren. He strengthens them by giving insight into what the Scripture says concerning the situation shortly behind them. Jesus's charge to strengthen the brethren (Luke 22:31–32) is now a reality. Peter is portrayed as leader and spokesman of the community.[16] "His denial of Jesus in the court yard of the high priest might well have discredited him irretrievably in his colleagues' eyes but the risen Lord's personal appearance to him and recommissioning of him rehabilitated him and ensured for him a position of leadership never to be forfeited."[17] Thus, the author characterizes Peter also as a restored leader.

In Acts 1:20 the author portrays Peter as interpreting (Ps 68:26 LXX [Ps 69:25 MT]), (Ps 108:8 LXX [Ps 109:8 MT]). David is referred to as a prophet here. David is speaking by the Holy Spirit and this place him among those whose statements can be relied upon in Acts narrative.[18] Peter directly applies David's Psalm to their situation at present. Judas's habitation or camp is referred to in the language of the wilderness camping (Num 2:1–31). Therefore, Judas represented a tribe, a camp in Israel among the followers of Jesus. According to BDAG, the accusative feminine singular τὴν ἐπισκοπήν could be rendered as "the office of watching over with special reference to being present, visitation, which manifests itself in protection care (Luke 19:44; 22:32) It is a 'position of responsibility' (Num 4:16) an engagement in oversight,

---

13. Marshall, *Acts of the Apostles*, TNTC, 64.

14. Marshall, 64.

15. Marshall, 64.

16. Craig Keener notes that Peter takes the lead here as his master had promised (Matt 16:18; Luke 22:32). He further observes that Jesus had accorded Peter a special resurrection experience. Keener, *Acts*, vol. 1, 754.

17. Lampe, "St. Peter's Denial," 346–68.

18. To mark out those speaking for God in Acts, one must be sanctioned by the Spirit.

supervision."[19] Since Judas and Peter are both called to the same office of apostle, the author consequently characterizes Peter as an overseer, a supervisor and inspector who functions as a protector and caregiver, responsibilities that are similar to the Mebaqqer in CD. It is noteworthy that though all the apostles were charged with the same responsibilities, Peter is portrayed as their leader, in essence overseeing the camps of the believers in Acts like the Mebaqqer in CD. The author's portrayal of Peter as interpreting Judas's act as a fulfillment of Scripture echoes a pesher interpretation, and this view provides a basis for us comparing the two communities in Acts and CD. The urgency of replacing Judas points to the significance placed on the camping of Israel in the wilderness where every tribe had a specific position around the tabernacle (Num 2) and any absence would be detrimental to the community as a whole (Judges 20–21).

The reader who is aware of the passion week activities, especially the details concerning Judas's betrayal, must be struck by the fact that Peter speaks about Judas's betrayal with no reference to his own denial of Jesus.[20] Judas's procurement of a field from the proceeds of his wickedness bears a resemblance to Ananias and Sapphira's act of keeping part of the proceeds of the sale of their piece of land in chapter 5. Peter highlights the punishment of Judas's wickedness as the curses enlisted in the Psalms, by describing the nature of his death and the stigma attached to the field he acquires that comes to be known known as Ἀκελδαμάχ "Field of Blood."[21] Peter proposes

---

19. *BDAG*, 379.

20. Spencer observes,

> Judas' failure provides an interesting counterpoint to Peter's. Both apostles turn their backs to Jesus – one through betrayal, the other through denial – but Judas is irrevocably lost while Peter is ultimately restored. Apparently, Peter's treachery is viewed as an isolated aberration, while Judas' is treated as a symptomatic of his total apostasy from Jesus' way.

Spencer, *Journeying through Acts*, 40. Spencer's position and others could be further argued on the basis of Luke's characterization of the two apostles' pre-aberration statements and activities. Peter on one hand, intentionally seeks to defend Jesus and show solidarity (Luke 22:33) while on the other hand Judas voluntarily confers with the Leaders of Israel and seeks for a perfect opportunity to hand Jesus over to them for a pay (22:1–6). Probably on the basis of these happenings Luke portrays Peter as forgiven and reinstated.

21. Luke depicts the dispensability of Judas, as an apostle. The choice of another may sound light but a far-reaching statement is made. The choices of God are not indispensable and can always find a replacement from other deserving followers or faithful. Israel particularly should be worried for betraying God to the world and like the rulers of the people who love money (Luke 16:14) should be warned through this act of reconstitution of Israel. Though Spencer

that the company of believers fill the vacancy left by Judas to complete the required number of witnesses, the camp of a renewed Israel. Qualifications are laid down, names proposed, prayer offered and the lots cast to determine God's choice, and with the appointment of Matthias the number required to constitute the team of witnesses is complete.

In sum, Acts 1 characterizes Peter as a restored and obedient leader, organizing the community of believers in Jerusalem to fit the expected standards of a Jewish community. He is further portrayed as an overseer providing protection and care, qualities that will clearly manifest in the narrative. The act of standing to address the believers, the concern for proper constitution of the community of believers, the pesher style of interpreting scripture and the eschatological expectations attested to in chapter 1, is a worthwhile basis for comparing the leadership and ethics of the two communities in Acts and CD.

4.1.3. Inauguration of the New Temple (2:1–13)

The tongues phenomenon in Acts 2 significantly advances the plot. The disciples are in one place at the time of this momentous occurrence. G. K. Beale writes,

> The appearance of "tongues as of fire" is an expression of the coming Spirit that reflects a theophany, which appears to be associated with the heavenly temple . . . This was the model theophany for most later similar divine appearances in the Old Testament, and to some degree, God's coming at Sinai stands in the background of the Spirit's coming at Pentecost.[22]

Beale (among other scholars[23]) proposes the Sinai experience as a model of successive divine experiences and a type of Pentecost. The Pentecost phenomena in turn become a model of successive divine experiences for the later similar divine occurrences in the book of Acts.[24] The apostles and the believers

---

argues that this is reinforces the significance of the twelve witness and as well reconstructs the idea opening the apostolic ranks to new members, it could be further observed as a warning to presumptuous Israel and her leaders that their position is being opened up for new members and creating space for the willing Gentiles as witnesses of Christ's resurrection. See Spencer, *Journeying through Acts*, 40.

22. Beale, *Temple*, 204.

23. Spencer, *Journeying through Acts*, 32; Keener, *Acts*, vol. 1, 801.

24. Acts 8 in Samaria, Acts 10 at Cornelius's house, Acts 19 at Ephesus.

in the upper room were heard speaking in other tongues. This act is enabled by the Holy Spirit. The multitudes present in Jerusalem were bewildered, for each one of them heard the believers speaking in their own language. Beale posits that the multitudes in Jerusalem and the tongues bring to mind the tower of Babel in Genesis 11. He views Pentecost as a reversal of Babel's sin of uniting against God's revealed will.[25] The tongues and confusion motif points back to Babel, but it also points forward to the spread of the gospel. The scattering that will erupt due to persecution of the believers in Jerusalem, and the scattered witnesses will take the message of the "mighty works of God"[26] wherever the Spirit-filled believers went (Acts 8:4; 11:19–23). The happening attracted two responses: one group seeking to understand the meaning and the other mocking the believers as full of new wine. They are respectively insiders and outsiders. The author's way of identifying insiders and outsiders again shows up in Acts. In Luke, it was how people responded to what they saw Jesus do and what they heard him say. Now it is what they see the Spirit do through the witnesses (the apostles, and specifically Peter as the leader of the group) and what they hear them say that will determine proper response in Acts. The two divergent groups will run parallel throughout the narrative, but this study will focus on how the audience responds to what Peter says and does (Acts 2:33), for this will determine for us who count as insiders and outsiders in Acts 1–12 and 15.

Peter as the leader of the emerging community stands up to clarify a misconception by the onlookers. Some were of the opinion that the disciples are drunk. Peter explains the significance of what is happening. Beverly Roberts Gaventa, however, strongly opposes this thinking focused on human agents (leaders) instead of the divine figure (the Spirit of God). Gaventa argues that reading Acts through the lens of leaders and heroes is to miss its purpose.[27] She counsels,

---

25. Beale, *Temple*, 202. It was God's plan that man should be fruitful, multiply, and replenish the earth. But the people in Babel united against this command, they wanted to dwell together and not be scattered.

26. μεγαλεῖα τοῦ θεοῦ as used in Acts 2:11 may also be attest in Job 37:14 in reference to creation, Psalm 65:5 and Psalm 78:7 in reference to miraculous acts, John 6:28 in reference to believing God, John 9:3 in relation to the healing of the blind man and Acts itself which could refer to prophecy.

27. Gaventa, *Acts of the Apostles*, 42.

Readers, who set aside the expectation that Acts is an institutional history, shaped and reshaped by human leaders, will
instead see God at work from the beginning until well past the
end. God is the one who glorifies Jesus and raises him from the
dead, who rescues the Apostles from the prison, who directs
Ananias to baptize Saul, and who insists upon the inclusion of
the Gentiles. . . . If readers of Acts find themselves in a journey,
the major sights are not those created by human hands; they
result from the actions of God alone.[28]

Gaventa's admonition is highly relevant to the twenty-first-century context,
especially in view of the resurgence of an overemphasis on the indispensability of charismatic leaders in relation to institutional success and the un-
checked "hero syndrome" that comes with it. For example, we live in a society
where members of churches and sects hold in high esteem their prophets and
apostles more than even God whom these men and women serve. Sometimes
these leaders are obeyed without thinking of the consequences. Marriages
are dissolved on the basis that the "man of God" has said it was not the will
of God in the first place, suicide and death is gladly embraced in obedience
to the "man of God". Gaventa's advise cannot be overstated, "It is God who
is at work from beginning to until well past the end."[29]

For example, consider this analogy. Eating fish in Africa is one of the most
risky yet delightful ventures especially to people who come from areas where
fish is not a traditional delicacy. Fish has flesh as well as bones. What benefits
our health most as human beings is the fillet and not the bones. Learners (and
sometimes even veterans by accident) have occasionally landed themselves
in difficulty by swallowing fish bones. It would be imprudent to reject fish
just because of the dangerous bones. Rather, it is wise to learn to separate
carefully flesh from bones. Thus, the apostles are witnesses as Gaventa rightly
posits, while on the other hand, the author characterizes them as providing
leadership to the church. On the one hand God is working in Acts, yet on
the other hand, God is using people to accomplish his purpose. These characters serve as models of God's accepted character norms. It is clear from the

---

28. Gaventa, 26.

29. Beverly Roberts Gaventa, *The Acts of Apostles*, Abingdon Old Testament Commentaries
(Nashville: Abingdon Press, 2003), 26.

Gospels that Jesus provided leadership to his disciples, and ultimately passed the responsibility to Peter and the apostles.[30] Therefore, human leadership in Acts, and God's work through leaders, should be celebrated without unduly emphasizing it over other themes.

4.1.4. Validation of the New Temple Symbols (2:14–41)

Apart from linking the tongues phenomena to Babel and Sinai, Beale also discusses tongues as a theophany from the heavenly sanctuary in Judaism. He sees a parallel between the "tongues of fire" in Acts 2:3 and *1 Enoch* 14:8–25. He points out that the Dead Sea Scrolls interpreted the Urim and Thummim stones as to having shone gloriously as "tongues of fire," "when God gave the prophetic answer in the midst of his theophanic cloud to the high priest's question about whether a prophet is true or false."[31] He further demonstrates that Pentecost was a fulfillment of prophecies by Isaiah, Joel, and John the Baptist.[32] Just as the Urim and Thummim was important in establishing the mind and will of God in a given situation or matter, the tongues phenomena is significant to this study because it shows the progressive establishment of a new community from one geographical location to the next and further helps us to identify characters that belong to the new community.

Peter interprets the episode of Acts 2:1–12 as the first phase of the fulfillment of Joel's prophecy (Joel 2:28–29; LXX 3:1–2). David W. Pao observes that Peter substitutes Joel's μετὰ ταῦτα (Joel 3:1 LXX) for Isaiah's ἐν ταῖς ἐσχάταις ἡμέραις (Isa 2:2 LXX) at the beginning of his quote.[33] His thematic pesher implies that the two prophets were speaking of what is happening in Jerusalem now. He fuses a time Isaiah envisions when the nations would be drawn to Israel with a time Joel envisions charismatic (operation of the gifts of the Spirit) service at the temple or Israel. The peaceful season is connected with charismatic service: ministries of prophecy, visions, and dreams would result in shalom. We must infer here that if indeed Isaiah is focused

---

30. Matt 16:17–20; Luke 22:31–34; John 21:15–19; Acts 1:13, 15; 2:14; Gal 1:19; 2:7–10.

31. 1Q29; 4Q376. "The Qumran text envisions the high priest discovering the prophetic revelation of the Urim and Thummim in the temple (presumably the innermost sanctuary or the holy place) and then revealing the prophetic answer to the congregation of Israel in the courtyard." See Beale, *Temple*, 207fn, 19.

32. Beale, *Temple*, 208–16.

33. Pao, *Acts*, 156–59.

on the restoration and renewal of Israel, then that connects his concerns to Eden, which could be the background of Isaiah's prophecy. Peaceful living will consistently accompany the Pentecost experience as witnessed in Acts, and it is a forerunner to phase two of Joel's eschatological prophecy as cited by Peter. Acts 2:19–21 of Peter's pesher seems to introduce the happenings that will usher in Jesus Christ's second advent. The angels have already alluded to this (Acts 1:10–11) and the Pentecost phenomena likewise point to this eschatological hope.

Peter argues that what is being witnessed in Jerusalem is the fulfillment of Yahweh's promise to his servant David. He points out that this Jesus who was crucified unjustly is the promised heir of David's thrown. Now that he has been "exalted to sit on the right hand of God, and having received from the Father the promise of the Holy Spirit, he has poured out this that you yourselves are seeing and hearing" (Acts 2:33). Since this is undisputed fact and Peter's audience have conceded that fact (Acts 2:37), Peter exhorts them to repent and be baptized for the remission of their sins. He emphasizes that if the conditions of salvation are met, they will receive the gift of the Spirit. The promise is for the audience, their children, and as many as the Lord shall call. Peter's assertion binds the Pentecost tongues phenomena to the preaching of repentance and forgiveness of sins with water baptism as a prerequisite to baptism in the Spirit and subsequent speaking in other tongues. Now the renewed Israel will be identified by the experience of the promise of the Father. Peter exhorts his audience to save themselves from "this crooked generation." It is not stated if they experienced the baptism in the Spirit and speaking in other tongues at that time, but many may have experienced Pentecost just like the apostles and the hundred and twenty at the upper room, for about three thousand souls were added to the community of believers at Jerusalem that day.

4.1.5. Description and Implications of the New Temple Space (2:42–47)

The author describes an environment of tranquility and peace. The believers devoted themselves to the word, fellowship, and prayers among other disciplines. The picture portrayed here is of a community of peace, evoking the environment where the first Adam lived in Eden. God does not only send the promise but restores humanity to a state similar to Eden. God had given to the first Adam his commandments, fellowship with God, the power to rule, and take care of the garden. Beale argues,

> Adam and Eve did not remember God's word, and they "fell,"
> and they failed to extend the boundaries of God's Edenic tem-
> ple . . . Christ succeeded in just those temptations where Adam
> and Israel failed because he remembered God's word and obeyed
> it. Therefore, Christ is the last Adam and true Israel who rules
> by his word as King over evil in the way Adam and corporate
> Adam, Israel, should have ruled.[34]

Consequently, through Christ, the church is the new Eden and Israel restored. The description of Eden in Genesis 2 points to an ideal community for the first Adam that was lost when he chose himself over God (Rom 5:12–17), but now restored through Christ. Thus, as God took time to describe his creation in Genesis, so is the author of Acts taking time to describe the state of the community of believers, as demonstrated in this summary statement and others to follow in the narrative.

Gaventa and Witherington link the major summary statements of Acts (2:42–47; 4:32–35; 6:7; 9:31; 12:24 etc.) to a description of an ideal Greek community.[35] However, Witherington notes that "the idea was already be-ing practiced in some form at Qumran."[36] The Christian community echoes an ideal community or space like the Eden of God. This understanding of the major summaries will create an even better stage for understanding the intrusions that follow in Acts 5. Satan intruded in the garden of Eden by in-fluencing the first couple, just as we see him intrude here in the new Eden by influencing Ananias and Sapphira. Pentecost inaugurates God's new temple, the community of believers became the dwelling place for God, and the true attendants, Israel, are the believers who experience Pentecost.

It is apparent that the functions of the temple and its attendants are be-ing replaced in the light of these new developments in Acts. We have seen the Lord descend upon his temple by his Spirit and take residence in the hearts of believers in Jerusalem. In the Old Testament, the Spirit rested upon

---

34. Beale, *Temple*, 396.

35. Gaventa, *Acts of the Apostles*, 81; Witherington, *Acts of the Apostles*, 162.

36. 1QS9:3–11; CD 9:1–15.

prophets, kings, and priests for special functions, but now he has filled the believers to prepare them for the task of witnessing. The apostles and believers are now portrayed as new representatives of God and his true temple. If this is true, then the functions and symbolism of the temple institution and related themes of the nation of Israel must have also shifted in the light of this transformation. God had promised Israel that when they prayed in his temple he will answer (2 Chron 7:13–15). However, he now responds to their prayers from wherever they pray (Acts 3:1–10; 4:24–31). This fact will soon become a point of conflict between the apostles and the leaders of the people. The fact that there was a community in Eden that failed to adhere to God's ordinances, then, there was a community in the nation of Israel and they failed. A new community is evidently formed on the day of Pentecost. This new community resembled the Qumran community, hence providing a suitable basis for comparing the leadership and ethics of the two communities in Acts and CD. This fact further demonstrates that God is a God of community (κοινωνία Acts 2:42).

In Acts 2, Peter is characterized as addressing not only the believers but the crowd also. The threads of pesher interpretation and eschatological expectations attested in Acts 1 are present also in Acts 2. Peter's role as an interpreter of the law in the Christian community portrays him as a teacher. He is also characterized as one persuading Israelites to save themselves from their crooked generation. It is noteworthy that Peter persuades them to join the renewed Israel as a way of salvation just as the community in CD believed that they were the renewed Israel through whom all Israel would be saved. Peter's interpretation of scriptures as being fulfilled in his time and his burden to persuade the Israelites are qualities attested of the Mebaqqer of CD and this provides similarities that sets grounds for comparing them (Peter and the Mebaqqer).

4.1.6. Conflict between the Apostles and the Leaders of the People (3:1–4:37)

Acts continues to highlight the significance of prayer in the lives of Jesus's followers. For instance, we are told that Peter and John go to the temple to pray at the ninth hour (Acts 3:1). In passing, it is noteworthy that Peter's name continues to take the first place narratively portraying him as the leader of the community. The apostles' commitment to prayer clearly portrays their dependence on God. This fact demonstrates the transformation they had undergone since they had struggled to watch with Jesus in Gethsemane (Luke 22:39–46).

4.1.6.1. Healing of the Lame Beggar (3:1–10)

The chapter opens with a reaffirmation of the apostles' involvement at the temple. Verse 1, connects chapter three to the previous narrative (Acts 2:46).[37] The physical setting of this episode as the temple is a foil of the new temple (the believers) and symbolizes the presence of God as well as the place of healing (Matt 21:12–17).[38] Peter and John are going to the temple with many faithful Jews for prayer.[39] In this temporal setting, the hour of prayer, it is interesting to note that Peter addresses the lame man directly "in the name of Jesus Christ,"(Acts 3:6–8) and he is miraculously healed. Peter is here portrayed as a channel of the miracle. This depicts Peter in the same light as the Mebaqqer in CD who taught the true Israel the mighty works of God.

A new character is introduced in the narrative, but we are given very little information about him. We are only told he was lame from birth and was carried daily to the gate of the temple to ask alms from those who entered the temple. We are given his age (forty years) at the end of the episode. The lame man is positioned at the gate to ask alms[40] from the worshippers who went in the temple. Peter as the leader of the new temple is presented as one devoted to prayer. This is depicted in the fact that it is the hour for prayer; the

---

37. Bock, *Acts*, 159.

38. The irony here lies in the fact that this man has been at this beautiful gate for a long time yet his story seems to portray little of the beauty represented in this setting.

39. Bock, *Acts*, 159.

40. "Alms giving was a responsibility that Judaism took seriously as an expression of compassion that honored God," Bock, *Acts*, 160. This is best demonstrated in Tobit 4:8–11:

> Give in proportion to what you own. If you have great wealth, give alms out of your abundance; if you have but little; do not be afraid to give alms even of that little. You will be storing up a goodly treasure for yourself against the day of adversity. For almsgiving delivers from death and keeps one from entering into Darkness. Almsgiving is a worthy offering in the sight of the Most High for all who practice it.

Peter responds to the guidelines of this passage appropriately. This is echoed in his address to the lame man. Peter and John have no silver and gold to demonstrate compassion to the lame man. However, like their master, they gave what they had as a worthy offering in the sight of God. This utterance is made in the sight of God and it must be construed so: silver and gold have we none but such as we have as an offering to God we give to you. For many years worshippers gave silver and gold but the apostles give the gift of God: healing.

multitudes present certainly must have come to pray just as Peter and John. Interestingly to note, even after the miracle, Peter and John are portrayed as entering the temple with the healed man (Acts 3:8). This thread of prayer runs through these first three chapters in Acts: in fact, the rest of the text under this study. This characterization of Peter and the people around the temple as devoted to prayer, provides another area similarity between Peter's leadership and ethics and CD community who described as highly regarding prayer (1QS 9:26–10:8).

Peter gives attention to the man as does John; they explain that they do not have anything to give in terms of traditional alms. In essence, they are stating that in terms of riches "we are on the margin like you. But by trusting the Lord Jesus Christ we have found a place in the society (community of believers) even though we have no silver and gold."[41] The author portrays Peter as one without money (wealth) but endued with the power of God to heal. Peter commands the lame man to rise up and walk and his feet were strengthened, and he walked.[42] Overjoyed, he entered the temple with them and all who saw him were utterly astonished (3:10). Here, the author characterizes Peter as a supportive and enabling leader (3:7).

It is very clear by this notable sign – the healing of the lame man – that the presence and power of God abide with the apostles. The presence of the God of Israel will not be limited to the physical temple as it was before. One needed to be in the geographical setting of Jerusalem to experience the presence of God, but now that presence dwells with people (Matt 1:23; John 1:14). Members of the renewed Israel do not need to be in the physical temple in Jerusalem to experience God's power to heal. For instance, Peter's shadow is able to heal the sick laid on the streets (Acts 5:14–16). Philip also heals in Samaria (Acts 8:6–8) and Peter in Joppa (Acts 9:32–35, 39–42). The narrator consistently persuades the reader of Acts to see and accept this change that has taken place concerning the temple as a place of God's presence. He

---

41. Peter professes poverty so to say and a promptness and readiness to show compassion to the needy. See Chung-Kim and Hains, *Acts*, 41.

42. Bock notes that the imperfect indicative περιεπάτει denotes a continuous act. The lame man has been asking for alms continuously but now has been commanded to continuously walk. He now joins those who walk and give alms as a result of receiving the gift of new life, Bock, *Acts*, 161.

continues to demonstrate that what the apostles are doing is consistent with what Jesus "began to do and teach" (Acts 1:1–2).

4.1.6.2. Peter's Address at Solomon's Portico (3:11–26)

The core message of Peter's address to the audience at Solomon's portico is not different from the one in chapter 2; however, he goes for different characters in persuading his audience this time.[43] Once again the author carefully selects his rhetorical instruments. The temple setting calls for a change of characters that are invoked in the rhetoric technique. It is most probable that the patriarchs and Moses will be the most appealing characters to use with this group at Solomon's portico. Peter demonstrates that the God of Abraham, Isaac, and Jacob, had raised Jesus from the dead and by faith in his name this lame man stands perfectly healed. The narrator quickly constrains his readers to shift their focus from people to God by having Peter clarify what had happened. Peter's humility and understanding is evident in the passage. He ascribes the glory of the miraculous act to God (3:12).[44] Gaventa rightly notes,

> Contrary to the conclusion that might have been drawn from the healing, Peter and John make no claim for themselves. This is no mere rhetorical flourish, since later episodes will provoke similar confusion in response to the miraculous (14:8–18; 28:1–6). In addition, the story of Herod's death demonstrates God's judgment against those who refuse to acknowledge their humanity (12:23; 28; 6).[45]

It was necessary that the source of this healing be stated in such a context that could construe it otherwise. Witherington suggests that Peter in choosing of the words, discounts the apostles' power, the author contrasts them with divine men (8:10).[46]

Peter notes the ignorance of his audience (3:17), and as the leader of the renewed Israel, he outlines the conditions of admission into the renewed

---

43. Myers, *Characterizing Jesus*, 42–52; George Kennedy, *Classical Rhetoric*, 202–7.

44. Bock, *Acts*, 168.

45. Gaventa, *Acts of the Apostles*, 86; Moule, "Christology of Acts," 159–85.

46. Luke clarifies that Peter and the other apostles are not like pagan religious "divine men" denoting a person of good character. It was imperative that the crowd understands that the apostles were not divine as pagan religious people would claim. See Witherington, *Acts of the Apostles*, 179.

Israel. Peter also alludes to the eschatological hope of Jesus's followers (3:21). He posits that the heavens will hold Jesus until the restoration of all things is complete as the prophets prophesied. He connects Jesus with the prophet Moses promised in Deuteronomy 18:15. Jesus is the fulfillment not only of Deuteronomy 18:15 for a prophet like Moses but also the promised seed of Abraham through whom all the families of the earth will be blessed (Gen 22:18). This promise made to Abraham in Genesis 12:1–3, and reiterated in 22:18, of land, offspring, kings, and a blessing has now found perfect fulfillment in Jesus Christ. The last of these promises had proved elusive and of a great concern during the Second Temple period. Now everyone anywhere in the world putting their faith in Jesus will experience these blessings and in turn, they will be blessings themselves. Peter candidly proclaims that any soul that does not listen to this prophet like Moses, Jesus Christ, will be destroyed from among the people (3:23). As a leader, he courageously lays the conditions for enjoying a new status in a renewed Israel. Disregarding the person of Christ and his message amounts to damnation.

It is at this crucial stage of his message that the leaders of the people come in and arrest them. Peter not only continues the message and miracles that Jesus "began to do" but also continues to experience the persecution the message and miracles attracted to Jesus's life. This portrays him as an obedient and courageous disciple of Christ. And now the motif of persecution and suffering moves the plot forward from here. If Peter's claims are true, then the following conflict in chapter 4 should be read in the light of 3:23.

4.1.6.3. Arrest and Trial of the Apostles (4:1–31)

The superiority of the apostles in countering the theological point of view as represented in the first three chapters of the narrative – the traditional and conformist theological point of view of the religious leaders of the day, that is the priests and the captain of the temple and the Sadducees – may be read as "wrongheaded, short-sighted, and contrary to the will of God."[47] The three groups are introduced as antagonists in chapter 4 and the offices they represent will be our focus in this section.

The arrest takes place in the evening, as the day darkens into night. It is late for the leaders to be working; they are in the dark about what is happening in

---

47. Resseguie, *Strange Gospel*, chapter 4 for a full discussion.

God's agenda. The readers, who have aligned their loyalty to Jesus as the new Moses, are armed with the understanding that anyone who disobeys Jesus and his followers (especially the apostles) is liable to destruction. The order of narration and the selection of the episodes (healing of the lame man, the people praising God) are meant to help the reader infer the divine verdict on what follows in chapter four, but also establish a new point of view. It is ironic that two men were put in custody yet five thousand people believe their witness. The Jewish leaders' effort to restrict and hinder the preaching of the apostles is portrayed as futile (4:3–4). Significant to note is the fact that the Sadducees did not believe in the resurrection, a theme that was core to the apostles' message. There is a clear rivalry unfolding between the priests and captain of the temple and the apostles. The apostles are portrayed as exercising priestly duties (2:38–41; 3:1–10) and 1 Peter and Revelation testify later that Christ has made us a royal priesthood (1 Pet 2:9; Rev 5:9–10).

The judicial bench in verse 5 is to be viewed in the light of verse 2. The priests, the temple captain, and particularly the Sadducees were annoyed that the resurrection of the dead was being taught and proclaimed in the name of Jesus. The group reacting in verse 2 should be the Sadducees who did not believe in resurrection.[48] Their question in Acts 4:7 does not make sense in the light of their reason for arresting the apostles (4:2), which perhaps indicates that they are not acting in an altogether rational way. The influential presence of the priestly family seems to denote or foreshadow what could be at stake. In Luke 20:1–2, the same groups allied together against Jesus, and the author here demonstrates the continuity of both volumes in employing the same response Jesus used in Luke 20:1–8. Still fresh in Peter's mind, he cites Psalm 117:22 LXX and Isaiah 28:16. Jesus is the cornerstone laid in Zion. The leaders knew well enough the implications of how one responded to this cornerstone. The rulers of the people are static characters in this Lukan narrative, they are still asking the same questions (Luke 20:1–2; Acts 4:7), they are still afraid of the people (Luke 20:19; Acts 4:14). Though in Acts the fear of people is not as explicit as in Luke, one could safely infer that they were

---

48. The Sadducees rejected the doctrine of resurrection (Luke 20:27–40). The witness of the apostles must have made them extremely uncomfortable especially in the case of Christ whom the Christians claimed to have concrete evidence. The apostles to be proclaiming this within the temple confines was a criminal offence and they were indeed culpable for the breach of peace in the temple precincts. See Marshall, *Acts of the Apostles*, New Testament Guides, 98.

constrained by the fact that people would react negatively if they punished the apostles for healing the lame man (4:16). The author shows his readers that the rulers of the people should have embraced Peter's leadership just as they should have embraced Jesus's leadership, and through this he demonstrates that the rulers of the people are unable to make sensible decisions. Up to this point, the groups confronted by the divine happenings and the message of Jesus have asked very resourceful questions that have enabled many of them to make choices and decisions that ultimately moved them to insiders in Acts narrative.

Peter, the leader of the group, is particularly portrayed as dynamic. In the Gospel of Luke he was fearful of the leaders of the people, he denied Jesus to save himself, but now is characterized as bold and courageous, he is filled with the Spirit and of course seeking to obey God rather than men (as before in Luke). Peter and the crowd are depicted as responding appropriately to what they heard and saw (Acts 2:8, 33).[49] The fact that Peter is presented as speaking under the influence of the Holy Spirit, placed him at the same level as the Old Testament prophets. The leaders of the people acknowledge that the boldness of the apostles must be as a result of Christ's influence, which is, of course, a contrast to their undecidedness. Narratively, we cannot rely on their observation, but the apostles' response to their threats is indeed a demonstration of their resoluteness and boldness. The apostles vow to obey God and stay true to what they heard and saw. Though angry and burning with a desire to punish, the priests, captain of the temple, and the Sadducees are overpowered by the many who are praising God for what had happened (4:21). Just like their Master in Luke 20, the apostles are found innocent, they found no legitimate grounds for punishing them, for people held them in high honor and they praised God for what he had done through them.

In Acts 4, the priests and temple hierarchy are against God's appointed leaders (the apostles). This is reminiscent of another priestly rebellion, in which Korah and his team had a dispute with Moses and Aaron (Num

---

49. In Acts 2:8, the devout men from every nation asked "what does this mean?" and after receiving an explanation, they asked "what shall we do?" Ironically the rulers after consulting asked among themselves, "What shall we do with these men." Whereas everyone is taking responsibility for their actions, the rulers after listening and now that they confess of the notable sign of the healed lame man, they still do not see themselves as faced with the burden of making things right by repenting and being baptized in the name of Jesus for the remission of their sins that they may experience the refreshing moments in the presence of God.

16:1–35). As Korah and his group rose against Moses and Aaron God's appointed priesthood (Exod 28:1) in Numbers 16, the leaders of the people have risen against Jesus – the promised Moses (Deut 18:15, Acts 7:37) – and his apostles as God's appointed priesthood sanctioned through the Pentecost experiences (Acts 2:1–4; 3:16; 4:8). The problem in Numbers is solved in two stages. In response to Korah, Dathan, and Abiram's opposition, God moves to destroy them but Moses and Aaron intercede for them before the Lord. Moses addresses Korah's group in the presence of the leaders with him and promises an unusual ending for the disobedient group. When Moses finished speaking (Num 16:31–35), the earth opened up and swallowed up Korah's group and their families (Num 16:32). Moses and Aaron are depicted as interceding, just as the apostles and the believers in Acts. God demonstrates who his true representatives are by first judging Korah; he opens the earth to swallow them, though in Acts the place where they were praying was shaken and were filled with the Holy Spirit. Then, God solves the priestly dispute by performing a notable miracle as a sign in both narratives. God instructs Moses that every house of Israel bring a labeled staff to be deposited in the tent of the meeting thus he will make the grumbling to cease (Num 17:1–12). Aaron's staff budded thus solving the priesthood problem permanently. The lame man's healing was equally a notable miracle that tamed the leaders of the people. Prayer continues as a setting for the baptism in the Holy Spirit and the bold witness as a characteristic of those who experience Pentecost.

4.1.6.4. The Ideal Community (4:32–37)

The restored humanity and Israel is portrayed as one in purpose; they shared their possessions and witnessed with power to the resurrection of Christ. There was sufficiency in the community, just like in Eden; the space described in Acts is an ideal habitation of the descendants of the second Adam (now represented by the Christian community). God had indeed created an ideal environment by his Spirit as the space for his redeemed people. In this space, selflessness and commitment to the purpose of God are significant, and the followers of Jesus contribute generously to the livelihood of the insiders.

In this setting, Barnabas is introduced into the narrative as Joseph, a son of encouragement, a Levite, and a native of Cyprus. The brief but packed introduction of this character attracts the close reader's attention. There is an indisputable threat facing the apostles and believers from the leaders (4:29).

Barnabas serves as a foil to Ananias and Sapphira in the selling of their field in chapter 5. However, discussing this multi-faceted character is clearly problematic. His descent from Levi reinforces his separation unto the Lord. Levi was sanctified unto God for his service and God was his portion. Just like we will see later these descriptions of Joseph portray who he is to the renewed Israel. Like Aaron the son of Levi came along with Moses to remedy Moses's speaking difficulties, Barnabas will be found to be to Saul and Mark's great encouragement. He is set apart as a true Levite for the work God had called him to do (13:1–3). Levi did not receive an inheritance with the rest of Israel and he depended on what the rest of Israel gave to God as offerings. The introduction of Joseph (Barnabas) at this point in the narrative prepares the reader for the divine intrusions that will follow in delivering the apostles, the high level of fidelity and holiness that will be required of the community members, and even the multi-ethnic inclusions that would follow thereafter.

Before we turn to Acts 5, it will suffice to make a comment on the narrator's defamiliarization technique in this Jerusalem narrative thus far. The narrator arranges his episodes to capture the attention of the reader and further persuade them to reject the dominant cultural point of view represented by the religious authorities. The crowd in chapter 4 is being drawn to the apostles; the author hints this by first reporting that the leaders were afraid of the people and second because people were praising God for the healing of the lame man (4:21–22). The insiders – made of "the powerful, wealthy, among others – shape the norms and values of the society and it is their ideological perspective that the narrator transforms."[50] The apostles are viewed in the society as outsiders and marginalized, they are poor (3:6; 4:13–14) and not rulers. Their actions and sayings deform and make strange the commonplace point of view expressed by the powerful religious leaders in Jerusalem.[51] The impact of this deformation can be noted in the questions posed by the powerful and ruling class: "by what power or by what name did you do this?" (Acts 4:7) The inverted social pyramid seems to throw out the society's acceptable insiders and move in the marginalized as the insiders. The reader is encouraged to espouse a new point of view of the true representatives

---

50. Resseguie, *Narrative Criticism*, 34.

51. Resseguie, 36.

and witnesses of God. This should be done in contrast to traditional norms of the society at Jerusalem.

In this section, the author continues to characterize Peter as one devoted to prayer (3:1–3; 4:24–31), one who is not rich (3:6), caring and supportive (3:7), humble (he does not take credit for the lame man's healing but ascribes the miracle to the power of God through Jesus's name). He is portrayed as explaining scripture, expounding the eschatological hope of those who believe (3:21–26). The author depicts Peter (and the apostles) as one filled with the Spirit, as courageous and bold (4:8–13), only fearing God and not people (4:19–20). By the threats and persecution directed to the apostles, they are shown as continuing in the sufferings of Christ as well as his message of the kingdom confirmed by healings and miracles.

4.1.7. Intrusion into the Eden Space (5:1–11)

The presence of δέ in verse 1, prepares the reader for a contrast of the character being introduced with the previous character, Barnabas. Ananias is simply introduced as a certain man. This man with his wife Sapphira sold a piece of property. The reader is by now accustomed to people selling their property and bringing the proceeds to the feet of the apostles to support the community (4:34–37). However, these two characters depart from the norms attested in the narrative so far. Ananias, with the knowledge of his wife Sapphira, keeps back some of the proceeds for himself. He brings part of the proceeds and lays it at the feet of the apostles. Peter is here portrayed as a leader. He takes the responsibility to interrogate Ananias. Peter indicates that Ananias's act is inspired by Satan. He clarifies that the lie or craftiness was not done to the apostles but to God, who through the Holy Spirit has made his abode among the Christian community in Jerusalem. At the mention of God, Ananias falls down and dies. Peter demonstrates the ability to understand the secrets of people; he confronts evil as God's representative.[52] He acts as a foil to the leaders of the people.

Ananias and Sapphira could be understood well through the analogy of Eden. For instance, Ananias and Sapphira could be read in the light of new

---

52. Marshall, *Acts of the Apostles*, 112.

Eden. Just as God judged Adam and Eve so he judged Ananias and Sapphira.[53] In this reading, they are characterized as outsiders (as they are outside the house where the apostles are operating). They are victims of Satan's craftiness just like Adam and Eve in Genesis. Adam and Eve desired something for themselves too. The principle of selfishness and craftiness is present in both narratives. Satan attempts to pollute the newly created community through a couple just as he did with the first couple (Adam and Eve). However, just as the second Adam (Jesus) overcame him in the wilderness after the baptism of water and the Spirit, his followers filled by the Spirit are able now to confront Satan in the power of the Holy Spirit and expose his lies and align themselves to God. Both the attempts to pollute Eden and the ensuing judgment meted out to the deceivers are very severe.[54]

A. E. Harvey provides "two other examples of similar experiments in communal living at about the same time."[55] The Qumran community dismissed such offenders from the community and due to the oaths that bound such; they ended up starving to death or received back out of compassion.[56] The gravity of the matter lies in the fact that the lie was made to the Holy Spirit. Harvey further observes,

> From early Old Testament times the attitude required of human beings by God was "faith," that is, readiness to accept wholeheartedly the demands and promises of God. The opposite

---

53. The setting shows Peter in the house and both Ananias and Sapphira are depicted as coming in from outside.

54. It is difficult to provide answers to all genuine questions that are posed in response to the severity of this judgment, even the disinterest in informing Sapphira of the husband's death. However, one thing is clear, that this new community is going to treat sin and wickedness seriously.

55. Harvey, *Companion to the New Testament*, 402.

56. See Josephus, *J.W.* 2.143–44:

> But for those who are caught in any heinous sins, they cast them out of their society; and he who is thus separated from, them does often die after a miserable manner; for as he is bound by the oath he has taken, and by the customs he has been engaged in, he is not at liberty to partake of that food that he meets with elsewhere, but is forced to eat grass, and to famish his body with hunger, till he perish.

It is apparent from Josephus that the idea of death for these grave falters was very present in the mode of their punishment. Harvey also highlights another model presented by a Greek historian writing a generation before Luke. Diodorus Siculus reports that the communal farming in Spain also punished by death anyone keeping back anything for private consummation. See Harvey, *Companion to the New Testament*, 402.

attitude was called "putting God to test": it consisted of question-ing whether God really intended a certain demand or whether he would really fulfill a certain promise. This kind of challenge to God was expressly forbidden (Deuteronomy 6.16, "Do not put the Lord your God to the test") and Peter was drawing attention to the seriousness of this offense when he asked how the couple had "agreed together to put the Spirit of the Lord to test." The punishment brought about by Peter was commensurate with the gravity of the sin.[57]

This contrary attitude was present in Eden in Eve and the Serpent's dia-logue, and was also persistent in the wilderness narrative and eventually cost the children of Israel a generation that died in the wilderness.

On the other hand, Ananias and Sapphira can also be read in light of Achan's greed in Joshua 7. Achan's greed for things dedicated to God, influ-enced his decision and consequently led to his stoning. It would be Luke's intention to show that the God of Abraham, Isaac, and Jacob (3:13) is still the same God, judging acts of faithlessness as severely as ever. Marshall sees similarities between the Ananias and Sapphira episode and the action of Achan in Joshua 7. He notes that the verb ἐνοσφίσατο in Acts 5:2 is identical with that used to describe Achan's action (Joshua 7:1).[58]

Peter is characterized here as a leader taking a firm position against decep-tion and greed of Ananias and his wife (Sapphira). Like Jesus in the wilder-ness, Peter resists the efforts of Satan to bring down what God is doing in the community of believers. Ananias and Sapphira seek to enjoy the honor that comes with giving yet are not keen on the spirit and principles that ac-company the exercise. This kind of severity to evil is also attested at Qumran in dealing with those who are caught in serious offenses.[59] Verses 12–16 sum up the activities as the interrupted narrative from Solomon's portico is resumed. Verse 11 provides the impression of the people, in the light of what happened to the couple, none dared to join them though they held them in high esteem. The apostles' defiance of the high priest and the Sadducees' prohibition is depicted in the miracles done even in a more spectacular way

---

of Peter's shadow healing those brought to the apostles (5:15–16). It is evident that the apostles are doing the works of God while the high priest and the Sadducees are plainly in opposition to what God is doing. However, it is ironical that the Sanhedrin purport by persecuting the apostles they are in essence serving God's purpose and will.

4.1.8. Persistent Opposition, Arrest, and Deliverance (5:12–33)

The leaders of the people again arrest the apostles and put them in prison. Initially, the names of the arrested are not given until later. The leaders are portrayed, as always, with negative emotions (here jealousy) and the same temporal setting (night) is attached to the actions of the leaders. An angel intervenes and opens the prison and instructs the apostles to go to the temple and speak to the people all the words of the new life. The narrator now clearly indicates that the Lord is on the apostles' side. Whereas the leaders impede the preaching of the words of this life, the instruction from above is to keep speaking. Thus, the apostles' position is strengthened and the reader is guided to choose the position of the apostles. The apostles' response to the charges by the leaders is brief but still provocative: "we must obey God and not people" (Acts 5:29). They further accuse the Sanhedrin for killing Jesus (5:30). The Sanhedrin respond with a desire to kill the apostles (5:33).

Gamaliel, a Pharisee, and teacher of the law intervenes and requests for the apostles to be put outside (5:34–35). He narrates to the leaders the history of movements of this nature in Israel and their fate and counsels the leaders to leave the apostles alone lest they find themselves fighting against God (5:37–39). The leaders consent to Gamaliel's advice but not without beating the apostles and threatening them not to speak in the name of Jesus (5:39b–40). Ironically the apostles leave the council rejoicing for having had an opportunity to suffer dishonor for Christ's name (5:41), and they continued every day in the temple and house to house to teach and preach Jesus as the Christ (5:42). What Jesus began to teach and do is irresistible. By his Spirit, the apostles are energized to witness boldly and perform signs and wonders in his name.

The author shows that Peter's shadow heals the sick laid on streets and he is used in delivering those possessed by the evil spirits. The priests (Sadducees) were filled by rage because of these great works. Peter and the apostles are evidently characterized as true representatives of God and his people. This is confirmed by the fact that God opens prisons and lets the apostles out to continue preaching the message of resurrection consequently demonstrating that God was evidently on the apostles' side. They are further characterized as leaders who fear God yet fearless of any man.

4.1.9. Growth and Its Challenges (6:1–7)

The expansion of the community at Jerusalem posed a challenge for the distribution of resources, with Greek speakers grumbling that they were being shortchanged. Γογγυσμὸς used in (6:1) is found in Exodus 16:7–9; Numbers 17:20, 25; John 7:12 among others. However, it is probable that the author reports here an episode similar to the one in Numbers 11.[60] The related verb γογγύζω is found in LXX Numbers 11:1, although the noun γογγυσμός is not used in Numbers 11, the cognate verb γογγύζω is used of the Israelites' grumbling about food, when they complain in the Lord's hearing. Gaventa points out:

> In Numbers, the Israelites complain unjustly against God because of the hardships of their life in the desert, and they incur God's wrath for doing so. In Acts 6, the grumbling is directed by one group to another group within the community rather than God, and the treatment of the complaint suggests that it is entirely appropriate. The widows within this community must receive care they need.[61]

The complaint of the Israelites is similar to the dissent in the Jerusalem community between Hellenistic Jewish widows and the Palestinian Jewish widows.[62] The initial problem in Numbers 11 is food, and the complaint is made in the Lord's hearing. Although the challenge in Numbers drives Moses to react before the Lord as the crowd does, the case in Acts receives a different response from the leadership (which is assumed to be Peter's leadership). The apostles, including Peter, prioritize the ministry of the word and prayer

---

60. Gaventa, *Acts of the Apostles*, 113.

61. Gaventa, 113.

62. Gaventa, *The Acts of Apostles*, 113. ; Joseph A. Fitzmyer, *The Acts of the Apostles*, 346–47.Basically, the difference between the Hellenistic Jews and the Hebrew speaking Jews was the language.

without neglecting serving on tables. Several details in this passage make it probable that the author is reporting something similar to Numbers 11. In both episodes, the leaders appoint other leaders to help in the situation (seventy in Numbers and seven in Acts). In Numbers, God did the transfer of the Spirit from Moses to the seventy and the confirmation that the Spirit had settled on the candidates was the ability to prophesy (Num 11:25).[63] Even two of them who did not come at the place ordination prophesied in the camp (Num 11:26–30). Though they never continued to prophesy it was evident that they shared in the Spirit of the prophet Moses. In Acts, the transfer of the Spirit is done differently, keeping in mind these men are already filled with the Spirit. However, the laying on of hands is done in the transfer of blessings or leadership. Just as the case in Numbers, two of the men become bold witnesses just like the apostles, although also they do not continue in this for long just like the elders in Numbers.

However, the line of thought where this passage is treated simply as an administrative challenge that required delegation has received great resistance from several scholars.[64] Joel Green takes it a notch higher, "rather than presuming that the Apostles are above reproach, we ought to wonder about the opposite." Green rightly states that "the apostolic task is simply *diakonia* (1:17, 25), and the same is true of Paul's commission (20:45; 21:19)."[65] However, it is critical to note that the primary assignment of the apostles is found in Acts 1:8 and not in verses 17 and 25 as Green purports. What the apostles do in Acts 6:1–7 is far from neglecting widows. Being Jesus's witness includes serving widows, but serving widows may not be witnessing for Christ per se. The leaders of the people in Acts had a program for serving widows yet they could never have claimed at all to be witnesses of Christ. Reading a theological problem in 6:1–7 would be reading too much too early in this text. Yes, we know that later challenges will emerge along that line but spotting them now would be too anxious. It is acceptable that Jesus presented himself, as "one who serves at tables,"[66] the measure of true greatness. However, a careful examination of the passages presented in support of

---

63. Kisau, *Acts*, 1310.

64. Spencer, *Acts*, 75–77. Spencer contends that "this narrow perspective marks . . . a reversion back to old habits of resisting Jesus' comprehensive ministerial program." Spencer, 76.

65. Joel B. Green, *Practicing Theological Interpretation*, 67.

66. Joel B. Green, *Practicing Theological Interpretation*, 66.

this view (Luke 22:4–27 and John 6:9–14)[67] indicate that Jesus did delegate some of those services. Further still, arguing that the apostles were wrong in prioritizing the word and prayer to serving tables, Green is not reading Acts 6:1–7 in light of Luke 10:38–42:

> Now as they went on their way, Jesus entered a village. And a woman named Martha welcomed him into her house. And she had a sister called Mary, who sat at the Lord's feet and listened to his teaching. But Martha was distracted with much serving. And she went up to him and said, "Lord, do you not care that my sister has left me to serve alone? Tell her then to help me." But the Lord answered her, "Martha, Martha, you are anxious and troubled about many things, but one thing is necessary. Mary has chosen the good portion, which will not be taken away from her."

Jesus clearly prioritizes attention to the word over serving. The apostles were cognizant of the fact and perceived how Jesus would have handled the two necessary functions. Therefore, reading social challenges and unrest in the widows' genuine concerns, which were adequately addressed, is unwarranted. Luke ends this section of the life and activities in the community in Jerusalem even with a clear summary statement (Acts 6:7) indicating the unity and progress of the new community.

In sum, Peter (represented among the Apostles) is characterized again as a leader who esteems the Word of God and prayer and he is not willing to relegate his responsibility for the word and prayer to second place in favor of serving tables. This characterization of Peter's leadership is similar to the emphasis given to prayer and the word in CD, therefore providing a good basis of comparison of Peter's leadership in Acts and the Mebaqqer's leadership in CD.

---

67. The apostles are literally imitating their master's philosophy of life. He spent time in prayer before the father, before he served people, and after his service he again retreated to prayer and listening to the father. It would be an overstatement to claim that the apostles neglected the widows to concentrate on prayer and the word. There must have been a clear balance on how the two important services were practiced and many times, like with Jesus, delegation may have been the way out.

4.2. Peter in Samaria and Judea (Acts 8–9)

In this second section of chapter 4, we will examine two settings: Samaria and Judea. Persecution aids the gospel in getting to Samaria. The message of the kingdom of God moves to fresh grounds – out of Jerusalem. The scattered believers find themselves among the despised half-breeds of Samaria.[68] Though the persecution may be viewed as a negative force against the church it is in essence serving the purpose of God, since the believers are scattered to areas that they are destined to be according to Jesus's program (1:8). Saul of Tarsus who was introduced in the narrative at the end of chapter 7 is portrayed as a threat to the believers. He is shown as ravaging the church. This introduction will serve as a contrast to his future life and ministry. Against the backdrop of these persecutions, Philip brings the message of Christ and the kingdom of God to Samaria. Looking at Acts 9:32–42 we will examine our topic around two characters in relation to Peter's leadership and ethics as portrayed at Lydda and Joppa. Aeneas in Lydda is bedridden (9:32–35) and experiences healing, whereas in Joppa Tabitha is dead and Peter resurrects her from the dead (9:36–43).

4.2.1. Peter and the Samaritan Community (8:1–25)

4.2.1.1. Philip Proclaims Christ in Samaria (8:4–8)

This portion of chapter 8, introduces a character connected to the persecution of Saul – Philip. Philip was among the seven deacons chosen in chapter 6. Stephen, his colleague, has been stoned to death, an act that sparked persecution in Jerusalem. Those who were scattered from Jerusalem went about preaching the word. Philip comes to Samaria and preaches Christ to the city; the crowd at Samaria with one accord pays attention to his message. Just like the crowds at Jerusalem, the crowd at Samaria is evaluated by how they respond to what they hear and see (8:6). They are also depicted as in one accord; the very qualities of the community at Jerusalem begin to form in Samaria also. Samaritans hear the message of Jesus as the Christ and see signs performed in the name of the risen Christ. Unclean spirits come out of many and also many who were paralyzed and lame received healing and that

---

68. Witherington, *Acts of the Apostles*, 280.

brought joy to the city of Samaria; for the first time the reader is introduced to the ministry of exorcism of unclean spirits in Acts.[69]

Simon the magician is introduced into the narrative as one who amazed the people of Samaria with his magic. Just as the message of Simon had an impact on these people so did the message of the Christ. It is noteworthy that Simon the magician is not contrasted to Philip but to Christ. The two authorities depicted here as influencing Samaria are the message of Simon and presently the message of Christ. The inhabitants of Samaria responded to Christ with the very attention and amazement they had earlier accorded to Simon who claimed to be "somebody great" (8:9), and the people testified of him saying "this man is the power of God that is called great" (8:10). In the light of the conjunction δὲ, signaling a new development, the contrast in verse 12, followed by the act of baptism, we can safely point to an inception of the triumph of the kingdom of God over the kingdom of Satan represented by Simon, who also is baptized. Simon's amazement at the signs performed by Philip after his baptism casts aspersions on his faith. This kind of response to the signs up to now in Acts is associated with onlookers who are yet to make a decision on how to relate to what they hear and see (Acts 2:12; 3:10). Simon, then, is characterized as undecided and an outsider, consequently shedding light on our understanding of his character in the following conversation. It is probable that the author seeks to demonstrate that becoming a member of the renewed Israel takes more than routine and outward activities; it is strictly a matter of a changed heart, as he points out later (8:21–23).

4.2.1.2. Peter and the Inauguration of the Community of Believers at Samaria (8:14–25)

The report of Samaria receiving the word reached the apostles at Jerusalem. The ideal Christian communal life is extended to other geographical locations as per the commandments of Jesus. It is not clear why the community in Jerusalem decides to send envoys to Samaria. Among other reasons, the need for the same quality of life and community may have informed the apostles' decision to send Peter and John to Samaria. Other scholars have interpreted this act to mean that Philip's work needed approval,[70] but Gaventa

---

69. Spencer, *Acts*, 95.

70. Fitzmyer, *Acts of the Apostles*, 400–401.

reads Peter and John's journey as an inspection trip.[71] Peter and John seem to know exactly why they were dispatched to Samaria.

On arrival, they prayed for the Samaritans to receive the gift of Holy Spirit. Prayer is closely associated with the apostles' undertakings. The author constantly characterizes the apostles as people of prayer, consequently portraying Peter in the same light, thus characterizing Peter as one who depends on God through prayer. Jesus's instructions to the apostles emphasized the place of the Holy Spirit in the life of his witnesses (Acts 1:4–8). The author further characterizes Peter and John as apostles who are keen to see the Holy Spirit take his position in the lives of believers.

Their prayer is specific, that "that they might receive the Holy Spirit for he had not yet fallen on any of them" (8:15–16). The tongues of fire viewed as a theophany of the heavenly temple descending on God's renewed Israel at Jerusalem is attested in Samaria, both authenticating and connecting the community in Samaria and Jerusalem. The community at Babel was scattered to fill the earth against their will but the renewed Israel of God by this phenomenon of tongues will be scattered to fill the earth with the message of life. The narrator clarifies that despite the deliverance and healings reported, the believers at Samaria have not yet been marked out as Jesus's disciples, who are distinguished by the baptism with the Spirit just as John's disciples were distinguished by the baptism in water. The sign of the heavenly temple descending on the Samaritan community is not witnessed as we saw it in Jerusalem, but the reliable narrator reports they received the Holy Spirit by laying on of hands. The Samaritans can now claim full rights as the true witnesses and representatives of Christ and God in this part of their world after receiving the Holy Spirit. Here also Peter and John are portrayed as men who desire the Spirit-filled life for the believers.

Despite Simon believing Philip's message, he is still portrayed as one outside of the community of the renewed Israel. In verse 18, the author employs irony as he records that Simon saw that the Spirit was given through the laying on of hands, and offered Peter and John money so that he may give the Holy Spirit. This act denotes Simon's defective understanding of the ways of God. At this point, Simon's mistaken response to what he hears and sees is demonstrated clearly. Several things come to the reader's mind at this point.

---

71. Gaventa, *Acts of the Apostles*, 138; Spencer, *Acts*, 79.

Peter's lack of silver and gold (3:6) come to play, in the light of Simon's offer, Peter is portrayed as a leader of integrity by rejecting to be compromised. Peter's ability to discern the activities of Satan again is manifest (5:3). He is presented here as a man of reliable spiritual discernment. A pattern seems to emerge, where Satan seeks to infiltrate the communities of the renewed Israel, as they get established. In Acts 5, through deceit and craftiness Ananias and Sapphira, who are portrayed as agents of Satan, attempt to gain a reputation as generous people in the community, following the Eden temptation model. However, in chapter 5, it is not an open affront like the one in the wilderness in Luke 4. Peter responds sternly to Simon condemning him to perish with his money.[72] He demonstrates his fidelity to the course of Christ by refusing to be corrupted or compromised. He states that the gift of God is not for sale and trying to do so is wickedness. Those who espouse Simon's point of view are agents of Satan and cannot be filled by the Spirit. The desire to be great and in control is still present in Simon whom the author mention as one who believes (8:13). It is apparent that Simon has not truly repented from his old ways – "your heart is not right before God" (8:21, 23).

The question of Simon's faith in Christ is rather troubling. Peter counsels him to repent of his wickedness and pray, perhaps he may be forgiven. To this Simon responds with a plea for Peter's prayer that none of the things spoken by him may affect him. The fact that Simon seems unable to participate in prayer, one of the common characteristics of the members of the renewed Israel in Acts, raises concern in regard to his conversion. Simon is reported as having believed and been baptized, it may be correct to infer that Peter and John may have laid hands on him, but he was not filled with the Holy Spirit like the rest of the believers at Samaria. Peter's language in Acts 8:20–24, "you have no part in this," "your heart is not right . . ." portray a Simon as an outsider. Marshall and Gaventa portray him as in opposition to the activities of the kingdom of God.[73]

---

72. Spencer has aptly discussed this exchange in the light of honor-shame context, observing that "To pretend to acquire the spirit as Simon has done marks the highest insolence against God on a level of abominable apostasy repeatedly denounced in Israel's deuteronomic-prophetic tradition ('your heart is not right before God'; you are in the gall of bitterness'; see Deut. 29:17–20)." He further states that the only remedy for Simon is to repent and pray though there is no guarantee for forgiveness. Spencer, *Acts*, 88.

73. Marshall, *Acts of the Apostles*, New Testament Guides, 160; Gaventa, *Acts of the Apostles*, 139.

Peter in chapter 8 is again characterized as the obedient messenger from Jerusalem, sent to supervise or inspect the work in Samaria. On arrival, the author shows him as one who relies on God through prayer and is focused on ensuring the promise of the Father is experienced among believers. Peter stands out as a bold and courageous leader in addressing abnormality in the body, a virtue enabled by his ability to discern the hearts of men just as in chapter 5. By the fact that he advises Simon the magician on how to avert judgment, repent and pray (8:22), Peter is portrayed as loving and caring; not willing that any one should perish. For more of these leadership traits and practices we will now examine Peter's leadership in the Judean region.

4.2.2. Peter and the Judean Communities (9:31–43)

Peter's activities are interrupted by the narration of Philip's ministry to the Eunuch and introduction of Saul, later known as Paul. This interruption is significant for it sets the stage for the ministry to the Gentiles. Just as Philip serves as Peter's forerunner at Samaria, so he does to the Gentiles in witnessing to the Ethiopian Eunuch. The author draws our attention to another protagonist (Paul, the apostle to the Gentiles) who will take Peter's place in the last half of Acts.

4.2.2.1. Summary and Community at Lydda (9:31–35)

The summary statement in verse 31 shows the state of the church: peace and growth characterize this new Eden community. It is true the church has grown from the one hundred and twenty disciples in Jerusalem at Pentecost to thousands in different regions (Jerusalem, Judea, and Samaria). The narrator is keen on portraying the obedience and success of the apostles in relation to Jesus's commandments in chapter 1. The renewed Israel is depicted as conducting herself in the fear of God and comforted in their sufferings and persecution by the Holy Spirit. Instead of diminishing due to the opposition as shown in chapters 6–9, the church is multiplying. Not even persecution could silence the church. The mission to witness that Jesus is Christ from Jerusalem to the uttermost parts of the world is unstoppable.

Peter has been missing since his confrontation with Simon the magician in chapter 8. He is reintroduced again in the narrative in Acts 9:32. Peter is characterized as traveling here and there among the saints in the churches in

Judea, Galilee, and Samaria.[74] He is depicted as an inspector or overseer in these communities. We saw him occupying a place of leadership in Jerusalem, he received by the converts at Pentecost, he was trusted with organizing Samaria's Christian community, and now he is seen as going here and there among these multiplied communities in Judea and Samaria.

Peter is shown as alone on this Judean trip. John, his regular companion, is now missing, as Peter visits the saints in Lydda.[75] Peter finds a man in Lydda called Aeneas. This brief episode employs repetition of actions in numerical series[76] to shape the reader's point of view in line with the narrator's. The author uses two-step progression for emphasis,[77] with the second step elaborating or amplifying the first step.[78] Peter addresses Aeneas by name and the source of his healing by name: Jesus. Peter is characterized as giving credit to Christ for the healing of Aeneas by stating: "Aeneas Jesus Christ heals you" (9:34). The people of Lydda and Sharon see the healing and respond appropriately by turning to the Lord. Apart from the healing, a sign that now is identified with the presence of the Holy Spirit, we are not told anything about the being filled with the Holy Spirit, though already we are told there were saints in Lydda who are seemingly familiar with Peter. The healing of Aeneas sets the stage for the Cornelius narrative, but also portrays Peter as an instrument of hope. The bedridden Aeneas's hope of experiencing life and health is fulfilled; this foreshadows the restoration of a people (the Gentiles) with no hope and without God. Although significant, the healing of Aeneas is accorded very little space; it seems simply to carry the motif of healing and the kingdom of God forward in Acts (9:35). Although Aeneas is a minor

---

74. Marshall, *Acts of the Apostles*, 178.

75. Τοὺς ἁγίους may refer to human beings belonging to God: Saints, God's people, believers (Acts 9:13); what is dedicated to God (Matt 7:6); as a place dedicated to God sanctuary, holy place (Heb 9:1); its plural ἅγια ἁγίων refers to most sacred place, inner sanctuary, very holy place (Heb 9:3), or holy of holies. This could be translated in reference to the community as place where the presence of God dwelled in the tabernacle or the temple or it could refer to the individual believers who now qualify as a habitation for the presence of God which had come down to tabernacle among his people but also in his people.

76. Resseguie, *Narrative Criticism*, 49.

77. This is a rhetorical technique that relies on repeated sequence of actions in a numerical series (twos, threes, fours, and so forth) the second step, or the subsequent step, is meant to clarify, elaborate, or amplify the first of the former step. See Rhoads, Dewey, and Michie, *Mark as Story*, 49–51; Resseguie, *Narrative Criticism*, 49.

78. Resseguie, *Narrative Criticism*, 49–51.

character, not even given an opportunity to speak, as a result of his healing, the residents of Lydda and Sharon are brought to the kingdom.

4.2.2.2. The Community at Joppa (9:36–43)

Tabitha (Dorcas) is introduced into the narrative at this point. The presentation of the Greek translation of her name foreshadows the Cornelius episode that follows. She is introduced as a disciple; it is not clear from the passage if Tabitha is a disciple of Peter or Jesus. However, it is apparent that she was a follower of the way, the Christian faith. Tabitha is like Mary the sister of Lazarus who chose to listen to Jesus. She chose that which cannot be taken from her as a disciple. We do not know whether she had a family or not. It is clear she was single but whether a widow or never married is not clear, but she is definitely among the voiceless and marginalized in the society (women, children, the poor, and Gentiles).

The two-step progression for emphasis continues in this episode too. She was full of good works, acts of charity. She became ill and died, they washed her and laid her in the upper room and immediately sent for Peter, requesting him to come to them hastily. The mention of upper room ties this episode not only to chapter 10, which reports Peter as ascending to the upper room, but it also harks back to chapter 1, in which Jesus's disciples were waiting in one accord for Pentecost in an upper room. Peter responds to their call promptly. On arrival, Peter is met with widows overwhelmed with grief, each weeping and waving tunics and other garments Dorcas had made while still with them.

Before exploring this further, let us consider the setting of this episode and its possible implications for the interpretation of the narrative. The author indicates that this happens in Joppa. Teresa J. Calpino states that "Joppa a plausible 'historical' setting for the narrative, it also held the symbolic significance of rescue from death,"[79] for it was the setting of the Greek myth of Perseus's rescue of Andromeda. She further notes that "Joppa not only had a cultural resonance through associations with Greek mythology but also through the book of Jonah . . . one of the major motifs of the book of Jonah

---

[79]. Joppa was one of the most familiar settings of the story of Perseus Andromeda. See Apollodorus, *Bibliotheca*, 2.3.4–5, and D. Ogden, *Perseus* (London and New York: Routledge, 2008), 149–52.

is rescue."[80] When Jonah was thrown in the sea the sailors were rescued. God rescued Jonah by sending a sea monster (Jonah 2:1 LXX) to swallow him. In the belly of τοῦ κήτους, Jonah cried to God and God rescued him. When Nineveh repented God spared the city (Jonah 3:6–10). And ultimately when Jonah asks to die out of his selfishness and frustrations, God equally spares his life as the Ninevites. The setting of Joppa provokes much more than rescue. It reminds the reader of the hatred and animosity that existed between Israel and the Ninevites. The setting foreshadows the struggles Peter will go through to accept what God is sending him to do just like Jonah, for Peter it will be a case of willing obedience to the heavenly vision. Calpino notes,

> Jonah in the boat and his rescue from the sea monster were the most ubiquitous images in the iconography of early Christianity. The sea monster (*Ketos*) had certain symbolic associations with death in both biblical and extra-biblical sources. Rather than strictly narrating the biblical story, the art and symbols evoke promises of deliverance and God's concern, assuring believers that hope exists even in the face of persecution, rejection, or danger.[81]

Returning to the narrative of Acts, Peter puts the widows who represent hopelessness outside and kneels down and prays. Peter's actions here portray him as a leader who is not willing to let his life and ministry be driven by what he can do for needy people rather than entirely depending on God in prayer and the power of the Holy Spirit. Tabitha's death was the cause of grief to the widows. Peter's action of turning to the body after prayer is actually facing the source of their sorrow. Prayer continues to occupy a special place in the life and composition of the Christian communities. When the disciples are waiting for the father's promise they prayed (Acts 1:12–14), when they were threatened by the rulers of the people they prayed (4:23–31), when setting forth leadership they prayed (Acts 1:24–26), and when faced with death challenges (Acts 4:23–31) and death itself (Acts 12:1–5) prayer was the way to confront life and its challenges. Peter turns from a place of prayer and commands Dorcas's body to rise and she opens her eyes and when she

---

80. Calpino, *Women, Work and Leadership*, 149.

81. Calpino, *Women, Work and Leadership*, 149. See also Snyder, *Ante Pacem*, 28, 54; Vermeule, "Sea Monster," 179–209; and Snyder, "Sea Monsters," 7–21.

sees Peter, she sits up.[82] Peter, again as he did with the lame man (Acts 3), gives her his hand and raises her up. Thus, several times when dealing with the weak Peter is shown to act in a supportive fashion. He presents her to the saints and the widows alive. The repetition of the word saints in this episode ties the two episodes (Aeneas and Dorcas) together and works to introduce chapter 10. Chapter 10 will speak of a man who was full of good works, and who sent two men to call Peter who was in the upper room praying.

The threads of prayer and healing attested earlier in Acts continue to characterize the life of Peter in Acts 8 and 9. Peter is further portrayed as traveling here and there overseeing and inspecting communities of believers (9:32), with a goal to see the communities experience the Father's promise expressed in communal life and works of God (healing and miracles). This characterization provides us with a reasonable basis for comparing Peter's leadership and ethics in Acts 1–12 and 15 with the leadership and ethics portrayed in CD.

The Greek name of Tabitha (Dorcas) prepares the reader for the Gentile world in chapter 10. Cornelius, a Gentile on the margin like Dorcas, can also receive life by faith in Jesus the Christ. Cornelius's good works and alms and devotedness are foreshadowed in the good work and charitable deeds and the sainthood at Joppa.

4.3. Peter among the Gentiles (Acts 10–12, 15)

The apostles in Jerusalem have the commandments of Acts 1:4–8) still fresh in their minds. It may have been easy for them to envision themselves saturating the familiar space of Jerusalem and Judea with the good news of Jesus the Christ who had risen from the dead for the forgiveness of sins and restoration of God's creational purpose. Things become a little complex as they begin to move to Samaritan and Gentile territories. Historic antagonism between the Jews and Gentiles is here felt. Peter and Cornelius know very well that they should not fellowship (Acts 10:28). Even with the good efforts of Cornelius trying to follow the God of Israel as a proselyte, the actions of Peter and his colleagues soon will require explanations. They will be put to task as to why they assumed the liberty to associate with outcasts. However,

---

82. The two-step progression for emphasis continues in this episode as well.

it will take the deliberate work of God through his Spirit to push the gospel over Jewish borders. Chapter 10 would have been well named the apostles' "Gethsemane" – especially for Peter whom God calls to go through this distressing experience, but he ultimately bows to God's will.

4.3.1. Peter and Cornelius (10:1–48)

In this chapter, a very important character is introduced in the narrative. The man is named Cornelius, a centurion, of an Italian Cohort. His involvement in prayer identifies him with the community of believers who are characterized as a praying community. About the ninth hour while in prayer Cornelius sees a vision. Cornelius is portrayed as involved in a major spiritual discipline of the people of God, prayer. The life of the communities of Israel revolves around prayer just as their master's did. Though traditionally a Jew would have difficulties in accepting a Gentile and an outcast like Cornelius, the God of the Jews chooses to accept what his people may have detested. The thread of prayer, which runs through Acts and here takes the narrative forward, provides a suitable similarity with the community in CD.

The author repeats "the ninth hour" in this narrative twice (Acts 10:3, 30). This emphasis probably points to the significance of the hour: the afternoon hour of prayer. It was also the ninth hour that Peter and John met the lame man at the beautiful gate (3:1) and Cornelius is praying at the ninth hour (10:3). The ninth hour at Golgotha may also be in view here. In Luke 23:44–49, Luke reports that the temple curtain was torn in the middle at the ninth hour. This symbolized the way Jesus made for his followers to the holy of holies through his body (Heb 10:20). Now, the time for the four corners of the earth (or the whole creation of God), symbolizing the inclusion of Gentiles, to come to him through the new and living way is complete. This idea is foreshadowed in the numerical repetition of threes and fours in the Cornelius narrative. The time is complete for the nations of the world to come to God by the way of Christ, who gave his life as a ransom for many. At this crucial hour, the angel of the Lord informs Cornelius that his prayers and alms have ascended as a memorial before God. Now Cornelius is to send for Simon,[83] who is called Peter. The author constrains the reader to adopt God's

---

83. Peter's Jewish name is used here, since his response and struggle will heavily be on those lines.

point of view. It is apparent that God registers his presence and point of view through the speech of the angel and visions and dreams repeated in Acts 10.

It is important to note here the presence of angels at Jerusalem at the inception of the renewed Israel (Acts 1:10–11) and now as the gospel transcends the borders of Israel (Acts 10:7). The fullness of time is inferred in the return to the three-progression emphasis used in verse 7 where Cornelius sends three men; two of his servants and a devout soldier. Cornelius's vision is repeated to the three men serving as messengers; this is only implied in καὶ ἐξηγησάμενος ἅπαντα αὐτοῖς ἀπέστειλεν αὐτοὺς εἰς τὴν Ἰόππην (10:8), and the fact that they were able to relay it to Peter later (10:22). The messengers are set forth on their way.

Peter feels hungry and goes up to the upper room for prayer as food is prepared at the sixth hour. Hunger is a normal human experience, thus portraying Peter as subject to normal human challenges. His going up to the house top to pray characterizes Peter as getting into a place of clarification. God is about to act in ways that requires explanation for human beings (Jews) to understand. The narrator mentions the noon-day meal here astutely to prepare the reader for the vision and the underlying issues in the Jewish and Gentile cultures. Peter's desire for food is contrasted with God's desire to save the Gentiles. Hence, the natural hunger for food is symbolic of God's deep desire to save Gentiles

The irony here is displayed in Peter's self-righteous response and understanding of ceremonial cleanliness. Whereas Peter focuses on the food, the Lord focuses on what that food represents. Jews could not eat and fellowship with Gentiles in their homes because they perceived them unclean. However, Peter's rejection of the food is synonymous with rejecting the Gentiles' redemption. Keener derides the fact that Peter would defend biblical kosher practices on a tanner's roof.[84] Due to dealing with dead animals, tanning was not held in favor by Jews for it was ceremonially defiling:

> Tanning was a complicated and smelly business. The hides of
> animals were tanned using tannic acid, which was extracted

---

84. Professional Jewish teachers shared such scruples especially with tanning which dealt with animal carcasses. See Jeffers, *Greco-Roman World*, 28. To observe the holiness in the camp, the Sages decided that none should recite the Shema standing beside a chamber pot, nor enter a bath or tannery with scrolls or phylacteries in hand. Keener, *Acts*, vol. 2, 1725.

from lime, from the juice of certain plants, or from the back of trees. Tanners often worked at seashore to facilitate the disposal of chemicals and because they used salt water in the tanning process. Because of the very unpleasant odors the work generated, its practice was not allowed in cities.[85]

Peter's willingness to be hosted in Simon's home characterizes him as humble and open-minded. Probably Luke wants to show that Peter has no problem with the Jewish scruples; other scholars suggest that Peter's staying with a tanner in a low-class area, and with one of a doubtful repute in Jewish eyes showed his humility.[86]

The angel had instructed Cornelius to send for Peter to explain the way of salvation, yet Peter's presupposition did not allow him to mix with the Gentiles. The voice commands Peter three times to kill and eat. This greatly disturbs Peter. As he ponders this matter, the three men sent by Cornelius had arrived and were inquiring at the gate if Simon Peter lodged there. The narrative clearly shows that the decision to go to Cornelius is purely a divine sanction.[87] The reluctant and soul-searching Israel may not have reached out to the despised Gentile world, to a cursed and defiled people.

Peter goes down to the men and says ἰδοὺ, ἐγώ εἰμι ὃν ζητεῖτε· τίς ἡ αἰτία δι' ἣν πάρεστε; (10:21) an action that characterizes him as accepting to the despised Gentiles. This crucial moment, which I have called Peter's "Gethsemane" above, seems to echo John 18:4–11. The text in John acknowledges that Jesus knew what would happen to him, just as Peter knew what he should do. They both (Jesus and Peter) voluntarily submit themselves

---

85. Jeffers, *Greco-Roman World*, 28.

86. Keener, *Acts*, vol. 2, 1725. Simon the Tanner was accepted in Christianity (Acts, 9:43; 10:6, 32) and Peter's abode there clearly speaks of his growing liberal-mindedness about ceremonial rules. Jeffers, *Greco-Roman World*, 28.

87. Gaventa points to this fact in observing that the conventional notion that this is the story of Cornelius conversion or Peter and Cornelius "threaten to eclipse the primary actor in the story namely– God." Gaventa, *Acts*, 173. It is God who reveals himself to Cornelius in a vision, instructs Cornelius to send for Peter, and prevails over Peter's underlying cultural scruples. Even further intervenes by pouring out the gift of his spirit to Cornelius household in breach of the emerging patterns (2:38–39; 8:17). Just the way the Holy Spirit fell on Jews on Pentecost without human agency so has he ordered events in the case of Gentiles. Indeed he shows no partiality . . . (10:34–35).

to parties that had an agenda that were contrary to their human desires.[88] As Jesus agonized over the issue of his death for humanity, Peter has same inner turmoil ἐν ἑαυτῷ διηπόρει (Acts 10:17). Peter is at a defining point in the matter of the Gentiles' inclusion in what God is doing as Jesus was in Gethsemane. Nevertheless, for him it may not translate to physical death, he is confronted by the decision to die to the fact that he was a Jew and thus superior to the Gentiles. In Gethsemane, Peter's flesh stood in his way of understanding what Jesus was called to experience at the time, leading him to cut off Malchus's ear (John 18:10). Now it is Peter's turn as a grain of wheat to fall to the ground and die in order to bear the fruit of Gentiles' inclusion to the kingdom of God (John 12:24). Peter is determined this time not to love his life more than the Lord lest he misses the harvest among Gentiles.

He presents himself to Cornelius's messengers and hosts them for a night before taking six brothers from Joppa to accompany him to Cornelius's house. A question lingers in the reader's mind as to how Peter's host may have responded to his decision of having Gentiles. The mention of Cornelius's devout soldier is reminiscent of the soldier in Gethsemane (Luke 22:50). Peter is portrayed as hospitable and accommodating to Cornelius messengers. Although the community in CD is known for being closed to foreigners, Peter's quality of being hospitable is similarly emphasized in the community in CD 13:9.

The next day, Peter embarks on the journey to Cornelius's house.[89] The journey is a metaphor of understanding and spiritual awakening.[90] For example the prodigal son came to his senses and journeyed back home (Luke 15:11–24). The two disciples walking to Emmaus were ignorant of the workings of God in Israel, but when their eyes were opened they changed direction (Luke 24:13–35). Noteworthy in this light is the transformation that Peter experiences in regard to his understanding of Gentiles. The journey also symbolizes a time of community formation.[91] This could be true of the inception of the Gentile community that is about to be inaugurated at Cornelius's house.

Cornelius is expectant; he has invited relatives and close friends. Three categories of people again emerge at Cornelius house. His own household is

---

88. In John, the Gentile delegation comes to arrest Jesus, they are not happy with his preaching, whereas in Acts they come to inquire of the way of life.

89. The new day may symbolize new things for both Peter and his host (Cornelius).

90. Resseguie, *Narrative Criticism*, 100.

91. Resseguie, 100.

implied, relatives and close relatives. He falls before his guest and worships him, but Peter lifts him up. It is now easy to identify this phrase, or one similar to it, with Peter's interactions.[92] Ὁ δὲ Πέτρος ἤγειρεν αὐτὸν (Acts 10:26) connects chapter 10 to the immediate passage and even the narrative of the lame man in chapter 3. The emphasis and completeness of his supportive and humble traits are here reiterated in characterizing him. It is worth noting that Peter has now established himself so far as a highly responsive and supportive leader that gives worship and glory only to God (Acts 3:3–5; 6:1–3; 8:14; 9:38; 10:29). The use of πολλούς or related words (10:27) connects this chapter to preceding narratives where πολλούς or πολλοί are used to describe expectant multitudes or those who believed the word.

Cornelius narrates his experience four days ago, at a time of prayer in his house. The time of prayer observed strictly at the temple is now equated to the time of prayer at Cornelius's house. This may be the breaking away from observing the time of prayer at the temple, validating house churches which are already alluded to in the house fellowships in 2:42. Cornelius's claim of having seen a vision of a man standing before him in bright clothing connects his narrative with chapter 1:10–12 Angels are now common agents of the divine message in the narrative. The prophecy and preaching of Peter on the dispensation of visions and dreams and the outpouring of the Spirit upon all flesh have now come upon the Gentiles too. However, the message must be mediated through Jewish instruments, and God has appointed Peter as his vessel and servant for this mission. Cornelius submits to what Peter has to say concerning his vision. "We are all here in God's presence to hear all you have been commanded by the Lord" (10:33).

The author thus portrays the space of Cornelius's house in the same light as the space of the temple. The temple in Israel was a symbol of God's presence. One wonders how the phrase "in the presence of God" here should be explained. God hears the prayers of Cornelius and receives his alms, now he sees visions just like the age described in Joel and Acts 2. This foreshadows the happenings that will follow. The servants and maidservants stated in Joel live on the margin. However, in the last days (this refers to the era of the

---

92. Peter is portrayed as either lifting someone up or exhorting or commanding them to stand up (Acts 3:7; 9:41; 10:26).

fulfillment of these prophecies) they will be acceptable to God and move to the center of God's purpose and activities.

In 10:34–40, the apostles are seen as continuing what Jesus began to teach and do (1:1–2). God sent the word to Israel (10:36); this possibly refers to "a non-vocalized communication," by metonymy the ὁ λόγος is perceived as a definitive expression of the person of Jesus Christ.[93] It is significant to note that Peter does not emphasize Jesus as the Christ, but as the judge of all. Since his audience is predominantly Gentiles the message of the Christ is irrelevant to them. Peter as a leader has repeatedly demonstrated a great understanding of his flock by engaging each group according to what is important to them. Yet, it is clear the message of the resurrection is relevant to all the groups he has addressed in the narrative. While Peter was still speaking the Holy Spirit fell on all who heard the word, to lift all that is happening out of human manipulation. The believers from among the circumcision are amazed that the Spirit fell even on Gentiles just as they themselves had experienced. The astonished believers are astonished as they always are when signs are done in the name of Jesus. The Pentecost narrative at Caesarea is here defamiliarized to get the attention of the readers who are used to the pattern in Acts 2:28–39 – repentance, baptism in water, and then receiving the Holy Spirit with speaking of tongues – are surprised to find the pattern broken here. In chapter 10, instead of repentance leading to water baptism, the baptism of the Spirit and speaking in tongues precedes.

Peter, who wrestled with God before he accepted the call to go to Cornelius to explain the way of salvation, is faced again with an unexpected turn of events. God as the key character in the narrative controls what happens. Peter who enjoyed an almost predictable process is thrown aback by God's interruption here. Peter's flexibility as a leader is also demonstrated here, and this may be held in contrast with the brothers at Jerusalem who seem to maintain a rigid position on the conversion of Gentiles and their receiving the gift of the Holy Spirit. Peter cements his growing liberty from cultural scruples in regard to the Gentiles' inclusion into the kingdom by accepting the invitation to stay for some days (10:48).

Chapter 10 describes Peter's growth and Cornelius's messengers are characterized as on a journey, denoting Peter's growth in understanding and the

---

93. Bock, *Acts*, 396.

formation of the Gentiles' community. The thread of prayer that has been running through the narrative is also attested to in chapter 10. The author continues to underscore the importance of prayer in Peter's life and the entire community of believers. This is consistent with the emphasis in Acts 1:4. Jesus insisted on their waiting in Jerusalem until they are clothed with power from on high. The author consistently uses prayer as a way of showing the apostles' dependence on and collaboration with God. Peter's humility is emphasized by his willingness to lodge at the tanner's house. He is portrayed as hospitable and accepting by the way he receives Cornelius's messengers; he is characterized as growing in experience and understanding of God, which is symbolized by the settings of house top (house as a place of encountering God or clarification) and journey to Cornelius. Because of the mighty works done through Peter, the author seeks to persuade his readers that Peter is a normal human being used by God as a vessel. This he achieves by portraying Peter as perplexed with the vision (10:17–19), he refuses to receive worship and confirms that he is also a man like Cornelius (10:24–27); as hungry (10:10). Significantly, in Cornelius's house as in Jerusalem, the Holy Spirit fills Cornelius and his people without the laying on of hands. Peter is seen again receiving Gentile believers in the Christian community just as he did at Jerusalem, Judea, and Samaria. He stays with them for a few days as per their request, denoting Peter's accepting attitude toward the Gentiles' community.

4.3.2. Defense for the Mission to Cornelius (11:1–18)

The inclusion of Gentiles is published far and wide. Not everyone in Jerusalem receives this news well, however.[94] The circumcision party[95] criticizes Peter for his involvement with the Gentiles (11:3). Διεκρίνοντο, which English translations have rendered as "contended, criticized or had issue" which may be as well defined as "distinguish on the basis of class or ethnicity" suggests the possibility of this circumcision group segregating from Peter for eating with the Gentiles. This is not explicit in chapter 10; it can be inferred on the basis of the invitation to remain with them for some days, thus possibly pointing to table

---

94. Gaventa, *Acts of the Apostles*, 172.

95. There seems to emerge two distinct groups at the community in Jerusalem, Peter representing one school of thought and the circumcision party representing the other. The former group learned to walk in liberty to dietary rules while the latter insisted on these rules.

fellowship. It is apparent that during the few days Peter stayed at Cornelius's house, these days were regarded as a time of fellowship. The author portrays Peter as having accepted the Gentiles by sharing their home and food.

Therefore, Peter is put on the defensive for his actions among the Gentiles. He retells his vision on the rooftop in Joppa. This further reiterates the importance of Peter's vision in the narrative. Peter and the apostles are acting on the commandments of Jesus through his Spirit (1:2). The reader who is now used to the apostles obeying these commandments from the Spirit already sees Peter as an obedient witness. He reports that he himself had a problem with the instruction but on the other hand knew that his was the place of obedience to the heavenly voice. Peter has witnessed the repercussions of those who choose to ignore God's way like Judas Iscariot (1:18–20). Peter presents God and his Spirit as witnesses of his actions. He further presents the six brothers who went with him. In chapter 10 we are not told the number of Peter's delegation but it is significant here to state the number. Peter also conveys Cornelius's vision and how the angel instructed him to send for him to instruct him in the way of salvation. Peter connects Cornelius's mission to the words of the Lord. He might be referring to Acts 1:4–5, which would have brought to memory the purpose of the baptism with the Holy Spirit. The Spirit was to empower the apostles to be witnesses in Jerusalem, Judea, Samaria, and the uttermost parts of the world (1:8). Peter wisely argues that his mission to Cornelius's house was within their mandate as Christ's witnesses; especially the witness that the Spirit is given to Gentiles just as it was given to the Jews. Rejecting Cornelius's and the Gentiles' experience is rejecting the works of God and disobeying the words of the Lord, and Peter is not willing to stand in God's way of blessing Gentiles. Peter is not ready to question what God is doing in his kingdom. Rather he is ready to follow even when he does not understand or he is not in favor (John 21:18–22).

It is worth examining verse 17, in the light of Acts 10:34. The Holy Spirit is God's promise, to as many as he will call and as long as he calls. God has the liberty to give to all who meet his conditions. Wherever and whenever he sees obedience to his commandments, he will bestow the promise regardless of the nation and gender. It is notable that the Holy Spirit is not the property of a few people or the leaders of the church. On the contrary, the church and its leaders are the property of the Holy Spirit. The Spirit is not programmed by people but he has the liberty to manifest himself to the people of God anytime and anywhere on earth. The author specifies the leader's limits. He clearly sets the gift and its bestowment beyond Peter's liberty and choice. He directs to whom the leader gives and how the leader gives it. What God intends with his promise is beyond humanity's stipulations and good intentions. For the kingdom to be preached to the ends of the earth, human involvement must be strictly subordinated to the divine sanctions. When the circumcision group was confronted by these facts they fell silent (11:18) and glorified God.

In 11:1–18, Peter is characterized as traveling. Chapter 10 ends while he is at Caesarea and chapter 11 begins by reporting that he is in Jerusalem; probably this is mentioned also to advance the narrative and the motif of missions – Peter traveling here and there as an overseer of the Christian communities (8:14; 9:32; 10, 11, 12:17; 15). He is portrayed as defending the truth and vision he received from God concerning the Gentiles. Peter contends that he heard a voice from heaven; hence what he teaches and does among Gentiles is a heavenly revelation and sanction.

This characterization is similar to the duties and responsibilities of the Mebaqqer in CD. He was the overseer of many camps; he valued truth to the extent of calling the community "sons of truth/light." He was also required to be experienced in dreams and visions, thus, Acts 11:1–18 provides another area of similarity between Peter's leadership in Acts and the Mebaqqer leadership in CD.

4.3.3. Insurgence of Persecution and Peter's Deliverance (12:1–25)

The sending and returning of Barnabas and Saul to Jerusalem frames the pride and death of Herod in chapter 12.[96] Acts 12 introduces Herod. Herod is portrayed as "laying violent hands on some who belonged to the church,"[97] as a contrast with "the laying on of the hands" by the apostles to bestow the gift of the Spirit. James son of Zebedee is killed, an act that pleases the Jews, and Peter is arrested pending execution after the Passover. Verse 5 shows Herod commits Peter to prison as the church commits Peter to prayer.

---

96. Resseguie, *Narrative Criticism*, 54–55.

97. Herod's laying on of hands produced death contrary to the life-giving laying on hands by the apostles.

The narrative of what happens to Peter is also framed by the two Herod episodes (12:1–5, 20–23). The description of Peter's manner of detention and the possibility of the death sentence the next day makes it unlikely for one to be deeply asleep, as he is depicted to be (12:7–8). Peter's ability to afford such deep sleep in this particular circumstance speaks of his trust in God. It is amazing that what is happening has not infiltrated Peter's peace. The second puzzling incident is that light shone in the prison and Peter's chains fell off without the soldiers noticing a thing, moreover they passed the first and second guard without the guards on duty realizing. The elaborate security around Peter makes his deliverance very difficult, if not impossible. Similarly, at the first Passover, it was not easy to deliver Israel from Egypt; during a more recent Passover, the tomb of Jesus was equally strictly guarded. If reading Peter's narrative in the light of the Passover festival is acceptable, then the most appropriate Passover setting to read this episode is the recent one during which Jesus was crucified.[98] But in all the Passovers (in Exodus, Jesus's, and now Peter's) there is a clear sense of divine intervention. The parallelism in the three episodes is notable.

	Exodus	Luke	Acts
Night	11:4; 12:8, 12, 28, 42	24:1	12:6
Angel revealed	3:2	24:4	12:7
Gird on sandals clothes make haste	12:11	24:12	12:7–8
Vision	3:3	24:11	12:9
Opens – sea, tomb, gate	14	24:1, 12	12:10
God rescues	18:8–10		12:11
Doubt			12:13–15

The prison setting is a place of restriction just as Egypt and Jesus's tomb were. The angelic messengers appear at both Passovers as shown above in the chart. It is evident that these happenings took the hand of God and it was not mere human schemes.

However, Peter's narrative finds a perfect analogy in the Jesus Passover episode, first in that both Jesus and Peter show themselves to their communities. Second, they are both first met by a woman and they both send the

---

98. Keener, *Acts*, vol. 2, 1879.

woman to pass the message of their deliverance to the others. One thing that is worth noting is the fact Peter's chains fell without being heard or noticed by the soldier (Acts 12:7–11), this was indeed a miracle just as Jesus was raised from the dead, leaving the linen clothing without tampering with them (Luke 24:12). Peter kept on knocking until they opened and when they saw him they were amazed. Though the church was praying for Peter's release, the believers had trouble believing that he was free (Acts 12:16). This act finds some similarity in Jesus's persistent revelation of himself to the doubting disciples after his resurrection.

The framing of this narrative with the Herod episodes implies that Peter's narrative should be understood in the light of how Herod treated Jesus and James. The author portrays Peter as a true disciple of Christ willing to follow his master even in his death. The characterization of his imprisonment as parallel to Christ's death may be foreshadowing his death.

The author ends chapter 12 by revisiting the state of the renewed Israel. The word of God increased, and the church multiplied even in the midst of this adversity. The narrative also serves to introduce Paul and Barnabas the main characters of the last half of Acts, along with their assistant (John) Mark. It is also apparent that Peter is exiting leadership, and this has been hinted repeatedly in the preceding chapters. Whether one favors the early or a later dating of Acts,[99] Peter must be at least sixty years old.[100] The mother church in Jerusalem is experiencing famine. Luke portrays the Christian community in Antioch as reaching out to help their brethren in Jerusalem, in contrast to the people of Tyre and Sidon who seem to heavily depend on Herod for survival, Luke portrays a renewed Israel as ably supplying the needs of her members in all places (Acts 11:27–30; 12:25). This confirms that the community is still sharing their property with each other.[101]

---

99. Keener, *Acts*, vol. 1, 383–401; Marshall, *Acts of the Apostles*, New Testament Guides, 46–48; Bock, *Acts*, 25–27.

100. This conclusion is based on assuming that Peter was around the same age as Jesus. Therefore, by the time Acts was written, Peter must have been at least 60 years of age, because at least thirty more years would have elapsed, whether one favors the early or later datings of Acts. This is the same period of time that he exits the scene of leadership just as it was required of the Mebaggar

101. It is apparent from this passage that some of the saints in Jerusalem still owned personal property like John Mark's mother, the church met for fellowship and prayer (12:12). This alludes to the fact that the selling done in the early chapters of Acts was purely voluntary.

The author continues to underscore the importance of prayer in the Christian community. Peter is characterized as in prison and the church earnestly offering prayer for him (obviously for his release). Peter is portrayed as being woken by an angel; the angel leads him out of prison as though in a dream. This act highlights his obedience, as he follows the angel's instructions without objections. He joins the believers who were praying for him and after explaining the miraculous deliverance from prison he departs to another place (12:17), which portrays him as still functioning as an overseer or inspector of the camps or communities of believers. Peter's last appearance in Acts will be to validate Paul and Barnabas's work among the Gentiles before the Jerusalem council in Acts 15. But here, the stage is set for Barnabas and Paul to take over the mission to Gentiles, notably inaugurated by Peter in Acts 10. We now turn to this final narrative in chapter 15 for further characterization of Peter's leadership and ethics in Acts.

In Acts 12, the author portrays Peter as a courageous disciple, who is not disturbed even in the face of imminent death. He is depicted as taking the persecution patiently and peaceful. The motif of prayer is advanced by his visit to Mary's house where believers are meeting for prayers. He is also portrayed as testifying of the mighty works of God in delivering him from prison in response to the prayer of the believers. He demonstrates his obedience and loyalty to the Jerusalem leadership under James, by requesting the believers to inform James of this happening. Luke advances the theme of overseer by indicating that Peter left for "another place."[102]

This characterization of Peter's leadership is similar to the Mebaqqer at Qumran and this provides a basis for comparing the two communities, but more so provides better lenses for understanding leadership and the ethics practiced in Acts.

4.3.4. Peter's Leadership and the Jerusalem Council (15:1–21)

The growth of the church continues to present both social and doctrinal challenges. Made up of both Jews and Gentiles, the early church begins to experience deep cultural conflicts that threaten to tear the group apart. Ben

---

102. Since the Mebaqqer was the Overseer of all camps CD 14:9, It is probable that he moved from one place to another just as Luke describes Peter in Acts 12;17

Witherington notes that Luke portrays the church as good at conflict resolution.[103] For instance, chapter 5 records the first conflict in the Christian community (church) by Ananias and Sapphira, which was thwarted by Peter through the revelation of the Spirit. The first intrusion was deceptive in nature best understood by the Eden narrative analogy. The second is found in chapter 6, the complaint by the Greek speaking widows concerning daily distributions. Indeed, the apostles (Peter) provide an amicable solution to this conflict that could have ripped the community along ethnic lines. Third, though chapter 8 is not good example of conflict resolution, it was clearly an effort to corrupt Peter by offering money to buy the gift of the Spirit by Simon the magician. Chapter 11 presents a fourth and personal challenge to Peter for having fellowship with the Gentiles. This is taken a notch higher by the same group in chapter 15. Verse 1 opens with another intrusion to the space of the renewed Israel or new Eden. The reference to the uncircumcised (11:3) and the insistence to circumcise the Gentiles (15:1, 5) and the similar response from Peter in both cases (11:18; 15:12) may suggest the need for the reader to read the two episodes together. Contrary to what the reader is accustomed to in Acts this far, he stumbles over a form of Jewish legalism that contradicts the gospel of salvation for people universally. The fifth intrusion seeks to have the renewed Israel embrace law observance and relapse into the acts of Jewish law that seeks to gain salvation through the works of the flesh. These five attempts to infiltrate the camp of believers and consequent victory by the apostles speak of the completeness of the church's triumph over the schemes of the enemy in the days of its inception.

Peter is portrayed as a leader wielding great authority in the church but not necessarily heading the Jerusalem community nor the budding center at Antioch. It is evident that leadership in Antioch is passing to Barnabas (11:22, 30; 13:2) and Paul (13:9, 13, 16, 46, 50; 14:9; 15:2) by the way the narrator refers to them.[104] At the same time the leadership of the church in Jerusalem is evidently passing to James. Representatives of the church at Antioch and the leaders at Jerusalem congregate to discuss these conditions

---

103. Witherington, *Acts of the Apostles*, 450. Witherington and Marshall argue that only a group within the church was causing all these disputes and difficulties – "the circumcision party" (Acts 11:2; 15:1). See Marshall, *Acts of the Apostles*, New Testament Guides, 243.

104. Marshall, *Acts of the Apostles*, New Testament Guides, 251; Spencer, *Acts*, 165.

of salvation held against the Gentiles (15:1, 5). The author shows that these conditions stem from "the party of Pharisees" from Judea. Circumcision was a sign of true children of Abraham, which was a physical sign. The priestly class contended against the authority of the apostles in Acts 4 and 5; now the believing Pharisees are depicted as challenging the message of Peter, Paul, and Barnabas (Acts 11 and 15), thus challenging the person and work of Christ in the Gentile believers. The author shows that the problem of circumcision arose only from the Jerusalem church. They went through Phoenicia and Samaria and the churches in those areas were at peace with what God was doing among the Gentiles. Peter stands up after a heated dispute (15:2, 7) among the groups involved. As always in significant moments (1:15; 2:14), Peter is portrayed in a leading position. He reiterates that God chose him as a mouthpiece in delivering the message to Gentiles. Peter's assertion, which is correct (15:14–18), places him at the same level with Old Testament prophets who spoke for God. Peter argues, that God knows the human heart (Jer 17:10) and on the basis of this knowledge he confirms who has satisfied the conditions of salvation and the baptism with the Holy Spirit. God himself is a witness to the salvation and the infilling of the Spirit among the Gentiles and proposing any other standards for them will amount to testing the Lord.[105] Peter reemphasizes the fact that God is not partial, and he sets the same standards for all Jews and Gentiles alike. Endorsing the conditions set by the "party of the Pharisees" for the entry of Gentiles will translate to putting a yoke of bondage on Gentiles, thus, putting God to test.

Peter's statement brings to memory unbelieving Israel in the wilderness. The group of people who tested the Lord died in the wilderness, and so the reader is being led to see the consequences of using lenses different to those that Peter, Barnabas, Paul, and God himself witness to for understanding the work of God among the Gentiles. The author allocates only one verse to Paul and Barnabas's witness, which may indicate the significance of Peter's witness concerning Gentile mission prior to this council. Paul and Barnabas may be carrying on the mission to the Gentiles but Peter is accredited for opening the door to the Gentiles in Chapter 10

---

105. Peter notes that advancing in the way of the party of circumcision is heading the way of Israel in Exodus 17:2 (see Larkin, *Acts*, 221; Barrett, *Acts 15–18*, 717); and 15:22–27; Numbers 14:22–23 (see Fitzmyer, *Acts of the Apostles*, 547); in Luke 4:2; 11:16, Acts 5:9 (see Bock, *Acts*, 500).

James sums up Peter's witness by implying that Cornelius's narrative was actually God's visitation to the Gentiles to take from them a people for himself.[106] James brings on board a third witness to this discussion, the prophets. God sent Peter to Cornelius's house, he confirmed the Gentiles' faith in his word by giving them the Holy Spirit, the new mark of the people of God, and third, even the prophets agree with this message.[107]

4.4. Conclusion

In summary, we have examined the characterization of Peter in Acts in three sections: Jerusalem 1–6, Samaria and Judea 8–9, among Gentiles 10–12 and 15. Tracing Peter's leadership in Acts 1–12 and 15 is easier than determining the ethical traits he espouses. We will summarize how the author portrays Peter chapter by chapter, and attempt to examine the character traits that are manifested in those leadership situations discussed.

In section one, chapters 1–6, the author characterizes Peter by means of several threads. He portrays Peter as a restored and an obedient leader, reorganizing the community of believers (1:15) to fit the expected standards of a Jewish community. He further highlights Peter's responsibility as a leader in explaining scripture for clarity to the believers (1:20; 2:16; 34–35; 15:16–17); the pesher style of interpretation is attested. Luke highlights his resilience, prayerfulness, confidence, conviction, honesty, faith, and compassion in these early chapters.

The healing of the lame man provides a fertile ground for many of Peter's traits. He is portrayed as continuing in prayer, demonstrating compassion to the lame man and caring by supporting him to his feet. His humility is demonstrated in explaining the source of the power that healed the man. In chapter 4, he is portrayed as a leader responding to the accusations laid

---

106. James refers to Gentiles by a term that priorly only described Israel λαός. They often referred to Israel as "the people of God" (Deut 26:18–19; 32:8–9; Ps 134:12 LXX; Acts 7:34; 13:17) but now Luke uses it in reference to Gentiles – see Polhill, *Acts*, 329. Although Bruce notes that this Gentiles are sheep not of this fold (John 10:16), William Larkin asserts that this was a messianic visitation among the Gentiles – see Larkin, *Acts*, 222.

107. Bock notes that Peter's teaching matches with the prophets. He renders συμφωνοῦσιν as "share the same sound" and thus "match" or "agree," Bock, *Acts*, 503. Bruce and Witherington note the cause of the difference in James' quotation, Witherington refers to this as "deliberate rhetoric." See Witherington, *Acts of the Apostles*, 456–57.

against the apostles. He displays respect to the authorities yet with great boldness refutes the accusations leveled against the team. Chapter 5 examines his leadership in terms of spiritual insight and the caring confrontational side of Peter. His ability to expose craftiness and reveal the secrets of the human heart is demonstrated. His commitment to truth and integrity is evident in the Ananias and Sapphira episode. Luke continues to portray Peter as a leader committed to prayer and ministry of the word. Peter displays great leadership in conflict management. His participatory style of leadership keeps the community intact in the face of a simmering ethnic tension. He blends great listening skills, participation, and delegation to respond to the Hellenistic Jewish widows' complaints. The threads of prayer, water baptism, and baptism in the Holy Spirit tie together this first section of Acts (1–6).

In section two (8–9), Peter is characterized as receiving the Samaritans into the kingdom by laying hands on them to receive the Holy Spirit. Faithfulness to God and his kingdom are depicted in rejecting Simon's offer to buy the gift of the Spirit. He displays a spirited fight as a guardian of truth and the trustworthiness of the gospel. Chapters 8 and 9 portray him as an inspector or overseer of the churches or communities of believers in Samaria, Lydda, and Joppa. He responds promptly and compassionately to the need in Joppa and Lydda respectively. He accepts humble accommodation in Joppa and demonstrates his ability to embrace all, especially the marginalized like Tabitha and Simon the tanner. The threads of traveling here and there (missions), healings (mighty works of God), and prayer, baptism in the Spirit and implicitly water baptism run through this second section of Acts.

The author presents Peter in chapter 10 as flexible and willing to change when confronted with the truth. His patience is the focus as he is put on defensive twice to account for his relationship with the Gentiles. He is not only patient but also consistent in relaying the story of how God brought in the Gentiles. The rest of the narrative (11–12 and 15) is tied together by the threads of prayer, water baptism, and the out pouring of the Spirit that run through all the communities: Jerusalem, Judea, Samaria, and Gentiles in this study. However, the threads of prayer, obedience (to God and the Holy Spirit), courage (boldness), and care in characterizing Peter is attested to in the communities he visits (Jerusalem, Samaria and Judea and the Gentiles).

On the basis of this characterization of Peter and his ethics in Acts, we will seek to draw parallels and contacts between Peter's leadership and ethics in

Acts and the overseer (inspector, Mebaqqer) of many camps and the ethics lived at Qumran community as provided in Damascus Document or where necessary the community rule and other early sources.

CHAPTER 5

Parallels: Peter and the Mebaqqer

In this chapter, we turn now to the heart of our study, drawing parallels between Peter's leadership and ethics in Acts and the Mebaqqer in the Damascus Document. This we will examine in the following order. First, we will examine the concept of parallels and its significance in the light of Samuel Sandmel's article on parallelomania, followed by a discussion on John the Baptist and Qumran. Then, we will examine general parallels between Acts and Qumran/CD, particularly Fitzmyer's parallels, before focusing on parallels between Peter and the Mebaqqer. These we will examine under two sections: the characteristics of the Mebaqqer that apply to Peter, and the characteristics of Peter that apply to both the Mebaqqer and the practices significant to community in CD. We will conclude this chapter by a summary of our findings.

5.1. Parallels and Parallelomania

The *Oxford Pocket Dictionary of Current English* defines parallel as "(of lines, planes, or surfaces) side by side and having the same distance continuously between them. . . . Occurring or existing at the same time or in a similar way; corresponding. . . . A person or thing that is similar or analogous to another."[1] As mentioned earlier, since the discovery of the Dead Sea Scrolls parallels with the early Christian community are constantly being explored in NT studies, though Sandmel's "Parallelomania" sternly cautions against any

---

1. The Oxford Pocket Dictionary of Current English, s.v. "parallel (adj.)," Encylopedia. com, https://www.encyclopedia.com/science-and-technology/computers-and-electrical-engineering/computers-and-computing/parallel-0

exaggerations. Sandmel defines parallelomania as "that extravagance among scholars which first overdoes the supposed similarity in passages and then proceeds to describe source and derivation as if implying literary connection flowing in an inevitable or predetermined direction."[2] Sandmel clarifies that he does not object to the drawing of parallels but he advocates for competence and precision in the exercise. He alludes to the possible relationship between John the Baptist with Qumran but disdains reasons given for his exit from Qumran.[3] Sandmel's efforts to restore sanity and aptitude to the exercise of drawing parallels should be greatly lauded. However, he concludes his article on an excellent note describing the ideal scholarly atmosphere present then:

> It is proper that our Society should be host to differences of opinion, and even acute ones. We do not want to arrive at some pallid unanimity, but rather to be the marketplace in which vigorously held viewpoints, freely expressed, vie with each other for acceptance. When one recalls the occasional fervid debate in this Society, it is notable that the issues have been primarily scholarly, and never to my recollection denominational.[4]

The tone and spirit of Sandmel's article clearly denote a desire for candid interactions in the academy. This study seeks to proceed with the same attitude and spirit. Therefore, his article remains significant to this study as we seek to move this discussion further by pointing out similarities between Peter's leadership and the ethics lived out in Qumran as reflected in the Mebaqqer.

James R. Edwards notes that "parallels can be determined by identical words, phrases, contextual similarities, and sequential arrangement."[5] These criteria will be followed in drawing parallels between the two communities. We will endeavor to be as clear as possible on points of contact in the indicated areas. The Dead Sea Scrolls are associated with a community believed to have existed from 150 BC–AD 70,[6] while the Christian community begins around

---

2. Sandmel, "Parallelomania," 1.

3. Sandmel, 5.

4. Sandmel, 13.

5. Edwards, "Parallels and Patterns," 485; Davila, "Perils of Parallels," refers to the same but with slightly different names – linguistic parallels (lexicography and translations), verbal parallels (quotations and use of technical language), conceptual parallels (parallels in structure and theme or ideas), and models.

6. Milik, *Ten Years of Discovery*, 133–36; Avigad, "Palaeography," 56–87.

AD 32–34. Therefore, all the parallels that will be drawn in this study will be guided by the understanding that it is the leadership and ethics of Qumran that will be used here as an analogy to understand Peter's leadership and ethics in Acts and not vice versa.

However, this study is not trying to establish dependence of Acts on the Qumran community. Fitzmyer argues,

> The sect, whose beliefs and way of life are made known to us in this literature [Dead Sea Scrolls] is revealed to be a community that is wholly Jewish, dedicated to the study and observance of the Torah, yet living a communal, religious, and ascetic mode of life for a considerable period before the emergence of Christianity.[7]

Moreover, this literature further highlights the leadership that inspired this community to such heights and profound commitments. One character that has received attention from scholars and had parallels drawn between him and his ministry and Qumran is John the Baptist. John, being a forerunner of Christ and a teacher of some of Jesus's disciples, is a crucial character because it is adduced that Peter may have been John's disciple or at least acquainted with John's ministry through his younger brother Andrew (John 1:40–42).[8]

5.2. John the Baptist and Qumran

It was Brownlee who first suggested an actual historical connection between John the Baptist and the Qumran community.[9] John was born of aging parents introduced to us in Luke 1:5–80. His father was a temple priest during a time of great expectation in Israel yet it was also a time of uncertainty. His parents had perplexing experiences before he was born. Zechariah, his father, representing Israel, was made dumb for doubting what God had promised, and Elizabeth his mother underwent a period of inexplicable withdrawal

---

7. Fitzmyer, "Jewish Christianity," 233.

8. Brown, Donfried, and Reumann, *Peter*, 130–31.

9. Brownlee, "John the Baptist," 71–90; Stendahl, "John the Baptist," 3–53. I say actual because the earliest one by Heinrich Graetz is highly controversial and assertive , for Graetz even believes that John means Essene: "The Essene who sent forth this call to the Israelites was John the Baptist (his name doubtless meaning the Essene, he who daily bathed and cleansed both body and soul in spring water)." Graetz, *History of the Jews*, vol. 2, 145–46.

from the public (Luke 1:24–25). After his birth, Luke does not give us much information other than in Luke 1:80. The wilderness referred to is the wilderness of Judea. Brownlee notes,

> Now in the territory most strictly defined as the Wilderness of Judaea are a series of caves from which have come the Dead Sea Scrolls, more accurately called the Qumran Scrolls after the name of the wady, or ravine, cutting through that section of cliff. Here some of the Essenes lived in tents and caves; and here they had a community building where they went for study, worship, bathing, eating, and fellowship one with the other.[10]

Robinson suggests that John was taken at an early age either by his parents or after they died to be nurtured in the desert discipline of the Qumran community.[11] Several reasons could warrant such a hypothesis. First, the Essenes routinely adopted orphans; Qumran is an Essene settlement, located close to John's hometown, the geographical point from which John the Baptist emerges preaching repentance and the kingdom in Matthew 3:1. John's parents were old when he was born, so he may have been orphaned at a relatively young age, thus being adopted by the nearby Essene community.[12] The Essene community had contacts with non-Sadducean priestly families such as Zachariah's.[13] Zachariah was not a Sadducee, since he was open to receiving a supernatural vision (Luke 1:11–13). However, it is also not possible that Zachariah belonged to Essenes sect because he was still serving at the temple yet the Qumran community did not have faith in the Jewish temple and sacrificial systems.

However, it is apparent that when John appears on the scene preaching the kingdom, he does not come as an Essene or any other Jewish leader group but as a voice crying in the wilderness (Matt 3:3). Robinson notes,

---

10. Brownlee, "John the Baptist," 72.

11. Robinson, *Twelve New Testament Studies*, 12; Brownlee, "John the Baptist," 73.

12. Josephus, in discussing marriage and adoption among the Essenes notes, "They neglect wedlock, but select other persons children, while they are pliable, and fit for learning, and esteem them to be of their kindred, and form them according to their own manners" (Josephus, *J.W.* 2.120).

13. Robinson, *Twelve New Testament Studies*, 12.

In some way or other he has by then broken any connexion he may have had with them. He is an individual prophet, who, though he gathered disciples and gave them the discipline of prayer (Luke 11:1; 5:33) and fasting (Mark 2:18 and pars), appears to have made no attempt to initiate them into any kind of order. In all that follows it must never be forgotten that John is a highly individual figure whom neither Josephus nor anyone in the Gospels ever associates with any other group. Whatever he may have received from his association, if there was one, with Qumran, he remolded into something quite distinctive and independent.[14]

John may have transformed himself into a leader in his own right, however, his sociocultural context still accounts for much of his distinctiveness. He re-emerges with the words of Isaiah "A voice cries: 'in wilderness prepare the way of the LORD; make straight in the desert a highway for our God" (Isa 40:3). The preparation here meant readiness for the messianic age. Brownlee opines,

> The idea was that if they were good enough God would honor them by sending them the Messiah. This Messiah was to be a prophet like Moses (cf. Deut. 18:18) and was expected to make his appearance in the wilderness in order to lead his people into the Promised Land (cf. Matt. 24:26) of the Messianic Kingdom.[15]

Robinson argues that John's ministry and teaching denote some form of connection with Qumran,[16] an idea advanced by Brownlee who states,

> One issue strongly debated among scholars is where John got his ideas for baptism. Does it represent a pagan influence, borrowed from some oriental mystery cult? Was it original with

---

14. Robinson, 12–13. The Gospel of John seems to associate Peter with John the Baptist through Andrew. Peter may have been John's disciple; he was introduced to Jesus by his brother Andrew who was handed to Jesus by John himself in a very dramatic introduction. So there is a possibility that Peter comes to Jesus with possible influence occasioned by John's connection to Qumran. However, it is not in the scope of this study to pursue the details of such a relationship now, albeit, an investigation in that direction could account for some of the problematic Petrine tendencies.

15. Brownlee, "John the Baptist," 72.

16. Robinson, *Twelve New Testament Studies*, 13.

John? Or was it an adaptation of some previous Jewish rite? We will be safer to assume the last position, for originality usually starts with ideas which are not entirely new, and John was not one to borrow directly from the Gentile world. Some have suggested that John adapted proselyte baptism as practiced in the synagogue. Proselyte baptism seems to have been introduced to wash away the defilement believed to cling to one who had not previously been a Jew, a defilement which had befallen him through failure to observe the Jewish ceremonial law. It thus marked his turning from paganism to the service of the true God, and his introduction into the community of God's people.[17]

John called Israel to repentance and baptism in preparation for the kingdom of God, just as the Qumran community emphasized separation from the rest of Israel in preparation for the coming kingdom. The Qumran community baptized strictly a choice group of people but John, other than demanding fruit demonstrating repentance baptized all that came to him at Jordan (Matt 3:5–10). John's baptism was so unique that it was used to identify him as "the baptist." It was not like the recurring washings done at Qumran[18] neither was it the proselyte type that was limited to non-Jews. He peculiarly demanded baptism even for the Jews who felt they did not need to be baptized.[19] This confirms his radicalness and sense of independence; even if he had any connections with Qumran, he never just mimicked every act seen and learned there. Instead, he transformed them to fit what God had individually called him to do. John's preaching comes in severe language (Matt 3:7–8) consonant with the Qumran community. Brownlee's comment captures this well:

> In demanding amendment of life, John attacked the sins of the mighty as well as those of the lowly. He did not hesitate to rebuke priests, Pharisees, or even Herod Antipas. Luke records a section of his teachings that sound remarkably like Jesus; but

---

17. Brownlee, "John the Baptist," 74–75.

18. Brownlee, 77.

19. John did not give conditions or classes for his baptism other than genuine repentance (Matt 3:6–10).

there is no need to deny this to John, for high ethical teaching existed among the Essenes.[20]

Remarkably, Jesus presented himself to John for baptism before commencing his ministry. John's objection to baptizing Jesus is in relation to his understanding of who Jesus was – the Messiah. Jesus sanctions the exercise as an act of fulfilling righteousness. John notes that Jesus will oversee a greater baptism. He baptizes for cleansing by water, but Jesus will baptize with the Holy Spirit and fire, motifs replete in the narrative of Acts. If then John had connections with Qumran, it is notable that he emerges as a prophet in his own right, with a distinct mission having similarities with the former but uniquely his own brand. John may have left Qumran, but they both shared the wilderness space and were influenced by the same culture and theological concerns. He may have practiced a different baptism from Qumran, yet they both believed in baptism although with a difference of emphasis laid on candidates, nature, and mode. While Qumran prepared a community of a renewed Israel for the coming Messiah, John seems to focus on a wider and more inclusive scope, as evidenced by the large numbers who went to him for baptism; even the very first of Jesus's disciples (including Andrew, Peter's brother) are identified as John's disciples (John 1:40–42). In sum, it is possible for someone to have contacts with a group and yet operate independently without mimicking them. It is possible to transform ideas from another group and present them as fresh and unsubordinated to previous acquaintances. Whether or not John the Baptist formed a direct conceptual link between Qumran and the early Christian community, it is relatively easy to observe parallels between the two communities.

5.3. General Parallels between Acts and Qumran

5.3.1. Overview

The similarities between the communities are the reason among others, why Qumran is the best analogy for reading Acts. It is true that the two communities saw themselves as living in eschatological times, with God intervening by sending to them charismatic leaders the Teacher of Righteousness and

---

20. Brownlee, "John the Baptist," 78.

Jesus Christ to prepare them for the day of their respective visitations. In this light, they both envisioned themselves as a renewed Israel.[21] They both believed in the centrality of the Scriptures and prayer, focused on holy living as the way of life.

The Qumran community, explicitly viewing themselves as a renewed Israel,[22] cites faithlessness as a reason for God abandoning old Israel to the sword (captivity) (CD 1:3–4). God abandoning old Israel and her temple to the sword and captivity, remembered his covenant, he renewed a relationship with the remnant that had separated themselves to the camps in the wilderness for holy and righteousness living in anticipation of his Messiah.[23] Hence, their community imitated Israel in the wilderness of Sinai and sought to improve in areas they felt old Israel had failed God. God raised for them a charismatic leader, the Teacher of Righteousness, who enforced the principles of holiness and taught them the ways of Yahweh.

Although Acts does not openly claim the designation true or renewed Israel, Luke portrays this new community of believers as though they believe themselves to be so. When Peter leads the community in reconstituting the leadership of the group (Acts 1:15–26), it is implicit that the community shares the concerns of an Israelite community.[24] Luke's portrayal of Peter in his speeches that apply the prophecies meant for Israel to the Christian community implies the community in Acts has the same sort of concerns in matters of interpretation (both adapted pesher style of interpretation). In Isaiah 43:10, God commands Israel to bear witness before humankind; the Lord controls history by proclaiming events beforehand and bringing them to pass. The old Israel, represented by the leaders of the people of Israel in Acts 4:1, is portrayed as unable to bear this witness. Luke indicates that the apostles now occupy the active role of being witnesses of the charismatic leader Jesus Christ in Jerusalem, Samaria, and to the nations of the world (Acts 1:8; 3:15). It is worth noting that the Christian community in Acts does

---

21. Schubert, *Dead Sea Community*, 150.

22. CD 1:4–5. Keener, *Acts*, vol. 1, 752; see Jeremias *Theology*, 171–72.

23. CD 1:3–9.

24. Haenchen, *Acts*, 163–65.

not separate itself physically from Israel and its temple services as did the Qumran community.[25]

Another area of similarity between Qumran community and the community in Acts is that there may have been multiple factions within each community. Several scholars[26] have suggested that there appear to be two groups at Qumran. Josephus alludes to the presence of ideological difference, not actual split. One group in the same community believed in celibacy whereas the other one married and had children. Josephus notes "that the marrying Essenes were in agreement with the others on 'the way of life, usages, and customs' except for the issue of marriage."[27] Boccaccini cites the Teacher of Righteousness' call for greater separation from Israel and the temple as a reason for the schism. Collins concludes,

> The two orders of the Essenes, one of which married, can be correlated with the distinction in the Damascus Rule between those who walk in perfect holiness and those who live in camps according [to] the order of the land and marry and have children (CD 7:4–8). Neither Josephus nor the Damascus Rule suggests that there was any schism; rather they suggest that the movement tolerated more than one lifestyle. In short, there is still a good case to be made that the movement initiated by the Teacher of Righteousness should be identified with the Essenes. There is no justification, in my view, for extending that label to the so-called "parent community" [motherhouse] that existed before his arrival.[28]

The Christian community in Acts begins as a group in prayer and one accord. This is the picture portrayed through the church in Jerusalem. However, after Peter's visit to the house of Cornelius in Caesarea, there emerges a difference in ideology (Acts 11:1–3). Prior to the Jerusalem encounter, God

---

25. The Sanhedrin persecuted the believers in Acts and eventually excommunicated them from the temple. It is noteworthy that the important difference between the Christians in Acts and the Qumran community is that Qumran rejected the temple, but the temple rejected the Christians.

26. Boccaccini, *Beyond the Essene Hypothesis*, 188; Collins, *Scriptures and Sectarianism*, 156–57; Collins, *Beyond the Qumran Community*, 50; Fitzmyer, "Jewish Christianity," 234.

27. Josephus, *J.W.* 2.160; Collins, *Scriptures and Sectarianism*, 155.

28. Collins, *Scriptures and Sectarianism*, 160.

confronts Peter in a vision that reveals Peter's underlying worldview. The circumcision party believed that it was not enough for the Gentiles to believe in Christ alone.[29] It required circumcision to give them the full identity of the true Israel; thus it was necessary for them to become Jews to perfect their salvation, by identifying themselves with the symbol of the Abrahamic covenant.

In Acts, the presence of these divergent ideologies culminates into a conflict.[30] The Jerusalem council is called and the two parties invited with a goal of resolving the debate. Witherington suggests that Greco-Roman background provides the best analogy for the Jerusalem council:

> The main way to resolve such conflict in antiquity was to call a meeting of the εκκλησια, the assembly of the people (cf 12, 22), and listen to and consider speeches following the conventions of deliberative rhetoric, the aim of which speeches was to overcome στασις and produce concord or unity. It is no accident, then, that Luke portrays both Peter and Paul as presenting deliberative speeches to resolve this conflict. Theophilus would have recognized the appropriateness of this procedure, and the need of calling a large assembly to settle the matter, regardless of how many spoke.[31]

Although the Greco-Roman analogy could fit with Acts 15, Luke's main interest in the book is establishing his readers in the certainty of the things Christ began to do and teach (Acts 1:1). Christ had set a procedure of how conflicts should be resolved among his followers (Matt 18:15–18).[32] Jesus's

---

29. Paul mentions this group in Galatians 2:15; 5:1; 6:15–16 as coming from James. This may be understood as coming by James's instruction and authority. Also in the Jerusalem council, it is only James who responds, seemingly on the behalf of the circumcision party; denoting his affiliation to their ideology.

30. It is apparent that James the brother of the Lord is with the circumcision party, while Peter, Barnabas, Paul, Mark, and the churches Phoenicia and Samaria are for the repentance of the Gentiles without circumcision as a condition.

31. Witherington, *Acts of the Apostles*, 450–51.

32. Matt 18:15–18:

> If your brother sins against you, go and tell him his fault between you and him alone. If he listens to you, you have gained your brother. But if he does not listen, take one or two others along with you, that every charge may be established by the evidence of two or three witnesses. If he refuses to listen to them, tell it to the church. And if he refuses to listen even to the church, let him be to you as a Gentile

model is similar to the judicial procedure at Qumran.[33] It is important to note that several efforts to solving the differences concerning Gentiles' inclusion in the community of believers have been made prior to the Jerusalem council. Peter and Paul discussed it in Galatians 1:11–15, Peter had been questioned concerning his relationship to the Gentiles in Acts 11:1–18.

The Qumran community literature portrays a strong commitment to justice and proper judicial process.[34] Josephus notes, "In their judgments, they are most scrupulous and just. He will cherish justice towards human beings."[35] Josephus indicates that the Essenes had a court of at least one hundred members.[36] Probably Josephus is referring to the assembly of many (1QS 6:8–13). Though the Qumran judicial procedure is a bit complex to delineate, the community's judicial system had several constituent parts: twelve laymen and two priests (1QS), four laymen and six Levites (CD 10), ten men (Community Rule), and the assembly of many. This judicial system may have developed over a span of time and perhaps practiced in different places among the camps. Nevertheless, the general judicial procedures practiced in Qumran and Acts are quite similar.[37] Another area of similarity is the witness of the two communities to those without (outside their communities).

The Qumran community was highly esteemed by the society living around them.[38] Josephus referring to the Essenes in general, states:

> It also deserves our admiration, how much they exceed all other men that give themselves over to virtue, and this in righteousness: and indeed to such a degree, that as it has never appeared among any other men, neither Greeks nor barbarians, no, not for a little time, so has it endured a long time among them. This is demonstrated by that institution of theirs, which will not allow

---

and a tax collector. Truly, I say to you, whatever you bind on earth shall be bound in heaven, and whatever you loose on earth will be loosed in heaven.

33. 1QS 6:27; CD 9:9–10, see 1QS 6:1, "Let no cause be brought before the many, by one man against another, unless reproof has been made before witnesses." It suggests one on one meeting before witness as the preliminary stage the judicial process before taking the matter to court which is referred to in CD 9:16–10:3.

34. Beall, *Josephus' Description of the Essenes*, 91.

35. Josephus, *J.W.* 2.145, 139.

36. Josephus, *J.W.* 2.145, 139.

37. Josephus, *J.W.* 2.145; cf. Acts 15:1–21.

38. Josephus, *J.W.* 2.119–20; Josephus, *Ant.* 18.1–2, 5, 11, 18–22.

anything to hinder them from having all things in common; so
that a rich man enjoys no more of his own wealth than he who
has nothing at all. There are about four thousand men that live
in this way.[39]

Though not in the exact words of Josephus, Luke describes similar admiration
for the community in Acts,

Now many signs and wonders were regularly done among the
people by the hands of the apostles. And they were all together
in Solomon's Portico. None of the rest dared join them, but the
people held them in high esteem. And more than ever believers
were added to the Lord, multitudes of both men and women.
(Acts 5:12–14)

Both Qumran and the believers in Acts were admired for their urge to pursue
godliness and righteousness. Moreover, the resolve not to let anything fracture
their communal life is witnessed in Peter's stern dealing with Ananias and his
wife Sapphira (Acts 5:1–11). Concerning wealth and possessions, Luke notes,
"Now the full number of those who believed were of one heart and soul, and
no one said that any of the things that belonged to him was his own, but they
had everything in common" (Acts 4:32).

The next area of similarity between the two communities is the way they
responded to pain and suffering. Josephus, in reference to how the Essenes
responded to the torture by Romans, notes,

And indeed our war with the Romans gave abundant evidence of
what great souls they had in their trials, wherein, although they
were tortured and distorted, burnt and torn to pieces, and went
through all kinds of instruments of torment, that they might be
forced either to blaspheme their legislator, or to eat what was
forbidden them, yet could they not be made to do either of them,
no, nor once to flatter their tormentors, or to shed a tear; but
they smiled in their very pains, and laughed [at] those to scorn
who inflicted the torments upon them, and resigned up their
souls with great alacrity, as expecting to receive them again.[40]

---

39. Josephus, *Ant.* 18.20.
40. Josephus, *J.W.* 2.152–53.

Luke reports similar fortitude in Acts:

> And when they had called in the apostles, they beat them and
> charged them not to speak in the name of Jesus, and let them
> go. Then they left the presence of the council, rejoicing that they
> were counted worthy to suffer dishonor for the name. And every
> day, in the temple and from house to house, they did not cease
> teaching and preaching that the Christ is Jesus. (Acts 5:40–42)

The Christian community in Acts responds to the persecution from the leaders of the people, in the same attitude and spirit portrayed at Qumran.

Furthermore, both communities had new markers of covenant identity. As
a symbol to the Abrahamic covenant, all his descendants were circumcised
the eighth day. According to Judaism, circumcision and careful observance of
the Torah were all one needed to lay claim on inclusion in the God's covenant.
However, Qumran introduces new terms of admission to the renewed Israel,
requiring a personal commitment and not just heredity. Contrary to the historical practices of Judaism, the Qumranites invited natural-born Israelites to
commit themselves to the sect. However, they rejected the lame, blind, and
those who had physical defects (CD 15:15–17).[41] In Acts, the apostles invite
everyone, Jew and Gentiles alike, to the community of believers. Whereas the
Qumranites' community seems to reject the physically challenged, it should
be understood that the head of the church – Jesus Christ – will not accept the
morally impure or unclean in the New Jerusalem (Rev. 21:8, 27).

Our final area of similarity between the two communities is baptism.
In Qumran, what we might call baptism is usually referred to as baths.[42]
Brownlee notes the presence of indoor pools in Qumran:

> Baths were taken regularly, by the membership, according to
> our ancient historians. Yet one's full admission into the com-
> munity was probably marked by a bath which marked him off

---

41. CD 15:15–17 read in the context of Rev 21:8, parallels the church's expectation that
nothing defective will be admitted into the New Jerusalem. The eschatologically obsessed
Qumranites may have mixed the conditions of preparing for the Messiah and those of his
final kingdom. Indeed, Qumran is similar here in principle but dissimilar in actual practice.
For the church in Acts, it is the new Jerusalem coming down from heaven at Christ's second
advent that will not admit defects in the sense of the morally unclean or impure, but for now
he is inviting all and asking his servants to compel everyone to come to the banquet.

42. We refer to them as "Baptisms" because we will look at water and spirit baptism.

henceforth as belonging to the "holy men." Anyone joining the true Israel had to come that way. This would be an exact parallel to John's extreme demand that everyone, not simply proselytes from the Gentile world, receive baptism. John's originality would be the great stress upon the once-for-all baptism of the initiatory rite and in extending a public invitation for all to repent and to be baptized.[43]

Qumran's baptisms (or baths) were done regularly and this distinguished them from John's. Therefore, we can certainly state, the baptism that marked the distinctiveness of the two communities could be experienced more than once.

In summary, there are many similarities between the Qumran community and the church in Acts. First, both had their focus on their eschatological assignment; second, they had two groups operating as one.[44] Third, they both operated similar judicial processes, though not in every detail of the procedure but distinctly different from the Greco-Roman standards of conflict resolution in the *polis*. Fourth, they both enjoyed honor and respect from the outsiders and they both responded similarly in matters of pain, suffering, and wealth. Fifth, they were both distinguished by a unique baptism, however only similar in the repetitiveness of the baptism, not in mode and nature. These similarities and many others to be pursued in this study provide a good window into understanding the leadership and practices of the early church in Acts.

Now, apart from George J. Brooke's use of the title Luke-Acts, a few comments on Acts 2:42 and 4:36–5:11, and his statements,[45] it is Fitzmyer who

---

43. Brownlee, "John the Baptist," 77.

44. Concerning these differences at Qumran, Collins concludes,

I see no reason to attribute the differences between the two rules to a schism. Since both rules continued to be copied, it would seem that the kind of family-based movement envisioned in the *Damascus Rule* was not simply superseded, but continued to exist in tandem with the more intensive communities of *yahad*.

Collins, *Beyond the Qumran Community*, 79. The decision at the Jerusalem council, just like Collins' conclusion, manages to keep the circumcision party and those in support of Gentiles' salvation by faith alone together, and it would be unprofitable to try and build any further on the dispute. For instance, arguing for the presence of two groups in the early church: those of the circumcision and those preaching the inclusion of Gentiles by faith.

45. Brooke in discussing parallels in Luke–Acts he asserts that "parallels between Qumran and the Gospel of Luke and the Acts of the Apostles have been pointed out frequently and in detail." He further asserts, "It is the third Gospel that has featured most in discussions of literary

has actually drawn parallels between Acts and Qumran.[46] Acts has a picture of Jewishness but is evidently manifesting a specific Jewish group's way of life, leadership, and organization.[47] Fitzmyer observes,

> The comparison of the early Jewish Christian church with Essene communities brings out fundamental differences far more than resemblances. These differences emerge when one considers the character and goal of the two groups. Even if we admit the difference of Qumran Essenism from that of the "camps" of Damascus, there is still a vast difference between the Essene movement and that of early Christianity. The difference is more manifest when the Jewish Christians are compared with the Qumran Essenes.[48]

For Fitzmyer, the differences between the two groups are significant and pervasive as he observes above. Dupont-Sommer, however, offers a corrective:

> It is a recognized fact in the history of religion that when a new sect comes into being it distinguishes itself from the old sect from which it emerges by certain innovations which are directly opposed to it, and yet at the same time betray its source of origin: this is the law of dissidence.[49]

Without repeating what has been amply discussed on the subject we will turn to some of the differences between the two communities and then

---

parallels . . . For the Acts of the Apostles the story has been the same. Numerous parallels have been noted." This claim cites Fitzmyer who seems to present a contrary opinion on the same. Brooke, "Luke-Acts," 72–73.

46. Fitzmyer, "Jewish Christianity," 233–57; Keck, Schubert, and Martyn, *Studies in Luke-Acts*, 233–57.

47. Parental experience will show that when a child is born it may be hard to determine whom the baby resembles, whether the child looks like the mother or the father. Those early days it may seem as the child looks like the father, mother or even sometimes both. But growth brings out the image and likeness of the baby not only physically but even in ways of thinking in general and approaches to life and eventually it can be confidently said they look like the mother but thinks like the father. Or even growth may reveal that physically the child does not resemble either of the parents. Therefore, Fitzmyer looking at Jewishness of the early church may arrive at different results from what this study finds since we are looking at different times and our scope is wider.

48. Fitzmyer, "Jewish Christianity," 239.

49. Dupont-Sommer, *Essene Writings*, 375.

discuss a few similarities in the communities before focusing on Peter and the Mebaqqer.

The perspective of every Jewish sect (Pharisees, Sadducees, Zealots, Essenes etc.) on what they believed to be wrong in Israel and the steps they took as a sect order to restore Israel to her God-given position always determined how each group lived. This approach to the theological and spiritual concerns of the Jews' community, still feeling exiled in the promised land, could account for the varied differences between the groups that share a similar heritage and environment yet have very diverse ways of approaching the future and matters of faith.[50]

Entry into the Qumran congregation's meetings was forbidden to any "one who is a fool or insane . . . and no simpleton or ignoramus or one with eyes too weak to see or lame or crippled or deaf or minor child, none of these shall enter the congregation, for the holy angels are in your midst"[51] (CD 15:15–17). Comparing these conditions to how the Christians in Acts admitted new adherents, reveals a stark difference. In Acts 2:41, three thousand souls were added to the community of believers; four thousand believed in Acts 4:4; and Acts 6:7 indicates the number of disciples multiplied greatly in Jerusalem. In Samaria (Acts 8), the conversion of Paul (Acts 9), and Cornelius (Acts 10) all do not indicate any set time of probation for the disciples before they were allowed to join the Christian community but rather they were immediately added to the disciples as shown in Jerusalem, Samaria, and at Cornelius's house.[52] In addition, Acts does not lay down physical conditions for its members other than the process of repentance, and baptism (2:38). It is not clear if the lame man at the beautiful gate believed but it can be inferred. Peter and John's attention to him and the precedents set in the Gospels indicate that the church in Acts admitted the lame, blind, and others marginalized by society (Matt 22:1–10; Luke 14:15–24).

---

50. It is like the story of two twins raised by an alcoholic father. One grew up to be an alcoholic and when asked what happened he said: "I watched my father" he was my model. The other grew up and never drank in his life. When he was asked what happened he said, "I watched my father see what alcohol has done to my father, how could I too walk that path in the full glare of these destructive evidence." These two boys, having the same father, develop two different perspectives to life. Our perspective in life has the capacity determine our trajectory.

51. CD 15: 15–17.

52. Acts 2:41; 8:4–25; 10:44–48.

At Qumran, to achieve their goal of preparing for the advent of the Messiah, it was imperative they separate themselves from the world and focus on a relationship with God This meant obligatory communal life away from the rest of society, which should be hated for being evil. They separated themselves from the temple and condemned its priesthood as corrupt. This contrasts with the church in Acts, especially within the scope of this study. There is the practice of voluntary communal life but not in a place secluded from the rest of society, and not obligatory (5:4). The apostles are portrayed as still attending prayers in the temple, although this will eventually change to house churches. Notably, the change was not because of separation from a wicked society but due to persecution and animosity that would ruthlessly force them out of the temple worship, since the temple leadership viewed the Christians as heretics.

At Qumran, the group looked forward to the coming of the Messiah; they were committed to a sect and set of rules. Failure to adhere to the rules meant fines and excommunication from the community of "true Israel."[53] Some of the Qumranites practiced celibacy and had a disdain toward marriage. There are echoes of celibacy in the church in Acts, Paul's marital status is left unclear in Acts, but celibacy is not mandatory in Acts and Paul only prefers it (celibacy) over marriage in his epistles (1 Cor 7:32–35). The church demonstrates a commitment to persons and a relationship rather than mere systems and laws. They are basically relational rather than the highly perfunctory system adopted at Qumran. Regardless of such observed differences between the two communities, there are a number of connections that can be drawn between them. We will address this subject later in this chapter.

5.3.2. Fitzmyer's Parallels

Fitzmyer begins by drawing parallels between Qumran and Acts in the way the two communities referred to themselves; he shows how the two communities used the designation "the way" as a mode of a life lived. At Qumran "the way" referred to a strict observance of the law. To the Qumran community, the Torah pointed to the way of life (CD 1:13; 2:6; 20:18). He notes that the designation is only found in Acts (9:2; 19:9, 23; 22:4; 24:14, 22) and nowhere else in the New Testament. This designation of "the way" and its use among

---

53. Josephus, *J. W.* 2.143–44; QS 7:1–2; 16–17; 22–25, 5:15–16, 8:24–9:2.

the two communities may be a borrowing from Isaiah 40:3, nevertheless he insists that the similarities of usage favor a Qumran influence. He also suggests that the communal meal in Acts 2:46 is similar to the religious common meal of the Essenes described in 1QS 6:4–5; 1QSa 2:11–22. At Qumran this meal was taken in anticipation of the messianic banquet (1QSa 2:14–20); nothing is mentioned in Acts in relation to this. However, we can confirm the institution of this meal based on the information available in the Gospels, but it is in Paul's epistle to the Corinthians that we see grounds to infer that the meal may have also pointed to the second coming of Christ (1 Cor 11:24–26).

Fitzmyer argues that the choice of Matthias in Acts 1:15 resembles more the Essene practice than the general Jewish custom of using lots. He observes that the language used to discuss Judas as having obtained the lot for this ministry and the process of having his replacement resonates with Essene custom; though it may not be asserted that this was an imitation of the Qumran since the Old Testament also has many such examples. He also identifies the style of interpretation in Acts as similar to the Qumran pesher. This method of interpretation sought to actualize or modernize the Old Testament texts as being fulfilled in the interpreter's time (CD 1:13).[54] The introductory formulas present in Acts are similar to Qumran. There are, evidently, a number of possible points of contacts that require further consideration. Nevertheless, we do not expect to unearth all the parallels that exist between Qumran and Acts. We commence our exercise by pointing out similarities between the two communities before specifically addressing contacts and parallels between Peter's leadership and ethics in Acts and the Mebaqqer and ethics lived in Qumran.

5.3.3. Parallels between Acts and Qumran

The similarity between the communities is the one reason among others, why Qumran is the best analogy for reading Acts. It is true that the two communities saw themselves as living in eschatological times, with God intervening by sending to them charismatic leaders (the Teacher of Righteousness and Jesus Christ) to prepare them for the day of their respective visitations. In

---

54. A good example is in CD 1:13. In introducing the prophecy of Hosea 4:16, the commentary says "this is the time about which it was written." Fitzmyer argues that this is the attitude repeatedly witnessed in Peter's use of the Old Testament in his speeches on Pentecost (Acts 2:16–21; 2:25–28, 34–35; 3:24) and at the upper room (1:20).

this light, they both envisioned themselves as a renewed Israel. They both believed in the centrality of the scriptures and prayer, focused on holy living as the way of life.

5.3.3.1. Renewed Israel

This parallel of a renewed Israel has been discussed in more detail elsewhere in this study. However, we cannot overemphasize the thought that the Qumran community explicitly viewed themselves as a renewed Israel.[55]

Although Acts does not openly claim the designation renewed Israel, Luke portrays this new community of believers as though they believe themselves to be so. When Peter leads the community in reconstituting the leadership of the group (Acts 1:15–26), it is implicit that the community shares the concerns of an Israelite community.[56]

5.3.3.2. Divisions within the Community

This similarity has been discussed in detail elsewhere in this study. However, it is worth mentioning here that the procedure of resolving conflict in the two communities were similar. Christ's guidelines on how conflicts should be resolved among his followers in Matthew's gospel are:

> If your brother sins against you, go and tell him his fault be-tween you and him alone. If he listens to you, you have won over your brother. If he does not listen, take one or two others along with you, so that "every fact may be established on the testimony of two or three witnesses." If he refuses to listen to them, tell the church. If he refuses to listen even to the church, then treat him as you would a Gentile or a tax collector. Amen, I say to you, whatever you bind on earth shall be bound in heaven, and whatever you loose on earth shall be loosed in heaven. (Matt 18:15–18)

These are is similar to the judicial procedure at Qumran.[57] The Qumran community literature portrays a strong commitment to justice and proper

---

55. CD 1:4–5. Keener, *Acts*, vol. 1, 752. See Jeremias, *Theology*, 171–72.

56. Haenchen, *Acts*, 163–65.

57. 1QS 6:27; CD 9:9–10, see 1QS 6:1, "Let no cause be brought before the many, by one man against another, unless reproof has been made before witnesses." It suggests one on one

judicial process.[58] Josephus notes, "In their judgments, they are most scrupulous and just."[59] Josephus indicates that the Essenes had a court of at least one hundred members.[60] With the complexities noted in the Qumran Judicial system, nevertheless, the general judicial procedures practiced in Qumran and Acts are quite similar.

5.3.3.3. Relations with Those outside the Community

The Qumran community was highly esteemed by the society living around them.[61] Though not in the exact words of Josephus, Luke describes similar admiration for the community in Acts.

> Now many signs and wonders were regularly done among the people by the hands of the apostles. And they were all together in Solomon's Portico. None of the rest dared join them, but the people held them in high esteem. And more than ever believers were added to the Lord, multitudes of both men and women. (Acts 5:12–14)

Both Qumran and Acts were admired for their urge to pursue godliness and righteousness. Luke notes, "Now the full number of those who believed were of one heart and soul, and no one said that any of the things that belonged to him was his own, but they had everything in common" (Acts 4:32).

5.3.3.4. Response to Pain and Suffering

Josephus refers to how the Essenes responded to the torture by Romans,[62] which is similar to Luke's fortitude report in (Acts 5:40–42). The Christian community in Acts' response to the persecution from the leaders of the people is similar to what Josephus describes of Qumran, and this provides a good window into understanding how both communities persevered in suffering and pain.

---

meeting before witness as the preliminary stage the judicial process before taking the matter to court which is referred to in CD 9:16–10:3.

58. Beall, *Josephus' Description of the Essenes*, 91.

59. Josephus, *J.W.* 2.145, 139.

60. Josephus, *J.W.* 2.145.

61. Josephus, *J.W.* 2.119–20; Josephus, *Ant.* 18.1–2, 5. 11., 18–22.

62. Josephus, *J.W.* 2.152–53.

5.3.3.5. Baptism

As most of the other similarities have been discussed in detail and here we only summarize our observations. Although baptisms (or baths) at Qumran were done regularly, they still provide for us a similarity necessary for this study.

In summary, there are remarkable similarities between the two communities. Most vividly in the composition of their communities, their eschatological concerns, and multiple factions in the community. They both operated similar judicial processes They both enjoyed honor and respect from the outsiders and responded similarly in matters of pain, suffering, and wealth among others. We will now examine further similarities between Peter's leadership and ethics in Acts and Mebaqqer and the ethics practiced in Qumran.

5.4. Peter and the Mebaqqer

Since this study relies mostly on CD, and most of the scholars regard the Padiq and the Mebaqqer as the same official,[63] we will proceed on the same assumption because their duties are the same. CD outlines the duties of the Mebaqqer as,

> He must teach the general membership about the works [8] of God, instruct them in His mighty miracles, relate to them the future events coming to the world with their interpretations; [9] he should care for them as a father does his children, taking care of all their problems as a shepherd does for his flock. [10] He should loosen all their knots, that there be no one oppressed or crushed in his congregation. [11] He shall observe everyone who is added to his group as to his actions, his intelligence, his ability, his strength, and his wealth [12] and write him down by his place according to his share in the allotment of Light. No members of the camp are allowed [13] to bring anyone into the group except by permission of the Overseer of the camp. (CD 13:7–13)

Additional duties are given in CD 14:6–12

---

63. Brownlee, *Dead Sea Manual*, 25n27; Wernberg-Moeller, *Manual of Discipline*, 107; Cross, *Ancient Library*, 176; Knibb, *Qumran Community*, 118

The priest who presides [7]at the head of the general membership must be between thirty to sixty years old, learned in the Book of Meditation [8]and in all the regulations of the Law, speaking them in the proper way. The Overseer of [9]all the camps must be between thirty and fifty years old, master of every [10]secret of men and of every deceptive utterance. At his command, the members of the congregation shall enter, [11]each in his turn. Anything that any man might have to say let him say it to the Overseer, including [12]any kind of dispute or legal matter. This is the rule of the general membership for meeting all their needs.

This study now will focus on drawing similarities between Peter's leadership and ethics in Acts and the Mebaqqer and the ethics lived at Qumran. We have established that Luke in Acts 1–12 and 15 portrays Peter as the leader of the church, though James takes over leadership from 15:13. More so, Peter is a leader depicting resemblance of duties and character traits similar to those emphasized in Qumran. For instance, at Qumran, it was the Mebaqqer alone who was permitted to speak without the permission of the many (1QS 6:12). Permission to speak at Qumran was basically requested by one standing up and when granted, nobody was allowed to interrupt. Peter is portrayed as standing up (Acts 1:15), standing with the eleven (2:14), addressing the people (3:12), defending the apostles before the leaders of the people (4:8), receiving property and confronting the owners of the property (5:1–11). Peter and John are sent to Samaria but it is clearly demonstrated that Peter is the leader (8:14–24). Peter is mentioned first before John and John does not speak at all throughout the mission. The disciples in Lydda and Joppa look to him as their leader and request him to come, in time of crisis and God instructs Cornelius to send for him to explain the way of salvation to him.

Then, these occurrences and others portray Peter as the leader of the group. we will now seek to demonstrate specific duties of the Mebaqqer that Peter is clearly portrayed as carrying out in Acts 1–12 and 15.

5.4.1. Characteristics of the Mebaqqer That Apply to Peter

Although Ernst Haenchen observes that it is wrong to say that Peter acts like the Mebaqqer in Acts 5:1–11, Menoud, Schmitt and Trocme suggest that Peter's leadership corresponds to the disciplinary function of the Mebaqqer of Qumran.[64] We have noted in this study that the list of names provided in Acts 1:13 narratively places Peter in a position of significance by naming him first.[65] Luke presents Peter as reconstituting the apostles' group by suggesting the replacement of Judas. Basing his proposal on the Pesher style of interpretation, he explains the importance of filling Judas's position.[66] It is worth noting that all members of the group (Christian community) up to now were received by Jesus. Therefore, Peter is simply reorganizing the group. The mention of 120 people paints a Jewish picture: a Qumran picture in this first camp in Jerusalem. It could be said that this is simply a Jewish idea depicting the wilderness camps in Israel. Taking into account that Israel's wilderness camps were built around the twelve natural sons of Jacob, but Qumran only kept the significance of the number yet organized the camps around priest, Levites, and a Mebaqqer of the camp.[67]

5.4.1.1. Admitting Members into the Community

CD states that the Mebaqqer

> shall observe everyone who is added to his group as to his actions, his intelligence, his ability, his strength, and his wealth and write him down by his place according to his share in the allotment of light. No members of the camp are allowed to bring anyone into the group except by permission of the Overseer of the camp. (CD 13:11–13).

The language in the passage above is one of scrutiny and careful consideration of members by the Mebaqqer. He was to examine the conduct of the new member, their intelligence, strength and wealth. All the findings were recorded on the new member's account in the allotment of light.

Peter stands up on Pentecost and gives a lengthy speech that culminates in guiding Israel on how to return to their God. There is no other human authority that could lay claim to the leadership of the church in Jerusalem at this point other than Peter – with many other words Peter bore witness to the crowd and exhorted them to turn away from the corrupt generation

---

64. Haenchen, *Acts*, 240.

65. Brown, Donfried, and Reumann, *Peter*, 40.

66. Brown, Donfried, and Reumann, 40.

67. There was the Mebaqqer of the camp (CD 13:13) and one for all camps (CD 14:8–9).

(Acts 2:40; cf. CD 6: 14–15). Just like the Mebaqqer, Peter explains the procedure of entering the kingdom of God, represented by the community of disciples. In essence, he facilitates the admission of the three thousand to the body of Christ at Jerusalem.[68]

The Mebaqqer in the Community Rule was assigned the task of administration of the candidates' property during the second year of probation (QS 6:20, CD 14: 13–16).[69] Luke notes that the property given by the believers was brought to the feet of the apostles.[70] Acts 4:35, 37; 5:2 generally refers to the apostles. However, the contentious Ananias episode has Peter responding to the couple. Since Peter is portrayed as the leader of the group in Jerusalem, he must have received the goods on behalf of the community, and in this light, Peter assumes the duties ascribed to the Mebaqqer. It may be inferred that the general reference to the apostles in Acts 6:1–2 also suggests that Peter serves as the leader to give direction on how food should be distributed among the needy widows, which also fell among the duties of the Overseer at Qumran.

Luke portrays Peter as not only traveling among the communities but also as receiving members in the Christian community. Philip, one of the seven

---

68. Conscious of the pitfalls of overdoing the supposed similarity in passages or figures, let me explain something here. This study is aware of the temptation to hunt for similarities in the face of glaring differences. However, in this parallel of admission of members by the two leaders, we will not be focusing on the process and methodology of admission, but the general principle that it had to be the Overseer of the camp not just anybody. We will demonstrate this truth as it runs through Acts that it is Peter who brings in the believers in all the inaugural stages of the church in new mission fields. The two communities lived at different times and cultural rituals are revised to fit the community's needs at the time yet maintain the underlying principles. A good example would be circumcision as a rite of passage to the next stage for a young man. A hundred years ago, it was done by crude instruments and at home with much singing and dancing throughout the month. Whereas today the community still maintains circumcision as a rite of passage to the next stage for boys, but it is now done in the hospitals, with female nurses assisting contrary to the tradition that prohibited even one's mother to appear at the circumcision scene. Due to social and economic changes, nobody has time to sing and idle the whole month observing this rite but they meet for one day to celebrate and admit these new men into manhood. The similarity between the two generations is they both use circumcision as a rite of passage to the next stage. Drawing parallels on the method of circumcision may indicate differences that are present yet not significant. Therefore, we limit our parallels in this section of admitting members on the officials not the process and methods involved and duration involved in the admission. See Dupont-Sommer, *Essene Writings from Qumran*, trans. G. Vermes, 375, on the relation of the new sect and the old sect.

69. Metso, "Qumran Community," 294; Keener, *Acts*, vol. 2, 1178.

70. The use of the term at "the apostles' feet" denotes submission. C. K. Barret observes that this has parallels sense of Qumran though not the wordings. Barrett, *Acts 1–14*, 255; Keener, *Acts*, vol. 2, 1178; Johnson, *Acts*, 87.

appointed to take care of the distribution of food takes the gospel to Samaria. The apostles at Jerusalem receive the information of Samaria receiving the Word. We have noted that baptism in the Spirit is the indicator for the presence of the kingdom of God in any new Christian community in Acts. Philip had a very successful ministry in Samaria to the extent of an exorcism of evil spirits and healing. However, it was not until Peter and John arrived and prayed for the believers that the distinguishing sign of the true disciples of Christ in Acts (the baptism into the Holy Spirit) came upon the Samaritans. It is not until Peter comes to Samaria that Luke portrays the Samaritans as receiving the Spirit. It remains problematic as to why the Spirit was not given through Philip, but it is apparent from what Luke presents that the church in Jerusalem sends Peter and John to inspect or authenticate (or both) the work in Samaria. This baffling situation at Samaria presents a setting in which Peter receives the Samaritans in the Christian family as the Mebaqqer would do at Qumran. This new community at Samaria also transforms Peter from just the leader of Jerusalem to the leader of two communities, hence, similar to the Overseer of many camps in Qumran. In Acts 9:32, Peter is portrayed as an overseer, inspecting the communities both in Jerusalem and Samaria to ensure the standards of the community are maintained and justice and holiness are upheld in every camp and procedure is adhered to in admission.

Thus, in the first half of Acts, Peter is intrinsically involved in receiving the initial converts, a duty similar to the Mebaqqer at Qumran. This survey evidently brings to light that Peter is performing a duty similar to the one the Mebaqqer performed at Qumran. Both leaders (Peter and the Mebaqqer) are performing similar duties in their respective communities, providing the necessary understanding required by readers into the leadership and practices of both communities (Acts and Qumran).

5.4.1.2. Teaching Members about the Mighty Works of God

Another duty of the Mebaqqer required that "He must teach the general membership about the works of God, instruct them in His mighty miracles," (CD 13: 7–8). The works of God could refer to his creation (Job 37:14) or how God works to manage and control his creation (Job 40:19). It could also refer to the acts of God in delivering Israel from Egypt and preserving her in the wilderness (Exod 11:9; Ps 78:7). In the New Testament, this could refer to teaching people to believe God (John 6:28), healing (John 9:3), or people declaring the greatness or the magnificence of God (Acts 2:11). In sum, this refers to teaching, training, or instructing about God's creation and what God does to maintain his creation. It also touches on training the camps in what God has done for them in history, that they may have faith in his works, experiencing healing and other spiritual graces that will culminate in their declaring the greatness and excellence of the Lord.

After the message on Pentecost, Peter is depicted as exhorting the people to believe in the works of God, who has raised Jesus Christ from the dead and exalted him above all authorities in heaven and earth. He reminds them that God has fulfilled what he promised Israel and the promise is valid for them, their children, and as many as the Lord will call. Luke portrays Peter as using words very similar to the language of the Qumran community to persuade men of Israel to save themselves from "this corrupt generation" (Acts 2:41; cf. CD 6:15). The healing of the lame man in Acts 3 depicts Peter as performing the works of God.

Brown attests to the fact that Peter was a miracle worker and his miracles resemble those of Jesus and Paul,[71] but he makes a problematic statement worth examining here:

> As we have indicated, the problem of Lukan redaction in the Matthias report severely limits our ability to reconstruct the historical scene. The other items allow more certainty. Peter is named first in the Marcan (3:16) and Matthean (10:2) lists of the twelve as well. That Peter had a prominent role in the Jerusalem church and that he was a missionary and a spokesman are at least partially supported by the Pauline letters, as we have seen. That Peter worked miracles and that he was the object of miraculous care are harder to verify as history, but we note that Paul associates "signs, wonders and mighty works" with apostleship.[72]

Brown concurs that Peter was a leader, missionary, and spokesman in the Jerusalem church. However, the efforts to reconstruct the historical Peter as a vicar of Christ on the basis of Pauline letters remain challenging. His reservations on Peter as a miracle worker should be viewed in the light of the

---

71. Brown, Donfried, and Reumann, *Peter*, 41.
72. Brown, Donfried, and Reumann, 42.

absence of information on Peter as a miracle worker in Pauline letters - not as a general challenge of reconstructing Peter as a miracle worker in New Testament, thus, affecting our study in Acts where Peter is evidently portrayed as an instrument of the mighty works of God. The incident in our text (Acts 3:1–10) does not only portray Peter as an overseer involved with the healing of an Israelite,[73] but also gives him an opportunity to explain the basis and significance of what is happening. The reaction of the people watching illustrates their obliviousness to what had transpired (3:12). Peter narrates to the crowd how the healing was made possible. Beginning with Abraham as the point of reference, he explains how the people of Israel (whom he will refer to as brothers in verse 17) had rejected Jesus before Pilate and asked Pilate to crucify him. Now God has raised the same Jesus up and by faith in his name, the lame man has received perfect health in the presence of them all (3:16).

The Ananias and Sapphira episode is a mighty act of God, perhaps a miracle of judgment. Two people meet their death for lying to the Holy Spirit. Although it may be hard to confidently ascribe the act to Peter, he is at least involved as the leader of the community, even if we cannot claim that he is the source of the act. Luke in Acts 5:9 tells us that Ananias and his wife Sapphira tested God. This statement provokes the memories of Israelites in the wilderness and God's indictment on them (Num 14:20–24). The end of those who tested God in the wilderness was tragic. Luke portrays that the end of those who opt to conduct their lives in ways that disregard God has not changed; it may be even more severe now.

In Acts 5:12–16, Luke records the mighty miracles performed by Peter, in that people laid their sick on the streets for Peter's shadow to fall on them for healing. The Lydda and Joppa episodes (Acts 9:32–43) provide another case of Peter being used to heal and resuscitate. We had prior made mention of him working among the disciples in Lydda and Joppa as an overseer and now we can see him as the overseer performing an act of healing to Aeneas and what is clearly a mighty miracle resurrecting Tabitha at Joppa.

Consequently, Peter is portrayed as an overseer in Jerusalem and Judea regions. As an overseer, he is making known to the members of those

---

73. In the Qumran community, the chances of the Overseer dealing with a lame man would have been very slim. Because according to their conditions of admission and may be association also, the lame man would have missed the opportunity for that healing (CD 15:15–17).

communities the works of God and his mighty miracles. This duty that was assigned to Mebaqqer also provides a parallel between the two leaders. Each functioned in his community as a teacher of the works of God and his mighty miracles (teaching, in this case, was conducted both by words and deeds).

5.4.1.3. Caring for Members as a Father and Shepherd

At Qumran, it was expected of the Overseer to relate to the members as a father would (CD 13:9), dealing with them compassionately and showing mercy yet demonstrating a high level of discipline and firmness in producing the necessary character of holiness and righteousness required of the community to please Yahweh (Ps 103:13). Though it is difficult to demonstrate clearly how fathers conducted themselves at Qumran in light of their varied understandings of family life, it would be assumed that any responsible father in a true Jewish home would have sought to train their children in the ways of God by emphasizing the significance of the Law and discipline.

Luke portrays Peter as indeed functioning as a father to the group of Christians in Jerusalem, Judea, and Samaria. He organizes them into an acceptable Jewish group (Acts 1:15–26), he clarifies issues and accusations leveled against the community (2:14–16), and points them to repentance (2:37–40). He has compassion on and shows mercy to the needy and neglected (3:1–10). He firmly confronts the erring (5:1–11), humbly listens to the needs of the weak and marginalized (6:1–2). He sets good standards for the members in resolving their conflicts and gives other members opportunity to shoulder responsibilities with him (6:2–6). He follows up to confirm that saints were progressing well (9:32), and he deals with issues that may be above them but vital for the community (8:14–25). He inspects the progress of the camp and community, and his promptness to the calls of the members is one thing everyone would love to see in a father (9:32–42). Peter's ability to accept change and adapt to God's worldview in chapter 10, is one of the specialties of a great father. As a father, children come with inevitable demands for change. This is true for both natural and spiritual children. The father-child relationship will definitely bring one face-to-face with issues related to change. As a father, Peter reckons with the fact that things will not always go the way he wants (John 21:18). And for the sake of the church and members, he embraces change for the good of the Gentiles' inclusion in the plan of God. As a father, he listens to the discussions and raises up at the opportune time to invoke wisdom and draw a judgment not provoking any to anger (Acts 15:7–12; Eph 6:4). He refers to what God had done in the past, bringing the younger ones into the picture of the divine undertakings (Acts 15:7–11). He clarifies issues and portrays the true picture of what is happening. What the council is discussing is the work of God among the Gentiles. This work was first committed to Peter, and he demonstrates to the members like a father how God confirmed his involvement with the mission to the Gentiles and warns that opposing it is directly opposing what is dear to the heart of God. This explanation brings the assembly to silence paving a way for the final resolution that is made. This brought the whole assembly to a mutual understanding of God's work among the Gentiles.

The Mebaqqer was also expected to take "care of all their problems as a shepherd does for his flock" (CD 13:9). Since the documents from Qumran do not tell us exactly how the Mebaqqer carried out this function as a shepherd, we may extrapolate from the relevant portions of the Jewish scriptures. We will limit ourselves to three essential roles of the shepherd-leader. From the ancient prophets, we learn that the shepherd seeks after his flock (Ezek 34:8–12), he rescues his flock (Amos 3:12), and keeps his flock (Jer 31:10).

These three areas are clear in Peter's leadership, as they were in Christ's leadership before him. Therefore, we will limit our comparison between him and the Mebaqqer to these three areas, namely seeking, rescuing, and keeping. Jesus had instructed Peter before his death to strengthen his brothers (Luke 22:31–32). This instruction was further emphasized and clarified after the resurrection, indicating that Peter was to feed Jesus's lambs and sheep (John 21:15–19). Luke records, "there was no needy person among them" (Acts 4:34). The basic responsibility of a shepherd is to feed his flock. It is apparent that there was no natural hunger among the members of the Christian community. The spiritual satisfaction is gauged by the increase of the word and the size of the community (Acts 6:7). He guards the flock against wolves and exterior intrusions (Acts 5:1–10). He maintains high standards of honesty in the community. The offer of Simon the magician to buy the Holy Spirit in Acts 8 would have corrupted the church and let it sink to deception and syncretism. It would have been hard for the Samaritans to distinguish genuine power from God and corrupt magic. The way Luke portrays Peter demonstrates him as a shepherd guarding his flock against deception and mischief. He is portrayed as going here and there among them. This great care resulted in peace, growth, and the fear of God and the comfort of the Spirit.

One other duty of the Overseer that depicts the shepherd as rescuing the flock is in CD 13:10, "He should loosen all their knots, that there be no one oppressed or crushed in his congregation." Since CD or the Community Rule does not state how this particular duty of the Mebaqqer was practically carried out, we will proceed by defining it here generally and mostly how it is used in the New Testament. However, In Daniel 5:12–16, קְטַר (knot) is translated as explain riddles or solve difficult problems in most of our English translations.[74]

Having explained what was entailed to loosen the knots of the members by the Overseer (in the New Testament), let us apply these to Peter as characterized in Acts. Peter and John are going to the temple for the time of prayer. A lame man was daily laid at the gate of this temple to ask for alms. Peter commands him in the name of Jesus to rise up and offers his hand and the lame man rises. Luke reports many more signs and wonders of this kind (Acts 5:12–16), where Peter's shadow heals many who were sick and afflicted with unclean spirits and they were healed (5:16). The same is true in Lydda at Aeneas's home (9:32–35). In healing this man the tradition of bringing him to the gate daily stopped from that day on. Peter is portrayed as having solved a situation that seemed like a riddle to the lame man. The man is loosed from his knot, thus, painting Peter in the light of what the Mebaqqer was expected to do in his community.

Immediately afterward, Peter is urgently called to Joppa because Tabitha is dead. She is portrayed as one loved and cherished greatly in Joppa, both acceptable to Jews and Greeks, hence the significance of translating her name. Death does grip, and in addition causes pain. Peter brings Tabitha back to life rescuing her or loosening her from the pain of death. Her characterization as Dorcas and her good works connects her narrative well with the Gentile centurion in chapter 10, who also is full of good works.

Cornelius may have been a proselyte, but the Jewish laws rated him as unclean. God reveals to Peter that what God has made clean, no one has the right to call unclean. Cornelius represents many who are limited by Jewish tradition. God sends Peter to Cornelius and explains the way of salvation, and while doing that the Holy Spirit fell upon them and they began to speak

---

74. See Strong, *Exhaustive Concordance of the Bible*, 80 (key word comparison).

in tongues as the apostles did. Thus, Peter frees Cornelius and the entire Gentile world symbolically from the legal obligations of the Jewish laws by explaining the way of salvation to them.

Therefore, the characterization of Peter's leadership portrays him as a caring father and shepherd as described in the duties of the Mebaqqer of Qumran. In the three analogies discussed for care as a father and a shepherd, with the supplement of untying their knots, we certainly find another similarity between Peter's leadership and the Overseer of Qumran. We acknowledge that there is not much detail from Qumran, but the general duties described in CD apply also to Peter. Although we do not know exactly how the duties were exercised, we have proceeded on the assumption that the Mebaqqer carried them out as stipulated in CD.

5.4.1.4. Disciplining Members and Dealing with Disputes

Now we turn to one of the most controversial duties of the Mebaqqer. As much as he was tasked with the responsibility to admit members, the reverse too fell under his duties, namely discipline and expulsion of members. "At his command, the members of the congregation shall enter, each in his turn. Anything that any man might have to say, let him say it to the Overseer, including any kind of dispute or legal matter" (CD 14:11–12). The Mebaqqer dealt with all discipline matters and legal issues in the community. Josephus notes,

> But for those who are caught in any heinous sins, they cast them out of their society; and he who is thus separated from them does often die after a miserable manner; for as he is bound by the oath he has taken, and by the customs he has been engaged in, he is not at liberty to partake of that food that he meets with elsewhere, but is forced to eat grass, and to famish his body with hunger, till he perish; for which reason they receive many of them again when they are at their last gasp, out of compassion to them, as thinking the miseries they have endured till they came to the very brink of death, to be a sufficient punishment for the sins they had been guilty of.[75]

---

75. Josephus, *J.W.* 2.143–44.

For us to understand what Josephus refers to as heinous sins that warranted a member to be expelled, several texts need to be consulted. The Community Rule records,

> Anyone who speaks aloud the M[ost] Holy Name of God, [whether in . . .] or in cursing or as a blurt in time of trial or for any other reason, or while he is reading a book or praying, is to be expelled, never again to return to the party of the Yahad. If anyone speaks angrily against one of the priests who are inscribed in the book, he is to be punished by reduced rations for one year and separated from the pure meals of the general membership, eating by himself.[76]

Similarly, 1QS 7:16–17 includes the offense of slandering the many, and 1QS 7:22–25 states that the one who betrays the community after ten years or more of membership should be expelled. Varying degrees of severity in discipline were meted out, also depending on the gravity of the offense in light to the laws of the community. Instructions on how to handle a judicial process are given in 1QS 6:24–7:2 and 1QS 8:20. On the basis of these guidelines, discipline was administered to the erring members at different levels. Two situations stand out that require expulsion of a member from the Qumran community with no provisions for restoration: backsliding spiritually and walking in a willful heart after being a member for ten years.[77]

How then, is Peter's leadership responsibility similar to this duty of the Mebaqqer? J. Schmitt points out that Peter's role corresponds to the disciplinary function of the Mebaqqer.[78] However, Ernst Haenchen categorically refutes this line of thought. He contests, "It is quite wrong to say that Peter acts like a Mebaqqer of Qumran: the Overseer did not execute judgements of God but 'shall have mercy on them as a father on his sons, and shall bring

---

76. 1QS 7:1–2; CD 19:13.

77. "Any man who, having been in the party of the Yahad for ten full years, backslides spiritually so that he forsakes the Yahad and leaves the general membership, walking in his willful heart, may never again return to the party of the Yahad. Also, any man belonging to the Ya[had who sh]ares with him his own food, his own wealth [or that of] the Yahad, is to suffer the same verdict: he is to be exp[elled.]" (1QS 7:23–25). "Any covenant member of the Yahad of Holiness (they who walk blamelessly as He commanded) who transgresses even one commandment from the Law of Moses intentionally or deviously is to be expelled from the party of the Yahad, never to return" (1QS 8:21–22).

78. Haenchen, *Acts*, 240; Conzelmann, *Acts*, 39.

back all their erring ones as a shepherd does with his flock' (CDC XIII. 7ff)."[79] He further insists, "If a member tells a lie about property, Qumran punishes him not with death, but with one-year reduction to the rank of a novice and the curtailment of one part in four of his food (1QS VI. 24f)."[80] Since these sentiments are made in reference to the Ananias and Sapphira narrative, let us begin to examine this similarity between Peter and the Mebaqqer here.

Peter confronts Ananias and Sapphira who knowingly conspire to lie about the proceeds of the sale of their property. Peter, by the Holy Spirit, discerns the deception and rebukes them. Scholars have questioned Peter's action, why he did not follow Jesus's procedure of dealing with a sinner (Matt 18:15)? Others have accordingly accused him of committing sin in the light of Jesus's approach (who did not kill Judas).[81] Haenchen makes two conclusions on this episode that we will examine further. First, he refutes that Peter cannot be compared to the Mebaqqer of Qumran here because "the Overseer did not execute judgments of God."[82] Fitzmyer rightly brings CD 13:9 ("he should care for them as a father does his children, taking care of all their problems as a shepherd does for his flock") into the discussion.[83] However, it is worth noting here that some of the expulsions done by the Overseer of Qumran may have led to death due to starvation. The expelled member could not receive food from other members and, due to the vow they had taken on admission, some of them may not have been free to beg food from outsiders, thus result-ing in death. Second, Haenchen argues, "If a member tells a lie about their property, Qumran punishes him not with death, but with one year reduction to the rank of a novice and the curtailment of one part in four of his food (1QS VI. 24f)."[84] It will suffice to read this alongside another rule of dealing with members at Qumran. It states, "Any covenant member of the Yahad of Holiness (they who walk blamelessly as He commanded) who transgresses even one commandment from the Law of Moses intentionally or deviously is to be expelled from the party of the Yahad, never to return. Further, none

---

79. Haenchen, *Acts*, 241.

80. Haenchen, 241.

81. Haenchen, 239–40.

82. Haenchen, 241.

83. Fitzmyer, *Acts of the Apostles*, 318.

84. Ernst Haenchen, *The Acts of the Apostles: A Commentary* (Philadelphia: Westminster Press, 1971), 241.

of the holy men is to do business with that man or advise him on any matter whatsoever." (CD 13:14–15)[85]

Other than lying concerning property, Ananias and Sapphira are guilty of contravening the law of Moses. Bearing false witness against the neighbor is not only in the negative sense but it could also be in the positive sense in that you support the neighbor's course as true when you know very well it is false. This is equally bearing false witness. Ananias and Sapphira supported one another in falsehood contra to the customary accusing your neighbor falsely. Breaking the law of Moses would have earned one permanent separation from the group. In view of the above, there was a tough penalty for some offenses and light penalty for others. Fitzmyer, on the other hand, argues, "There is no indication in Acts that Ananias and Sapphira had 'fraudulently' taken a 'vow' of dispossession in some 'inner circle' of Christians, which might resemble the Essene obligation."[86] However, although there was no formal vow of poverty among the early Christians, the only way to become part of the community was through radical repentance, turning from and renouncing sin. As far as we can tell, if Ananias and Sapphira had been honest about donating only a portion of their property to the community, they would not have been sinning. Their sin was in lying and trying to make themselves look more generous than they really were.

Fitzmyer, and Haenchen among other scholars, seek to understand Ananias and Sapphira's action in the light of the judgment on Achan's action (Josh 7), or Aaron's two sons (Lev 10:2).[87] Without pursuing the original sin reading of the passage yet partially in consonant with its point of departure, we have stated in chapter 4 that another suitable analogy to this episode is the fall narrative. The restored temple represented by the Christian community provides a similar setting to Eden.[88] Beale states,

> Jesus' resurrection from the dead demonstrates the inauguration of a new order, with Jesus as the new temple, from whom flow the rivers of life, and through whom the temple veil is opened so that peoples from all nations might enter in. God's original

---

85. CD 13: 14–15

86. Fitzmyer, *Acts of the Apostles*, 318–19.

87. Fitzmyer, 319.

88. Beale and Kim, *God Dwells*.

purpose for the temple in Eden – that it would be a place to expand and fill the whole earth – begins to be fulfilled in Jesus, the new temple.[89]

With Beale's view on Eden as the sanctuary or dwelling place, it is noteworthy that the Christian community represents the temple of Christ (1 Cor 3:16). Thus, Ananias and Sapphira should also be read in light of Adam and Eve a couple that allowed Satan's intrusion into the sanctuary of God. An assault on Edenic shalom attracted one consequence and that still stands to date: death, which also comes to Ananias and Sapphira.[90]

Therefore, we see Peter portrayed as dealing with discipline and dispute issues in Acts 5:1–11, 8:18–24 and 15:6–12. The council in Jerusalem is characterized as resolving a dispute around the legality of the Gentiles' salvation. Notwithstanding the fact that Peter does not make the final decision in Acts 15, his counsel provides the wisdom and basis upon which the assembly draws its conclusions. Thus, these three episodes serve to portray Peter as dealing with discipline and disputes in Acts.

5.4.1.5. Discerning the State of the Hearts of Men (and the Overseer's Age)

The Damascus Document records that "The Overseer of all the camps must be between thirty and fifty years old, master of every secret of hearts of men and of every deceptive utterance" (CD 14:9–10). Peter was probably born about 1 BC and died sometime around AD 67.[91] These dates place Peter in the same age bracket as Jesus. Thus, if Jesus died at thirty-three years old, consequently Peter also began leading the Christian community at Jerusalem around that age of thirty-three. Based on the dates of his execution, during the reign of Nero (AD 54–68), he was slightly above sixty years old. Peter is reported to have been a part of the Jerusalem council AD 50–51.[92] It is

---

89. Beale and Kim, 98.

90. It not only comes to Achan (Jos. 7:24–26) and Aaron's sons (Lev. 10:1) but is equally witnessed in Korah and Dathan (Number 16:31–35), whom the ground swallowed up. Pharaoh's army (Exo. 14:26–31), and the unnamed prophet in (1 Kings 13:14–25) who got mauled by the lion are among the narratives where this consequence is attested.

91. This date is informed by the fact that Peter experienced a judicial execution during the reign of Nero in Rome (AD 54–68).

92. Lightfoot, Acts, 189.

apparent that Peter was within the age bracket required of a Mebaqqer of between thirty and fifty years[93] (mostly this would be the age bracket required of leaders in Jewish circles).

To examine the second part of the Overseer's qualification – "master of every secret of men and of every deceptive utterance" – we will center our conversation on two episodes in Acts; the narratives of Ananias and Sapphira (5:1–11) and Simon the magician (8:18–24). Acts 5:1–11 portrays Peter as "a man of supernatural insight."[94] Marshall notes, "Peter is assumed to have the power of spiritual insight and to be able to recognize when he is being told lies, God's power to see into men's hearts (Heb 4:13) is given to the apostle."[95] When Ananias and Sapphira lie about withholding part of the proceeds from the sale of their property, Peter attributes this act to the inspiration of Satan.[96] The Semitic idiom "filled your heart" suggests that it is Satan who gave them the courage to act in this manner. However, Peter, enabled by the Holy Spirit, confronts the couple. The incident depicts Peter as one who knows the secrets of people's hearts, first Ananias and then his wife Sapphira.

The next episode in this light is that of Simon the magician in Samaria (8:18–24). Peter and John are sent to the thriving Samaria community, to validate Philip's work among the Samaritans. Simon the magician, who also has believed the gospel preached by Philip, offers money to buy the gift of the Spirit; Peter confronts him and rebukes him for imagining that what was happening could be bought. Peter declares that Simon's "heart is not right before God." Simon does not object, which confirms Peter's utterance. Peter again is presented as one who has the ability to detect deceptive utterances of the people around him.

The duties and qualities of the Mebaqqer of Qumran we have compared with Peter's leadership in Acts – namely admission of members in the community, teaching members the mighty miracles and works of God, care of members as father and shepherd, relating and interpreting future events

---

93. After Samaria we see Peter as more of an overseer of many camps reporting to Jerusalem where James may have been the leader of the community at Jerusalem now. Though tradition has information of his existence, however, Peter fades from active leadership after the Jerusalem council tentatively at the age of fifty.

94. Marshall, *Acts of the Apostles*, TNTC, 110.

95. Marshall, 112.

96. Marshall, 112.

coming to the world, and the Overseer's age and ability to discern the secrets of man's hearts and the deception of their utterance – have shed significant light on how Peter's leadership is characterized in Acts. These qualities and duties provide evidence for similarities between Peter's leadership in Acts and the Mebaqqer at Qumran. Although there are a few differences between the two, these do not outweigh the many similarities between Peter's leadership and the Overseer at Qumran. We will now seek to draw similarities or parallels between Peter's ethics and the ethics at Qumran.

5.4.1.6. Prophecy, Vision, Dreams and Their Interpretations

The Mebaqqer had the duty to "relate to them the future events coming to the world with their interpretations" (CD 13:8). This particular duty points to the Overseer's prophetic function. Josephus notes in his writings that the Essenes had the ability to foresee the future: "There are also those among them who undertake to foretell things to come, by reading the holy books, and using various sorts of purifications, and being perpetually conversant in the discourses of the prophets; and it is but seldom that they miss in their predictions."[97] In defending the sensibility of the accuracy of the Essenes' prediction, Josephus refers to examples of these kind of predictions.[98] The numerous copies of the Old Testament prophetic books, as well as the large number of citations from these materials, indicate the interest in and popularity of the prophetic writings in the community.[99] In this light, the pesharim at Qumran become very significant. Dupont-Sommer defines a pesher as "the explanation of the hidden significance, a revelation of the secrets concealed in the divine books, which only inspired commentators, prophets, or initiates were able to discover."[100] These explanations involved interpretation of dreams and visions too. The community believed that the prophetic mysteries could be only interpreted by the Teacher of Righteousness and other leaders in that capacity to follow him (1QpHab 7:4–5).

---

97. Josephus, *J.W.* 2.159.

98. Josephus, *J.W.* 1.78–80.

99. Beall, *Josephus' Description of the Essenes*, 110. For a list of the copies of the prophetic writings found at Qumran as well as citations for such writings in other Qumran literature see Fitzmyer, *Dead Sea Scrolls*, 163–70.

100. Dupont-Sommer, *Essene Writings*, 255. Dupont-Sommer's definition helps us to bring out clearly the characteristics of the pesher interpretation that are similar to how Peter interprets Scripture.

Now, how is Peter's leadership similar to this responsibility of the Mebaqqer of Qumran? We will attempt to trace how Luke portrays him within our scope of study. First, we will compare Peter's use of Old Testament passages in Acts to the approach of the pesharim. This conviction that they are living in the end times enables both groups to refer to the sayings of the Old Testament prophets and writings to events or tenets in their own history or beliefs.[101] Fitzmyer observes,

> This attitude underlies the constant actualization or modern-
> ization of the Old Testament texts being used either in the *pe-*
> *sharim* or in isolated quotations in other writings. See CD 1:13
> ("This is the time about which it was written," introducing Hos.
> 4:16); 10:16; 16:15 ("For that is what it [or: he] said"); 1QM 10:1;
> 11:11. It is this same attitude that underlies the use of the Old
> Testament in Peter's speech on Pentecost, as the prophet Joel is
> quoted . . . The introductory formulas often reveal this attitude
> more than anything else.[102]

We will now turn to some of these passages to confirm Peter's interpretations are similar to those in the pesharim. We wish to point out here again that Luke presents Peter as one speaking under the direction of the Spirit, plac-ing him at the same level as the Old Testament prophets (Acts 4:8). The first place Peter manifests the pesher style and approach is Acts 1:20 (CD 11:20) in discussing the replacement of Judas. He links the Judas episode with two Psalms (Pss 69:25; 109:8). Peter applies these two Psalms to their situation that what David spoke in the past is applicable to the replacement of Judas (Acts 1:19–22). Thus, implying its fulfillment in Judas's betrayal of Christ and even the need for his (Judas) replacement (Acts 1:18). The same interpretive strategy is witnessed in CD 10:16; 16:15, (cf. CD 6:6–8, 13), CD 4:20, and CD 4:13–14 as clarifying the Pentecost incident.[103]

---

101. Fitzmyer, "Jewish Christianity," 251.

102. Fitzmyer, 252.

103. However, it is important to note Dupont-Sommer's caution on pesher. He notes that:
    "all concerns for an objective interpretation disappears from an exegetical system
    of this sort . . . the text is only a pretext; the commentator tears it out of its context,
    transposes, transforms, isolates and forces it in order to make it express his own
    obsessive ideas." See Dupont-Sommer, Essene Writings, trans.G. Vermes, 255. I
    wish to state that this is not what is happening with Peter because he is portrayed as

This kind of interpretation required the Overseer to demonstrate a high level of commitment to the study of the law (1QS 6:6–7). Dupont-Sommer writes,

> The spirit of these ascetics drew its nourishment therefore from the unceasing study of the biblical books: all their speculations, even newest and boldest, were ingeniously and subtly linked to biblical texts, even when this required a real *tour de force*. For them, the Bible was the book of God, and as such, all truth was thought to lie hidden there. The remains of the biblical commentaries from Qumran are witness to immense exegetical labor which the Essenes pursued without respite, day and night, for almost two centuries.[104]

This sheds light on important information concerning what may have informed Peter's position in Acts 6:1–3, when he states that it is not right for the apostles to give up the ministry of the word and prayer to serve tables. As an Overseer, Peter demonstrates the importance of God's word in which there are hidden mysteries of God. It was especially the responsibility for the Mebaqqer to read, search, and interpret this hidden truth to his community. Peter's commitment to the word and prayer does not wane throughout Acts. Therefore, Peter is characterized as a Mebaqqer who diligently commits himself to study and prayer as a pre-requisite for an approved pesher exegete.

In chapter 10, Luke portrays Peter as still committed to prayer and the word. He is lodging at the tanner's house, yet even when he is away from his familiar context he finds a place of prayer. Peter receives a vision, and the conversation in the vision paints Peter as an astute student of the law. This was also required of course from the Overseer. However, our focus here is to highlight Peter's ability to see visions and the responsibility of explaining Cornelius's vision. It is noteworthy that God himself instructs Cornelius to send for Peter to explain the vision and guide him in the way of salvation (Acts 10:5–6, 30–33). In Peter explaining the vision to Cornelius, he is also, in essence, explaining what God is beginning to do among the Gentiles.

---

filled with the Holy Spirit the author of the text and consistently his interpretation is validated by God and the spirit by signs and wonders.

104. Dupont-Sommer, *Essene Writings*, trans. G. Vermes, 256.

One of the most contentious issues in Acts is the inclusion of Gentiles in the community of faith. There is an apparent conflict between the circumcision party and Barnabas and Paul's party. The circumcision party insists that, according to the promises made to Abraham (Gen 17:9–14), circumcision was the sign of the covenant between God and Abraham and his offspring. Everybody who claims a connection to the Abrahamic covenant must be circumcised. The Gentiles, however, were flouting the dictates of the Abrahamic covenant. Now, Barnabas and Paul, on the other hand, preach that Gentiles are saved by grace apart from the works of the law, including circumcision, and this engenders a hot debate. A council is called as noted earlier; this was similar to the Essenes' judicial courts. After a heated discussion in Acts 15:7, Peter stood up and explained how God chose him to evangelize the Gentiles, probably referring to Acts 10. He explains to the council this mystery and in essence interprets the events of Amos 9:11, 12. The silence recorded in verse 12, is an indication of the end of the contention. James in summarizing puts Peter at the same level as the Old Testament prophet. He asserts that the words of Peter agree with the Prophets. Now, if what Peter has stated agrees with the prophets (Amos), then, the inclusion of Gentiles, which Peter points out as happening in their time, is another demonstration of his pesher style of interpretation.

Again, this examination of how Peter is characterized in Acts shows that Peter prioritized study of the word and engaged in his duty through prayer. It is evident that he is portrayed as a prophet and he received and interpreted visions. This parallels the duties of the Mebaqqer in the Damascus Document, thus giving us yet another area of similarity or parallel between Peter's leadership and that of the Mebaqqer at Qumran.

5.4.2. Characteristics of Peter That Apply to the Mebaqqer

In this second section of drawing parallels, we will now focus on the ethics that characterizes Peter in Acts and compare that with the ethics in Qumran. We will consult both CD and the QS and where applicable refer to Josephus in order to capture the similarities in the moral principles lived in the two communities. We will analyze our characters by the means of characterization or scales of means, in ascending order of explicitness and certainty.[105]

---

105. Alter, *Art of Biblical Narrative*, 116–17; Williams, *Other Followers of Jesus*, 54–66.

5.4.2.1. Prayerfulness

The Qumran leadership laid stress on the discipline of regulated prayer, study, and esoteric interpretation of the Torah.[106] The leadership at Qumran was charged with the responsibility to keep the law and prayers alive for it was believed to be the way to please God and cause restoration of his glory to a renewed Israel. In Peter prioritizing prayer and ministry of the word (Acts 6:1–4), he was enforcing the leadership ideals of the Mebaqqer at Qumran.[107]

The community of believers in Jerusalem is portrayed in Acts as a praying community. The narrator of Acts presents them praying in the process of replacing Judas (1:24), they lived together in prayer (2:42) and they faced their threats through prayer (4:23–31; 12:5). Other than the corporate prayer in the community, of which we can safely infer that he was a part, Peter is portrayed individually as one who prays. Peter and John are shown going to the temple at the hour of prayer, presumably to pray (3:1). It can be inferred that as the spokesperson of the community he, together with the other apostles, prioritized prayer and the ministry of the word (6:4). He prays for the Samaritans to receive the Holy Spirit (8:15). Before the miracle of resurrecting Tabitha, he is depicted as praying before he turns to speak to the dead body (9:40). He received the vision of the "great sheet" symbolic of the ingathering of the Gentiles while in prayer at Simon the Tanner's house in Joppa (10:9). Last, he appears at a prayer meeting and shared a testimony of how God rescued him from the prison before leaving for another place (12:17–19).

At Qumran, Josephus notes, "As for their piety toward God, it is very extraordinary; for before sunrising they speak not a word about profane matters but put up certain prayers which they have received from their forefathers as if they made a supplication for its rising."[108] We will not get into the conversation of the sun worship at Qumran.[109] It was a norm for the Qumranites to begin the day with prayer early before the sun rose. Though Josephus comments

---

106. Fitzmyer, "Jewish Christianity," 239.

107. We must reiterate that the process of admission may not be perfectly identical in every aspect of the word but our emphasis in the similarities is largely focused on the responsibility of admitting per se.

108. Josephus, *J.W.* 2.128.

109. For more on the sun worship see, Hengel, *Judaism and Hellenism*, and Beall, *Josephus' Description of the Essenes*, 52–54.

on morning prayer, the evening custom is witnessed in both the Community Rule and the war scroll (1QS 10:1–3, 10, 13–14; 1QM 14:13–14).

In sum, prayer was a custom taken seriously at Qumran. The language Josephus uses "as if they made a supplication for its rising" could simply be indicative of the passion and intensity of the prayers that were made, evidently anticipating something significant like causing the rising of the sun. The same seriousness of this norm is witnessed in Peter's life, giving us a similarity of ethics between Peter's ethics and the ethics practiced at Qumran.

5.4.2.2. Honesty (Justice, Trustworthiness, Righteousness)

The healing of the lame man at the beautiful gate provides a setting from which several of Peter's character traits will be demonstrated. The lame man draws the attention of Peter and John as they go to the temple at the hour of prayer. Peter equally calls for his attention, and the lame man responds expectantly. However, Peter informs the man that he does not have silver and gold (Acts 3:6). The narrator portrays Peter as one saying the truth and his confession will be helpful later (8:20). Peter's word is reliable and so the lame man can trust him, thus when he commands him to rise and walk in the name of Jesus Christ of Nazareth it indeed happens.

This trait is highlighted even further when Peter confronts Ananias and Sapphira. Luke presents Peter and Ananias and Sapphira in the same circumstance to reinforce Peter's value of honesty. Ananias and Sapphira are portrayed as dishonest with the proceeds of the sale of their parcel of land. Peter is portrayed as one who values truth and honesty.

The narrator again highlights Peter's honesty through the episode of Simon the magician.[110] The two Simons are presented in the similar circumstances, so as to emphasize the distinctiveness of their traits through their responses to what the Spirit is doing.[111] In Acts 3 Peter not only acknowledges his lack of money but also his having the Holy Spirit. Simon the magician acknowledges his lack of the Spirit but he has money. Peter is associated with the life-giving Spirit, the Spirit of truth, righteousness, and joy (Rom 14:17). Simon the

---

110. Williams, *Other Followers of Jesus*, 65. See also Berlin, *Poetics and Interpretation*, 40; Gowler, *Host, Guest, Enemy*, 73; Rimmon-Kenan, *Narrative Fiction*, 67–69; Sternberg, *Poetics of Biblical Narrative*, 479–80.

111. Williams, *Other Followers of Jesus*, 65.

magician is portrayed as deceptive, wicked and bitter (Acts 8:21–23). Simon's offer seeks to overturn Peter's moral values, but Peter is portrayed as established in honesty and righteousness.

The inclusion of the Gentiles in the Christian community proved to be highly contentious. The elders and apostles gather in Jerusalem to consider the matter (15:6). After much debate, Peter stands up to address the council. Peter is now known for saying the truth, trustworthy and righteous in his judgment. He relays the history of how God began to work among the Gentiles and warns of the danger challenging what is happening among the Gentiles. Peter's testimony stills the assembly, an indication that they were satisfied by his explanation. The narrator indicates the importance and reliability of Peter's message by according him more space than Barnabas and Paul in this passage. James is accorded equal attention as Peter, making what James says highly significant. Peter is elevated to the same level as the Old Testament. James notes that what Peter has narrated is in agreement with Amos.

The significance of justice (or righteousness) at Qumran is attested to by the preeminence it receives in the Damascus Document by being the first thing a reader encounters in the first sentence: "So listen, all you who recognize righteousness, and consider the deeds of God" (CD 1:1). The Manual of Discipline echoes the same words (1QS 1:5–6; 2:24; 5:3–4). Josephus comments,

> observe justice toward men; and that he will do no harm to anyone, either of his own accord, or by the command of others; that he will always hate the wicked, and assist the righteous . . . that he will ever show fidelity to all men . . . that he will be perpetually a lover of truth, and propose to himself to reprove those who tell lies; that he will keep his hands clear from theft, and his soul from unlawful gains.[112]

This characterization of Peter's ethics in Acts compared to the ethics lived at Qumran reveals a similarity. Peter is presented in Acts as an honest, righteous, trustworthy and reliable character, a character trait that is strongly stressed at Qumran. Though this was the general expectation of godliness and proper dealing among observant Jews in this period, it is significant to note

---

112. Josephus, *J. W.* 2.139–41.

that both communities emphasized the qualities whereas they were evidently missing in other Jewish sects (e.g. Pharisees, Sadducees etc.).

5.4.2.3. Compassion

Our analysis of the character trait of compassion begins again at the beautiful gate. Almsgiving is an act of showing compassion and kindness. Jesus demonstrated in the Gospels that the miracles and healings he performed stemmed from a compassionate heart (Matt 14:14; 15:32; 20:34, Mark 1:41; 5:1–20; Luke 7:13–15). Peter's compassion is expressed in the desire to have the man healed in the name of Jesus Christ of Nazareth (Acts 3:6). Though Peter did not give alms, his compassion was expressed in a better way, healing. The lame man breaks out in celebration of the miracle, and Peter and John are portrayed as agents of God's mercy as the lame man clings to them (3:11). The man is shown to have received immense goodness from God through the apostles.

Peter's compassion is again depicted at the home of Tabitha (9:36). He responds to the urgent call promptly. The scene is highly moving, the widows stood beside him weeping showing acts of kindness done to them by the deceased Tabitha. The state of the widows, needless to say, calls for sympathy. Peter sends them out of the room, not to dismiss them, but so that he prays to "the Father of mercies and God of all comfort" (2 Cor 1:3). Tabitha is raised from the dead and presented alive to the widows and the saints at Joppa (Acts 9:40–41). Tabitha has an opportunity to continue with her acts of kindness to the community and Peter is portrayed as one who contributes to this kindness.

Compassion and hospitality seem to go hand in hand in Acts 10. Peter is lodging at Simon the tanner's house, and he receives guests from Cornelius (10:21). He invites them in to be his guests in Simon's home (10:23). Luke points back to the communal spirit, which began in Jerusalem (3:32). The two Simons are presented together to establish their distinct character trait of hospitality and compassion. Peter is portrayed as traveling and living with saints, who must have taken care of his needs as portrayed in 10:10.

This is similar to the admonitions in CD: "Each one must love his brother as himself and support the poor, needy, and alien. They must seek each the welfare of his fellow, never betraying a family member" (CD 6:20–7:1; 14:12–16). The Qumranites did not need to carry anything when traveling, for in each city they were welcomed as friends by their brothers and were provided with everything they needed just as we presume is the case with Peter in the tanner's home. Josephus also attests to this norm,

> They have no one certain city, but many of them dwell in every city; and if any of their sects come from other places, what they have lies open for them, just as if it were their own; and they go in to such as they never knew before, as if they had been ever so long acquainted with them. For which reason they carry nothing at all with them when they travel into remote parts . . . Accordingly, there is, in every city where they live, one appointed particularly to take care of strangers and to provide garments and other necessities for them.[113]

Therefore, Peter's acts of mercy and hospitality portray him as compassionate, character traits that were stressed in the Qumran community as confirmed above.

5.4.2.4. Godliness (Piety)

After the lame man was healed, the crowd of utterly astounded people gathered in Solomon's portico call for Peter and John to explain the incident at the beautiful gate. What kind of men are these? Has this been made possible by their powers or holy living? Such supernatural acts can only happen by an act of the divine or his intermediaries. Peter's response alludes to his piety (3:12), but it is not their godliness that has healed the man, but rather faith in the name of Jesus Christ of Nazareth.

It is apparent that Peter is portrayed in Acts as character devoted to godliness. His rejection of Simon the magician's offer to sell the Holy Spirit was an act of godliness (8:20). Chapter 10 is a good example of characterization of Peter's piety in Jewish culture. He challenges God that he has not eaten anything unclean (10:14). Peter is devoted to the law of God and prayer, disciplines that enhance his piety (6:4).

Qumran literature stressed piety (1QS 1:1–2; 3:9–11; 5:8–10). Thus, again a character trait depicted in Peter's life is similar to the ethics of Qumran.

---

113. Josephus, *J.W.* 2.124–25.

5.4.2.5. Humility and Obedience (Submission)

The leaders of the people of Israel refer to the healing of the lame man at the beautiful gate as "a notable sign" (4:16). However, Peter and John understood the snare it can present to the human ego. Therefore, they quickly explain to the crowd that the healing power is not something they own (3:12–16). The act of acknowledging God as the source of the healing through Jesus's name not only presents Peter as honest but as humble too. Peter and John are humble enough to ascribe the glory to the true source of the miracle.

Peter is the spokesperson and leader of the Christian community at Jerusalem. This is a position of honor in human terms, leading the group his master founded and handed over to him, a group that is highly esteemed in the city of Jerusalem and its environs. However, it is interesting to note that Peter is sent out by the apostles at Jerusalem (8:15). The normal thing would have been Peter sending the other apostles, "as the Gentiles do" (Matt 20:25–28). His willingness to carry out assignments is both an act of obedience and humility. This trait becomes evident even when he is asked to go to Joppa and Caesarea. The saints in Joppa make an urgent call for him as their overseer and he responds immediately (Acts 9:38). Furthermore, we have discussed his sense of humility displayed in accepting to stay with Simon the tanner. As a true Jewish believer, living at the tanner's house would have impinged on Peter's ceremonial purity. He accepted the tanner as his brother, making his home his operations base in the area. Being at Cornelius's house for a Jew would have been even more defiling than associating with a tanner. Peter's humility is highlighted best when he lifts Cornelius up when he fell down to worship him (10:25). He acknowledges exactly who he is, "But Peter helped him up and said, 'Stand up! I myself am also a man'" (10:26).

These two traits, humility and obedience, were highly valued at Qumran. Contentment and a simple life was viewed as an act of love to God. Josephus rightly notes, "Nor do they allow the replacement of garments or of shoes till they be first torn to pieces or worn out by time."[114] Clothing is one way someone's sense of modesty or humility can be adduced. For instance, a proud person would probably want the latest fashions, while the humble would be content with an old but still usable garment. Peter himself in addressing the subject of submission or obedience, encourages modesty in dressing

---

114. Josephus, *J. W.* 2.126.

coupled with a gentle and quiet spirit as pleasing and acceptable before God (1 Pet 3:5). This he demonstrates in his life when submits to the brethren at Jerusalem and the council and Jerusalem (Acts 11:1–17; 15: 6–11)Peter's humility, submission, and obedience resemble the Qumran practices in the same area as noted by Josephus.

5.4.2.6. Boldness (Courageousness)

Luke, in his first volume, paints Peter in the image of a coward who is unable to follow through his promises. When Jesus predicted Peter's denial, connecting it with satanic influence, Peter emphatically promised that he was ready even to die with Christ (Luke 22:33). Jesus knows Peter's heart and what will happen in the future. Yes, in future, Peter will go to prison and even die for Christ's sake. However, at present, Peter denies Jesus vehemently (Luke 22:56, 58, 60) and decides to go back to his fishing profession (John 21:3). His post-resurrection experience at Pentecost depicts a transformed Peter. He demonstrates courage and boldness before the confused crowd on Pentecost and clarifies what is happening (Acts 2:14–21), he boldly identifies himself as a witness of Christ's death and resurrection (2:40; 3:15). His bold witness is attested to by the Sanhedrin (4:13). He boldly confronts unrighteousness in the community (5:1–11; 8:20) and eventually goes to prison as per his prior promise (5:17–18). The apostles defy the council's command regardless of the perceived consequences (5:29–32). They rejoice over the fact that they "were counted worthy to suffer dishonor for the name [of Christ] even in the face of a severe beating" (5:40–41). Peter displays an unfathomable state of peace that – even expecting to die the next day death (12:1–5) – he enjoys deep sleep, all the while chained between two soldiers and a heavily guarded prison.

Fearlessness in the face of trial receives significant attention in Qumran literature.[115] The Community Rule admonishes the new converts, "to act according to all [God's] commands and not turn back from him on account of any fear or fright or trial during the dominion of Belial." (1QS 1:16–17). "One who allowed fear to influence his actions was disciplined by being separated from the council of the community" (1QS 7:1). Suffering at Qumran like the Christian community was considered an integral part of the saints' lives (1QS 8:4, cf. Mark 10:29–30). Josephus attests to the fearlessness of pain and death

---

115. Beall, *Josephus' Description of the Essenes*, 102.

of the Qumranites: "They condemn the miseries of life, and are above pain, by the generosity of their mind. And as for death, if it will be for their glory, they esteem it better than living always."[116]

In this section, we have demonstrated that Peter is portrayed in Acts as bold and fearless (Acts 4:13; 5:1–11; 8:20 etc.), character qualities that resonate with the ethics practiced in Qumran, thus providing another area of contact in ethic between the characters of the two communities.

5.4.2.7. Despising Riches

Luke portrays the community of believers in Acts as communal. Those who owned land and property are shown as doing that in trust of the larger community and many availed their houses and property to meet the needs of the believers. Peter manifests little interest in owning wealth and property in Acts contrary to his concern in the Gospels, where he confronted Jesus, "See, we have left everything and followed you. What then will we have?" (Matt 19:27). On his way to the temple in Acts 3, he confesses that he does not have silver and gold but his tone suggests contentment, not complaining. He willingly hands over the management of the daily distribution of food in the community to the seven and chooses to devote himself to prayer and ministry of the word (6:4). But the best example of Peter's despising wealth is in Acts 8:20 when Simon offers Peter money in exchange of the Holy Spirit. Clearly Luke portrays Peter as one who is not interested in money or wealth for that matter. Peter perceives Simon as an agent of Satan and wickedness.

In discussing the three nets that Belial uses to trap Israel, the Damascus Document records riches as the second net (CD 4:17). Riches are condemned and shown as of little significance. Members of the Qumran community are encouraged "beyond the will of God he (they) shall desire nothing" (1QS 9:21–24). This disdain for riches at Qumran could also be the basis of their reference to the community as "poor ones" or "the poor of grace" (1QH 5:22, QM 11:9, 13; 13:12–14).

Therefore, Peter's reprimand to Simon for offering money read in light of the attitude espoused to riches and wealth at Qumran definitely strikes a clear parallel between the characterization of Peter's ethics and the ethics at Qumran.

---

116. Josephus, *J. W.* 2.151.

5.5. Conclusion

In this chapter, we have first examined parallels and parallelomania, John the Baptist and Qumran; general connections between Acts and CD at Qumran, particularly Fitzmyer's parallels; characteristics of the Mebaqqer that resonate with Peter's actions in Acts; and character qualities of Peter and the early Christians that resonate with Qumran. Similarities have been pointed out between the communities themselves (of believers in Acts and Qumran). The community in Acts is portrayed as renewed Israel, an identity claimed by Qumran too. Both communities may have had multiple factions, they both enjoyed high reputation from those outside their communities. They responded to pain and suffering with courage and boldness, they had similar judicial processes, and last, they both emphasized baptism although exactly not the same kind.

We have pointed out similarities in the duties of the Mebaqqer that resonate with Peter's leadership and ethics in Acts. There are similarities in admission of members, teaching about mighty works of God, care for members as a father and shepherd, prophecy, vision, dreams and their interpretation, and the Overseer's age and his ability to discern the hearts of men. Further, we have highlighted similarities between character qualities of Peter and the early Christians that resonate with Qumran, in the area of prayerfulness, honesty, compassion and hospitality, piety/godliness, humility, boldness, and a disdain of riches.

Collins and Evans correctly argue, "We find that the very structure of the early Christian community grows out of a typology (or set of typologies) rooted in the sacred scriptures of Israel. This structure cannot be adequately understood without a careful and nuanced appreciation of the Dead Sea Scrolls."[117] These similarities will serve not only in understanding the structure of the early church but also provide clear lenses for understanding the leadership and practices of the early Christian church. Although there are a few instances where the similarities are overweighed with differences, the many areas that point out similarities between the leadership and ethic in Acts and that in CD at Qumran are numerous.

---

117. Collins and Evans, *Christian Beginnings*, 62.

CHAPTER 6

Conclusion

Peter as a character in Luke-Acts, has received minimal attention in comparative studies done in the New Testament, particularly on the subject of characterization and parallels drawn between him and Qumran Leadership. Generally, writers have examined characters like Jesus, John the Baptist, John, Herod, and Pharisees on this subject. This study has discussed the characterization of Peter's leadership and ethics in Acts 1–12 and 15 in the light of Qumran leadership and ethics. We now provide a cycloramic summary of this Lucan character as we highlight the most outstanding features of Peter's characterization.

Chapter 1 presented the problem statement, methodology, survey of previous study on the topic, and our proposal. Chapter 2 examined methodology, narrative criticism as the key approach to this study, supplemented by intertextuality. Chapter 3 examined our proposed analogy for studying Acts and the Damascus Document. Here we examined the suitability of Mebaqqer and the ethics lived at Qumran in understanding Acts 1–12 and 15. In the fourth chapter, this study examined how Luke portrays Peter. We focused on his characterization in areas of expansion of the community of believers, handling of scriptures (by Peter), the works of God (miracles, healings, and visions), and values he demonstrated. This examination demonstrated that Luke portrays Peter as an overseer; moving from Jerusalem (Acts 1–6), to Samaria/Judea (8–9) and to the Gentiles (10–12, 15), admitting members in the Christian community (2:37–41; 8:14–17; 10:44–48), and inspecting the state and progress of the members (9:32). During these interactions, Peter's devotion to prayer and the word (3:1; 6:4; 8:15; 9:40; 10:9), and his character traits of humility (3:6; 4:13; 8:14; 10:6; 15:6–21), boldness (2:14; 4:13; 5:1–11;

8:20–24), and compassion (3:3–8; 6:1–3; 9:36–43), were highlighted. Peter opens Scriptures to the members (1:20; 2:16–21, 25–28; 10:34–48; 15:6–11), interprets visions (ch. 10) and discerns the contents of hearts (5:1–11; 8:20–24). In this study, several differences between the communities were also highlighted. However, in chapter 5, we evidently demonstrated that there are similarities between the two communities and their leaderships.

We established that Acts 1–12 and 15 represent Peter as a leader. This has been depicted in various ways: listing his name first on the list of apostles, presenting him as the spokesperson of the group, and his role in organizing the new communities (Jerusalem, Samaria, and Gentiles). Moreover, the donations to the community were brought under the apostles' feet and he represented the apostles by interrogating the inconsistencies. All these portrayed him as the leader of the group appointed by Jesus. Peter's position of teaching and performing miracles, his visits to the believers and participating in significant leadership meetings, and his presence in key conflict and dispute resolution forums greatly contribute to these findings.

6.1. Peter and the Mebaqqer

This study has shown similarities in the following leadership roles accredited to Peter and the Overseer at Qumran. First, they admitted members in the community. Peter guided the first three thousand believers (Acts 2:38–41) into the fold. Though Philip preached first in Samaria, it is not until Peter and John went over and prayed for the Samaritans that they received the Holy Spirit (8:15–16), and we have argued that the presence of a Christian community is marked by the giving of the Holy Spirit. The Ethiopian eunuch seems to have heard the gospel and been baptized before Cornelius. However, it is not until Peter visits Cornelius and explains his vision that the Holy Spirit falls on the Gentiles. Peter's involvement with the disciples in Lydda and Joppa alludes to the possibility that Peter may have been integral to the inception of the church in Judea also. The authority of admitting members to the community was exclusively ascribed to the Mebaqqer at Qumran (CD 13:13).[1]

---

1. No members of the camp are allowed to bring anyone into the group except by permission of the Overseer of the camp.

Second, both taught their members the mighty miracles and the mighty works of God. Luke portrays Peter as continuing Jesus's teaching and actions. He performs mighty acts (Acts 3:6–8; 5:1–11, 15–16; 9:34, 40–41), also explains the mighty works of God (2:16–21; 4:12–16; 10:34–48; 12:17). This also was the role of the Mebaqqer at Qumran (CD 13:7–8).[2]

Third, they both cared for their communities as a father cares for his children and the shepherd his flock. Peter is depicted as a caring father (Acts 6:1–4) and a shepherd (9:32–41), ensuring their freedom from any kind of knots (9:40–43; 10:38–48), a role reserved for the Overseer of Qumran (CD 13:9–10).[3]

Fourth, they were responsible for enforcing discipline and resolving disputes. Peter is portrayed as administering discipline (Acts 5:1–11; 8:20–24); and involved in resolving disputes (6:1–4; 15:6–12), a duty similar to one exercised by the Mebaqqer at Qumran (CD 14:11–12). Fifth, they both related the future and its interpretation to their contemporary communities (Acts 10 cf. CD 13:8). Last, the age prescribed for the Overseer and the condition on his ability to discern the hearts of men and their secrets is also like the age Peter served and his ability to discern men's hearts and their deception is evident (Acts 5:1–11; 8:20–24 cf. CD 14:9–12).

6.1.1. Peter's Ethics and the Ethics Lived at Qumran

We have also pointed out similarities in the discipline of prayer,[4] compassion, hospitality,[5] piety,[6] and disdain of riches,[7] coupled with the values of honesty,[8] humility,[9] and boldness.[10] These practices attested to in the life of Peter and

---

2. He must teach the general membership about the works of God, instruct them in his mighty miracles.

3. He should care for them as a father does his children, taking care of all their problems as a shepherd does for his flock. He should loosen all their knots, that there be no one oppressed or crushed in his congregation.

4. Acts 1:24; 2:42; 3:1; 4:23–31; 6:4; 8:15; 9:40; 10:9; 12:5, 17–19; cf. 1QS 10:1–3, 10, 13–14, 1QM 14:13–14.

5. Acts 3:6; 9:36, 40–41; 10:21–23; cf. CD 6: 20–7:1; 14:12–16; Josephus, *J. W.* 2.124–25.

6. Acts 3:12; 6:4; 8:20; 10:14; cf. 1QS 1:1–2, 16–17; 3: 9–11; 5:8–10; 10:1–11:22.

7. Acts 5:1–11; 6:4; 8:20; cf. CD 4:17; 1 QS 9:21–24; 1QH 5:22, QM 11:9, 13; 13:12–14.

8. Acts 3:6; 8:20; cf. CD 1; 1QS 1:5–6; 2:24; 5:3–4.

9. Acts 3:12–16; 8:15; 10:25–26; cf. Josephus, *J. W.* 2.126.

10. Acts 2:14–21, 2:40; 3:15; 4:13; 5:1–11, 17–18, 29–32, 40–41; 8:20; 12:1; cf. 1 QS 1:16–17; 7:1; 8:4; Josephus, *J. W.* 2.151.

the community of believers, are virtues and practices highly valued at CD and the community it represents.

6.2. Implications

Fitzmyer had concluded that "the influence of Qumran on Acts is not as marked as it is in other New Testament writings (e.g., John, Paul, Matthew, [and] Hebrew). The parallels that do exist, striking though they may be, are not numerous."[11]

Brooke, however, objected, confidently asserting, "For the Acts of the Apostles the story has been the same. Numerous parallels have been noted."[12] It is evident that Fitzmyer's opinion would have to be modified in the light of these findings. We can therefore confidently conclude that Luke portrays Peter's leadership and ethics in Acts 1–12 and 15 as similar to the Mebaqqer at Qumran and the ethics practiced there.

We propose that with these numerous connections, future research should focus on studying the possibility of literary dependence between Acts and CD (or DSS). Whereas we posit that there is a possibility that the church Luke is writing about may have been influenced by Qumran, or even that the members may have been adherents of Essenes' camps that were within the environs of Jerusalem. An examination should be attempted to establish the possibility of Acts literary dependence on the Qumran (DSS). Research in this direction will be a worthy course for biblical studies scholarship. For it will provide a perfect window into understanding the leadership and practices of the early church.

In sum, this study has demonstrated a clear resemblance between Peter's leadership and that of the Mebaqqer at Qumran and between Peter's ethics and those lived out at the Qumran community. I, therefore, offer these findings in confident belief and hope that future research will enable more confident and sober interactions in the area of literary dependence. Research should be done on the large numbers of believers converted in Jerusalem area (2:41; 4:4; 6:7) to establish whether they have any connections with the Essenes who are believed to have had settlements in the vicinity of Jerusalem.

---

11. Fitzmyer, "Jewish Christianity in Acts Light of Qumran Scrolls," 253.

12. .Brooke, "Luke-Acts," 72.

Bibliography

Abegg Jr., Martin G. "Paul and James on the Law in Light of Dead Sea Scrolls." In *Christian Beginnings and the Dead Sea Scrolls*, edited by John J. Collins and Craig A. Evans, 63–74. Grand Rapids: Baker Academic, 2006.

Abram. M. H. *A Glossary of Literary Terms.* 7th ed. Fort Worth: Harcourt Brace College Publishers, 1999.

Alkier, Stefan. "Intertextuality and Semiotics of Biblical Texts." In *Reading the Bible Intertextually*, edited by Richard B. Hays, Stefan Alkier, and Leroy Andrew Huizenga, 2–21. Waco: Baylor University Press, 2009.

Alter, Robert. *The Art of Biblical Narrative.* New York: Basic Books, 1981.

Aune, David E. *The Westminster Dictionary of New Testament and Early Christian Literature and Rhetoric.* Louisville: Westminster John Knox, 2010.

Avigad, N. "The Palaeography of the Dead Sea Scrolls and Related Documents." *Scripta Hierosolymitana* 4 (1958): 56–87.

Baigent, Michael, and Richard Leigh. *The Dead Sea Scrolls Deception.* London: Corgi Bks, 1992.

Bal, Mieke. *Narratology: Introduction to the Theory of Narrative.* 2nd ed. Toronto: University of Toronto Press, 1997.

Bar-Efrat, Shimon. *Narrative Art in the Bible.* Journal For the Study of the Old Testament Supplement Series 17. Sheffield: Sheffield Academic Press, 1989.

Barrera, Julio Trebolle. "The Qumran Texts and the New Testament." In *The People of the Dead Sea Scrolls: Their Writings, Beliefs and Practices*, Florentino García Martínez and Julio Trebolle Barrera, 203–20. Leiden: Brill, 1995.

———. "The Essenes of Qumran: Between Submission to the Law and Apocalyptic." In *The People of the Dead Sea Scrolls: Their Writings, Beliefs and Practices*, Florentino García Martínez and Julio Trebolle Barrera, 50–76. Leiden: Brill, 1995.

Barrett, C. K. *Acts 1–14: A Critical and Exegetical Commentary on the Acts of the Apostles.* International Critical Commentary. London: T&T Clark, 1994.

———. *Acts 15–18: A Critical and Exegetical Commentary on the Acts of the Apostles.* International Critical Commentary. London: T&T Clark, 1998.

Beale, G. K. *The Temple and the Church's Mission: A Biblical Theology of the Dwelling Place of God*. New Studies in Biblical Theology 17. Downers Grove: InterVarsity Press, 2004.

Beale, G. K., and Mitchell Kim. *God Dwells Among Us: Expanding Eden to the Ends of the Earth*. Downers Grove: InterVarsity Press, 2014.

Beall, Todd S. *Josephus' Description of the Essenes Illustrated by the Dead Sea Scrolls*. SNTSMS 58. Cambridge: Cambridge University, 2004.

Bennema, Cornelis. *A Theory of Character in New Testament Narrative*. Philadelphia: Fortress Press, 2014.

Bennis, Warren G. *An Invented Life: Reflections on Leadership and Change*. Reading, MA: Addison-Wesley, 1993.

Berlin, Adele. *Poetics and Interpretation of Biblical Narrative*. Bible and Literature Series 9. Sheffield: Almond Press, 1983.

Black, David Alan, and David S. Dockery, eds. *New Testament Criticism and Interpretation*. Grand Rapids: Zondervan, 1991.

Boccaccini, Gabriele. *Beyond the Essene Hypothesis: The Parting of the Ways between Qumran and Enochic Judaism*. Grand Rapids: Eerdmans, 1998.

———, ed. *Enoch and Qumran Origins: New Light on a Forgotten Connection*. Grand Rapids: Eerdmans, 2005.

Bock, Darrell L. *Acts*. Baker Exegetical Commentary on the New Testament. Grand Rapids: Baker Academic, 2007.

Bockmuehl, Markus. *The Remembered Peter: In Ancient Reception and Modern Debate*. Wissenschaftliche Untersuchungen Zum Neuen Testament (Wunt I) 262. Tübingen: Mohr Siebeck, 2010.

———. *Simon Peter in Scripture and Memory: The New Testament Apostle in the Early Church*. Grand Rapids: Baker Academic, 2012.

Bond, Helen K., ed. *Peter in Early Christianity*. Grand Rapids: Eerdmans, 2015.

Booth, Wayne C. *The Rhetoric of Fiction*. 2nd ed. London: Penguin Books, 1993.

Brawley, R. L. *Centering on God: Method and Message in Luke-Acts*. Currents in Biblical Interpretations. Louisville: Westminster John Knox, 1990.

Brooke, George J. "Luke-Acts and the Qumran Scrolls: The Case of MMT." In *Luke's Literary Achievement: Collected Essays, edited by Christopher M. Tuckett*, 72–90. Sheffield: Sheffield Academic Press, 1995.

———. "The Amos-Numbers Midrash (CD 7 13b–8 1a) and Messianic Expectation." *Zeitschrift für die Alttestamentliche Wissenschaft* 92, no. 3 (1980): 397–404. https://doi.org/10.1515/zatw.1980.92.3.397.

Brown, Raymond E., Karl P. Donfried, and John Reumann, eds. *Peter in the New Testament: A Collaborative Assessment by Protestant and Roman Catholic Scholars*. Minneapolis: Augsburg, 1973.

Brownlee, William Hugh. *Dead Sea Manual of Discipline*. New Haven: American Schools of Oriental Research, 1951.

————. "John the Baptist in the New Light of Ancient Scrolls." *Interpretation* 9, no. 1 (1955): 71–90.

————. *The Meaning of the Qumrân Scrolls for the Bible: With Special Reference to the Book of Isaiah*. New York: Oxford University Press, 1964.

Calpino, Teresa J. *Women, Work and Leadership in Acts*. Wissenschaftliche Untersuchungen Zum Neuen Testament, 361. Tübingen: Mohr Siebeck, 2014.

Capper, Brain. "Community of Goods in the Early Jerusalem Church." In *Aufstieg Und Niedergang Der Römischen Welt*, vol. 26, no. 2, edited by W. Haase and H. Temporini, 1730–74. Berlin: Walter de Gruyter, 1995.

————. "The Palestinian Cultural Context of Earliest Christian Community of Goods." In *The Book of Acts in Its Palestinian Setting*, edited by Richard Bauckham, 323–56. The Book of Acts in Its Ancient Literary Setting, vol. 4. Grand Rapids: Eerdmans, 1995.

Charles, Robert. *Apocrypha and Pseudepigrapha of the OT*. Vol. 1. Oxford: Oxford University Press, 1963.

Chatman, Seymour. *Story and Discourse: Narrative Structure in Fiction and Film*. Ithaca: Cornell University Press, 1978.

Chung-Kim, Esther, and Todd R. Hains. *Acts*. Reformation Commentary on Scripture: New Testament (VI). Downers Grove: InterVarsity Press, 2014.

Cohn, Robert L. *The Shape of Sacred Space: Four Biblical Studies*. Chicago: Scholars Press, 1981.

Collins, John J. "Apocalyptic Theology and The Dead Sea Scrolls." In *Christian Beginnings and the Dead Sea Scrolls*, edited by John J. Collins and Craig A. Evans, 129–33. Grand Rapids: Baker Academic, 2006.

————. *Beyond the Qumran Community: The Sectarian Movement of the Dead Sea Scrolls*. Grand Rapids: William B. Eerdmans Publishing Company, 2010.

————. "An Essene Messiah? Comments on Israel Knohl, The Messiah before Jesus." In *Christian Beginnings and the Dead Sea Scrolls*, edited by John J. Collins and Craig A. Evans, 37–44. Grand Rapids: Baker Academic, 2006.

————. *Jewish Wisdom in the Hellenistic Age*. Edinburgh: T&T Clark, 1998.

————. "A Messiah before Jesus?" In *Christian Beginnings and the Dead Sea Scrolls*, edited by John J. Collins and Craig A. Evans, 15–35. Grand Rapids: Baker Academic, 2006.

————. *Scriptures and Sectarianism: Essays on the Dead Sea Scrolls*. Wissenschaftliche Untersuchungen Zum Neuen Testament 332. Tübingen: Mohr Siebeck, 2014.

Collins, John J., and Craig A. Evans, eds. *Christian Beginnings and the Dead Sea Scrolls*. Acadia Studies in Bible and Theology. Grand Rapids: Baker Academic, 2006.

Conzelmann, Hans. *Acts of the Apostles: A Commentary on Acts of the Apostles.* Translated by James Limburg, A. Thomas Kraabel, and Donald H. Juel. Philadelphia: Fortress, 1987.

Cross, Frank M., Jr. *The Ancient Library of Qumran and Modern Biblical Studies.* The Haskell Lectures.Garden City: Doubleday, 1976.

Cullmann, Oscar. *Peter, Disciple, Apostle, Martyr: A Historical and Theological Study.* Translated by Floyd Filson. London: SCM Press, 1953.

Culpeper, R. A. *Anatomy of the Fourth Gospel: A Study Literary Design.* Philadelphia: Fortress, 1983.

Daniélou, J. *Les Manuscrits de La Mer Morte et Les Origines Du Christianisme.* Paris: Éditions de l'Orante, 1957.

Danker, Frederick W., William Arndt, and Walter Bauer. *A Greek-English Lexicon of the New Testament.* Chicago: University of Chicago Press, 2000.

Darr, John A. *Herod the Fox: Audience Criticism and Lukan Characterization.* Journal for the Study of the New Testament Supplement Series 163. Sheffield: Sheffield Academic Press, 1998.

———. *On Character Building: The Reader and the Rhetoric of Characterization in Luke-Acts.* Literary Currents in Biblical Interpretation. Louisville: Westminster John Knox, 1992.

Davies, Philip R. *The Damascus Covenant: An Interpretation of the "Damascus Document."* Journal for the Study of the Old Testament Supplement Series 25. Sheffield: Sheffield Academic Press, 1983.

Davila, James R. "The Perils of Parallels." University of St Andrews, April 2001.

Dunn, James D. G. *The Acts of the Apostles.* Epworth Commentaries. London: Epworth Press, 1996.

Dupont-Sommer, A. *The Essene Writings from Qumran.* Translated by G. Vermes. Gloucester, MA: Peter Smith, 1973.

———. *The Essene Writings from Qumran.* Meridian Books MG44. Cleveland: World Publishing, 1973.

———. *The Jewish Sect of Qumran and the Essenes: New Studies on the Dead Sea Scrolls.* London: Valentine, 1954.

Dupont-Sommer, A., and E. M. Rowley. *The Dead Sea Scrolls: A Preliminary Survey.* Oxford: Blackwell, 1952.

Edwards, James R. "Parallels and Patterns between Luke and Acts." *Bulletin for Biblical Research* 27, no. 4 (2017): 485–501.

Eshel, Hanan. *The Dead Sea Scrolls and the Hasmonean State.* Grand Rapids: Eerdmans, 2008.

Evans, Craig A. "Jesus, John and the Dead Sea Scrolls: Assessing Typologies of Restoration." In *Christian Beginnings and the Dead Sea Scrolls*, edited by John J. Collins and Craig A. Evans, 45–62. Grand Rapids: Baker Academic, 2006.

Ferguson, F. *Backgrounds of Early Christianity*. 3rd ed. Grand Rapids: Eerdmans, 2003.

Fitzmyer, Joseph A. *The Acts of the Apostles*. Anchor Bible Commentary Series 31. New York: Doubleday, 1998.

———. *The Dead Sea Scrolls and Christian Origins*. Studies in the Dead Sea Scrolls and Related Literature. Grand Rapids: Eerdmans, 2000.

———. *The Dead Sea Scrolls: Major Publications and Tools for Study*. Sources for Biblical Studies 8. Missoula: Scholars Press, 1977.

———. *The Impact of the Dead Sea Scrolls*. New York: Paulist Press, 2009.

———. "Jewish Christianity in Acts in Light of the Qumran Scrolls." In *Studies in Luke-Acts: Essays Presented in Honor of Paul Schubert*, edited by Leander E. Keck and J. Louis Martyn, 233–57. Nashville: Abingdon Press, 1966.

Flessen, Bonnie J. *An Exemplary Man: Cornelius and Characterization in Acts 10*. Eugene: Pickwick, 2011.

Forster, E. M. *Aspects of the Novel*. San Diego: Harcourt Brace, 1955.

Gaventa, Beverly Roberts. *The Acts of the Apostles*. Abingdon New Testament Commentaries. Nashville: Abingdon Press, 2003.

Gowler, David B. *Host, Guest, Enemy, and Friend: Portraits of the Pharisees in Luke and Acts*. Emory Studies in Early Christianity 2. New York: Peter Lang, 1991.

Graetz, Heinrich. *History of the Jews*. 6 vols. Philadelphia: Jewish Publication Society of America, 1893.

Green, Joel B. *Practicing Theological Interpretation: Engaging Biblical Texts for Faith and Formation*. Grand Rapids: Baker Academic, 2011.

Haenchen, Ernst. *The Acts of the Apostles: A Commentary*. Philadelphia: Westminster, 1971.

Harvey, A. *A Companion to the New Testament*. 2nd ed. Cambridge: Cambridge University Press, 2004.

Hengel, Martin. *Judaism and Hellenism*. 2 vols. London: SCM Press, 1974).

Hochman, B. *Character in Literature*. Ithaca: Cornell University Press, 1985.

Howlett, Duncan. *The Essenes and Christianity: An Interpretation of the Dead Sea Scrolls*. New York: Harper and Brothers, 1957.

Iser, Wolfgang. *The Act of Reading: A Theory of Aesthetic Response*. Baltimore: Johns Hopkins University Press, 1978.

Jeffers, James. *The Greco-Roman World of the New Testament Era: Exploring the Background of Early Christianity*. Downers Grove: InterVarsity Press, 1999.

Johnson, Luke Timothy. *The Acts of the Apostles*. Sacra Pagina Series 5. Collegeville: Liturgical Press, 1992.

Josephus. Translated by Henry St. J. Thackery et al. 10 vols. LCL. Cambridge, MA: Harvard University Press, 1926–1965.

Keck, Leander E., Paul Schubert, and J. Louis Martyn, eds. *Studies in Luke-Acts: Essays Presented in Honor of Paul Schubert*. Nashville: Abingdon, 1966.

Keener, Craig S. *Acts: An Exegetical Commentary*. Grand Rapids: Baker Academic, 2012.

———. *Acts: An Exegetical Commentary*. Vol. 1. 4 vols. Grand Rapids: Baker Academic, 2012.

———. *Acts: An Exegetical Commentary*. Vol. 2. 4 vols. Grand Rapids: Baker Academic, 2013.

Kennedy, George. *A New History of Classical Rhetoric*. Princeton: Princeton University Press, 1994.

———. *Progymnasmata: Greek Textbooks of Prose Composition and Rhetoric*. Writings from the Greco-Roman World 10. Atlanta: SBL Press, 2003.

Kermode, Frank. *The Genesis of Secrecy: On the Interpretation of Narrative*. The Charles Elliot Norton Lectures, 1977–1978. Cambridge, MA: Harvard University Press, 1979.

Kingsbury, J. D. *Matthew as Story*. 2nd ed. Philadelphia: Fortress Press, 1988.

Kisau, Paul Mumo. *Acts*. In *Africa Bible Commentary*, edited by Tokunboh Adeyemo. Nairobi: Word Alive, 2006.

Kittel, Gerhard, Gerhard Friedrich, and Geoffrey W. Bromiley. *Theological Dictionary of the New Testament*. Grand Rapids: Eerdmans, 1964.

Klein, William W., Craig L. Blomberg, and Robert L. Hubbard. *Introduction to Biblical Interpretation*. Edited by Kermit Allen Ecklebarger. Dallas: Word Publishing, 1993.

Knibb, Michael A. *The Qumran Community*. Cambridge: Cambridge University Press, 1987.

Kurz, W. S. *Reading Luke-Acts: Dynamics of Biblical Narrative*. Louisville: Westminster John Knox, 1993.

Lane, Belden C. *The Solace of Fierce Landscapes: Exploring Desert and Mountain Spirituality*. New York: Oxford University Press, 1998.

Lampe, Geoffrey William Hugo. "St. Peter's Denial." *Bulletin of the John Rylands Library* 55, no. 2 (1973): 346–68.

Larkin, William J. *Acts*. The IVP New Testament Commentary Series. Downers Grove: InterVarsity Press, 1995.

Lied, Liv Ingerborg. "Another Look at the Land of Damascus: The Spaces of the Damascus Document in the Light of Edward W. Soja's Thirdspace Approach." In *New Directions in Qumran Studies: Proceedings of the Bristol Colloquium on the Dead Sea Scrolls, 8–10 September 2003*, edited by Jonathan G. Campbell, William John Lyons, and Lloyd K. Pietersen, 101–25. Library of Second Temple Studies 52. London: T&T Clark, 2005.

Lightfoot, J. B. *The Acts of the Apostles: A Newly Discovered Commentary*. Edited by Ben Witherington and Todd D. Still. The Lightfoot Legacy Set, vol. 1. Downers Grove: IVP Academic, 2014.

Lowe, John. *Saint Peter*. Oxford: Clarendon Press, 1956.

Maddox, Robert. *The Purpose of Luke–Acts*. Edinburgh: T&T Clark, 1982.

Malbon, Elizabeth Struthers. *In the Company of Jesus: Characters in Mark's Gospel*. Louisville:Westminster John Knox, 2000.

Marguerat, Daniel, and Yvan Bourquin. *How to Read Bible Stories: An Introduction to Narrative Criticism*. Translated by John Bowden. London: SCM Press, 1999.

Marshall, I. Howard. *The Acts of the Apostles: An Introduction and Commentary*. TNTC. Leicester: Inter-Varsity Press, 1980.

———. *The Acts of the Apostles*. New Testament Guides. Sheffield: Sheffield Academic Press, 1997.

Martinez, Florentino Garcia. "The Dead Sea Scrolls." In *The People of the Dead Sea Scrolls: Their Writings, Beliefs and Practices*, Florentino Garcia Martinez and Julio Trebolle Barrera, 3–16. Leiden: Brill, 1995.

Martinez, Florentino Garcia, and Julio Trebolle Barrera. *The People of the Dead Sea Scrolls: Their Writings, Beliefs and Practices*. Leiden: Brill, 1995.

Mauser, Ulrich W. *Christ in the Wilderness: The Wilderness Theme in the Second Gospel and Its Basis in the Biblical Tradition*. SBT 39. London: SCM Press, 1963.

Maxwell, John C. *Developing the Leader within You Workbook*. Nashville: Nelson, 2001.

———. *The 21 Irrefutable Laws of Leadership: Follow Them and People Will Follow You*. Revised and updated 10th anniversary ed. Nashville: Nelson, 2007.

Merenlahti, Petri, and Raimo Hakola. "Reconceiving Narrative Criticism." In *Characterization in the Gospels: Reconceiving Narrative Criticism*, edited by David M. Rhoads and Kari Syreeni, 13–48. JSNTSup 184. Sheffield: Sheffield Academic Press, 1999.

Metso, Sarianna. "Qumran Community Structure and Terminology as Theological Statement." In *The Bible and the Dead Sea Scrolls: The Second Princeton Symposium on Judaism and Christian Origins*, edited by James H. Charlesworth, 283–300. Waco: Baylor University Press, 2006.

Milik, J. T. *Ten Years of Discovery in the Wilderness of Judea*. Studies in Biblical Theology 26. London: SCM Press, 1959.

Moule, C. F. D. "The Christology of Acts." In *Studies in Luke-Acts: Essays Presented in Honor of Paul Schubert*, edited by L. E. Keck and J. L. Martyn, 159–85. Nashville: Abingdon Press, 1966.

Munck, J. *The Acts of Apostles*. Anchor Bible 31. New York: Doubleday, 1967.

Myers, Alicia. *Characterizing Jesus: A Rhetorical Analysis on the Fourth Gospel's Use of Scripture in Its Presentation of Jesus*. Library of New Testament Studies. London: T&T Clark, 2012.

Nolland, John. *Luke*. Word Biblical Commentary. 3 vols. Dallas: Word Books, 1993.

Pao, David W. *Acts and the Isaianic New Exodus*. Grand Rapids: Baker
    Academic, 2002.

Parkes, James. *The Conflict of the Church and the Synagogue: A Study of the Origins
    of Antisemitism*. Cleveland: World Publishing, 1961. ACLS Humanities
    E-Book, http://www.columbia.edu/cgi-bin/cul/resolve?clio8861159.

Parsons, Mikeal C. *Acts*. Paideia Commentaries on the New Testament. Grand
    Rapids: Baker Academic, 2008.

———. *The Departure of Jesus in Luke-Acts: The Ascension Narratives in Context*.
    Journal for the Study of the New Testament Supplement Series 21. Sheffield:
    Sheffield Academic Press, 1987.

Pate, C. Marvin, J. Scott Duvall, J. Daniel Hays, E. Randolph Richards, W. Dennis
    Tucker, and Preben Vang. *The Story of Israel: A Biblical Theology*. Downers
    Grove: InterVarsity Press, 2004.

Perkins, Pheme. *Peter: Apostle for the Whole Church*. Studies on Personalities of the
    New Testament. Columbia: University of South Carolina Press, 1994.

Peterson, David G. *The Acts of The Apostles*. Grand Rapids: Eerdmans, 2009.

Philo. *The Works of Philo: Complete and Unabridged*. New updated ed. Translated
    Charles Duke Yonge. Peabody: Hendrickson Pub, 1993.

Polhill, John B. *Acts*. New American Commentary 26. Nashville: Broadman &
    Holman, 1992.

Porter, Stanley E. "Literary Approaches to the New Testament: From Formalism
    to Deconstruction and Back." In *Approaches to New Testament Study*, edited
    by Stanley E. Porter and David Tombs, 77–128. Sheffield: Sheffield Academic
    Press, 1995.

Powell, Mark Allan. *What Is Narrative Criticism? Guides to Biblical Scholarship*.
    Minneapolis: Fortress, 1990.

Price, M. *Forms of Life: Character and Moral Imagination in the Novel*. New Haven:
    Yale University Press, 1983.

Priest, J. F. "Mebaqqer, Pāqîd, and the Messiah." *Journal of Biblical Literature* 81,
    no. 1 (1962): 55–61.

———. "The Messiah and the Meals in 1 QSa." *Journal of Biblical Literature* 82, no.
    1 (1963): 95–100.

Rabinowitz, Isaac. "A Reconsideration of 'Damascus' and '390 Years' in the
    'Damascus' ('Zadokite') Fragments." *Journal of Biblical Literature* 73, no. 1
    (1954): 11–35.

Rackham, Richard B. *The Acts of the Apostles: An Exposition*. 5th ed. London:
    Methuen, 1910.

Resseguie, James L. *Narrative Criticism of the New Testament: An Introduction*.
    Grand Rapids: Baker Academic, 2005.

———. *Revelation Unsealed: A Narrative Critical Approach to John's Apocalypse*.
    Biblical Interpretation Series 32. Leiden: Brill, 1998.

———. *Spiritual Landscape: Images of the Spiritual Life in the Gospel of Luke.* Peabody: Hendrickson, 2004.

———. *The Strange Gospel: Narrative Design and Point of View in John.* Biblical Interpretation Series 56. Leiden: Brill, 2001.

Rhoads, David. "Narrative Criticism and the Gospel of Mark." *Journal of the American Academy of Religion* 50, no. 3 (1982): 411–34.

———. "Narrative Criticism: Practices and Prospects." In *Characterization in the Gospels: Reconceiving Narrative Criticism,* edited by David Rhoads and Kari Syreeni, 264–85. Sheffield: Sheffield Academic Press, 1999.

Rhoads, David, Joanna Dewey, and Donald Michie. *Mark as Story: An Introduction to the Narrative of a Gospel.* 3rd ed. Philadelphia: Fortress, 2012.

Rimmon-Kenan, S. *Narrative Fiction: Contemporary Poetics.* 2nd ed. London: Routledge, 2002.

Robbins, V. K. *Exploring the Texture of the Texts: A Guide to Socio-Rhetorical Interpretation.* Valley Forge: Trinity Press International, 1996.

———. *The Tapestry of Early Christian Discourse: Rhetoric, Society and Ideology.* London: Routledge, 1996.

Robinson, John A. T. *Twelve New Testament Studies.* Studies in Biblical Theology, 34. London: SCM Press, 1962.

Sandmel, Samuel. "Parallelomania." *Journal of Biblical Literature* 81, no. 1 (March 1962): 1–13.

Schiffman, Lawrence H. *The Eschatological Community of the Dead Sea Scrolls: A Study of the Rule of the Congregation.* SBLMS 38. Atlanta: Scholars Press, 1989.

———. "The Law of Vows and Oaths (Num. 30:3–15) in the *Zadokite Fragments* and the *Temple Scrolls.*" *Revue de Qumrân* 15, no. 1/2 (1991): 199–214.

———. *Reclaiming the Dead Sea Scrolls.* Philadelphia: Jewish Publication Society, 1994.

Scholes, Robert, James Phelan, and Robert L. Kellogg. *The Nature of Narrative.* 40th anniversary ed., revised and expanded. Oxford: Oxford University Press, 2006.

Schubert, Kurt. *The Dead Sea Community: Its Origin and Teachings.* Westport: Greenwood Press, 1959.

Seymour-Smith, Charlotte. *Macmillan Dictionary of Anthropology.* London: Macmillan, 1986.

Smith, Charles Foster, trans. *Thucydides: History of the Peloponnesian War Book I and II.* Vol. 1. 4 vols. Cambridge, MA: Harvard University Press, 1935.

Snyder, Graydon F. *Ante Pacem: Archaeological Evidence of Church Life before Constantine.* Macon: Mercer University Press, 2003.

———. "Sea Monsters in Early Christian Art." *Biblical Research* 44 (1999): 7–21.

Spencer, Aída Besançon. "Literary Criticism." In *New Testament Criticism and Interpretation*, edited by David Alan Black and David S. Dockery, 225–51. Grand Rapids: Zondervan, 1991.

Spencer, F. Scott. *Acts*. Sheffield: Sheffield Academic Press, 1997.

———. "Acts and Modern Literary Approaches." In *The Book of Acts in Its Ancient Literary Setting*, edited by Bruce W. Winter and Andrew D. Clarke, 381–414. The Book of Acts in Its First Century Setting 1. Grand Rapids: Eerdmans, 1993.

———. *Journeying through Acts: A Literary-Cultural Reading*. Peabody: Hendrickson, 2004.

———. "Sacred to Death: The Rhetoric of Fear in the 'Tragedy' of Ananias and Sapphira." In *Reading Acts Today: Essays in Honor of Loveday C. A. Alexander*, edited by Steve Walton, Thomas E. Phillips, Lloyd K. Pietersen, and F. Scott Spencer, 63–80. Library of New Testament Studies 427. London: T&T Clark, 2011.

Springer, M. D. *A Rhetoric of Literary Character: Some Women of Henry James*. Chicago: University of Chicago Press, 1978.

Stendahl, K. "John the Baptist in the New Light of Ancient Scrolls." In *The Scrolls and the New Testament*, edited by K. Stendahl, 3–53. London: SCM Press, 1958.

Sternberg, M. *Expositional Modes and Temporal Ordering in Fiction*. Baltimore: Johns Hopkins University Press, 1978.

———. *The Poetics of Biblical Narrative: Ideological Literature and the Drama of Reading*. The Indiana Literary Biblical Series. Bloomington: Indiana University Press, 1985.

Strong, James. *The Exhaustive Concordance of the Bible*. Nashville: Abingdon, 1980.

Talmon, Shemaryahu. "The 'Desert Motif' in the Bible and in Qumran Literature." In *Biblical Motifs: Origins and Transformations*, edited by Alexander Altmann, 31–64. Cambridge, MA: Harvard University Press, 1966.

Tannehill, Robert C. *The Narrative Unity of Luke-Acts: A Literary Interpretation*. Foundations and Facets. Philadelphia: Fortress, 1986.

Thiede, Carsten Peter. *The Earliest Gospel Manuscript? The Qumran Papyrus 7Q5 and Its Significance for New Testament Studies*. Exeter: Paternoster Press, 1992.

———. *Simon Peter: From Galilee to Rome*. Exeter: Paternoster Press, 1986.

Tuckett, C. M., ed. *Luke's Literary Achievement: Collected Essays*. JSNTSup 116. Sheffield: Sheffield Academic Press, 1995.

Tyson, Joseph B. "The Gentile Mission and the Authority of Scripture in Acts." *New Testament Studies* 33, no. 4 (1987): 619–30.

Verheyden, J., ed. *The Unity of Luke-Acts*. Bibliotheca Ephemeridum Theologicarum Lovaniensium Betl 142. Leuven: Peeters Publishers, 1999.

Vermes, Geza. *Scripture and Tradition in Judaism: Haggadic Studies*. Studia Post-Biblica, vol. 4. Leiden: Brill, 1961.

Vermeule, Emily. "Sea Monster, Magic, and Poetry." In *Aspects of Death in Greek Art and Poetry*, 179–209. Berkeley: University of California press, 1979.

Walton, Steve. "Where Does the Beginning of Acts End?" In *The Unity of Luke-Acts*, edited by J. Verheyden, 447–67. Bibliotheca Ephemeridum Theologicarum Lovaniensium Betl 142. Leuven: Peeters Publishers, 1999.

Wernberg-Moeller, Preben. *The Manual of Discipline: Translated and Annotated with an Introduction*. Leiden: Brill, 1957.

Wiarda, Peter. *Peter in the Gospels: Pattern, Personality and Relationship*. Wissenschaftliche Untersuchungen Zum Neuen Testament 2. Reihe 127. Tübingen: Mohr Siebeck, 2000.

Williams, David John. *Acts*. New International Biblical Commentary 5. Peabody: Hendrickson, 1990.

Williams, Joel F. *Other Followers of Jesus: Minor Characters as Major Figures in Mark's Gospel*. JSNTSup 102. Sheffield: Sheffield Academic, 1994.

Wilson, Jonathan R. "The Dead Sea Scrolls and Christian Theology." In *Christian Beginnings and the Dead Sea Scrolls*, edited by John J. Collins and Craig A. Evans, 121–28. Grand Rapids: Baker Academic, 2006.

Wise, Michael Owen, Martin Abegg, and Edward M. Cook, eds. *The Dead Sea Scrolls: A New Translation*. San Francisco: HarperOne, 2005. https://www.academia.edu/28913750/The_Damascus_Document_CD_2005_

Witherington, Ben. *The Acts of the Apostles: A Socio-Rhetorical Commentary*. Grand Rapids: Eerdmans, 1998.

 Langham
PARTNERSHIP

Langham Literature, with its publishing work, is a ministry of Langham Partnership.

Langham Partnership is a global fellowship working in pursuit of the vision God entrusted to its founder John Stott –

> *to facilitate the growth of the church in maturity and Christ-likeness through raising the standards of biblical preaching and teaching.*

Our vision is to see churches in the Majority World equipped for mission and growing to maturity in Christ through the ministry of pastors and leaders who believe, teach and live by the word of God.

Our mission is to strengthen the ministry of the word of God through:
• nurturing national movements for biblical preaching
• fostering the creation and distribution of evangelical literature
• enhancing evangelical theological education
especially in countries where churches are under-resourced.

Our ministry

Langham Preaching partners with national leaders to nurture indigenous biblical preaching movements for pastors and lay preachers all around the world. With the support of a team of trainers from many countries, a multi-level programme of seminars provides practical training, and is followed by a programme for training local facilitators. Local preachers' groups and national and regional networks ensure continuity and ongoing development, seeking to build vigorous movements committed to Bible exposition.

Langham Literature provides Majority World preachers, scholars and seminary libraries with evangelical books and electronic resources through publishing and distribution, grants and discounts. The programme also fosters the creation of indigenous evangelical books in many languages, through writer's grants, strengthening local evangelical publishing houses, and investment in major regional literature projects, such as one volume Bible commentaries like the *Africa Bible Commentary* and the *South Asia Bible Commentary*.

Langham Scholars provides financial support for evangelical doctoral students from the Majority World so that, when they return home, they may train pastors and other Christian leaders with sound, biblical and theological teaching. This programme equips those who equip others. Langham Scholars also works in partnership with Majority World seminaries in strengthening evangelical theological education. A growing number of Langham Scholars study in high quality doctoral programmes in the Majority World itself. As well as teaching the next generation of pastors, graduated Langham Scholars exercise significant influence through their writing and leadership.

To learn more about Langham Partnership and the work we do visit **langham.org**

Milton Keynes UK
Ingram Content Group UK Ltd.
UKHW022320020424
440481UK00015B/687